Book of American Types
Standard Faces

Foreword to the New Edition

PROPONENTS OF WORD PROCESSING WOULD HAVE US BELIEVE that there is nothing to be gained from the slow, painstaking art of hand printing, the obsolete process that took literacy itself from the European aristocracy and monastery to the common man. But setting movable type, difficult a process as it was, was once the most promising technology in the world. Metal letters, some no thicker than a stick of chewing gum, and no longer than a push pin, were aligned backwards and upside-down in a tight-fitting composing stick, spelling out works as long as *The Bible* and *The Iliad*. Massive blocks of words were inked on a hand press, a sheet of paper lifted a precise impression of ink with one gentle pass, and ideas finally found a way to reach the world.

BUT JUST AS MOVABLE TYPE did not eradicate the need to master handwriting, neither did the introduction of digital type leave movable type irrelevant. In fact, digitization may have made an appreciation of the art of letterforms more important than ever before. These days, digital methods of typography have produced successful and not-so-successful logos, headlines, and body copy, and the determinant of success seems to always be the same: in the unsuccessful designs, the new ease with which letterforms can be manipulated took precedence over traditional standards of readability. In our desire to let the type play, we are forgetting to make it work. The age of digital typography gives new importance to a book like this 1934 standard typeface catalogue; the ability to alter letterforms at the click of a mouse creates a need to understand and preserve fundamental design elements that enable human eyes to successfully perceive letters. Understanding letterforms involves consulting the masters, the giants of the industry, who revolutionized type and the way it was printed. In America these masters were the type designers of The American Typefounders Company.

CONTEMPORARY TYPE was born in the twenty-six worldwide branches of ATF, whose typefaces would find their way into the metal forms of hundreds of manuscripts, onto the presses of thousands of publishing houses, and into the hands of millions of readers. ATF catalogues, like the one reprinted in this edition, showcased the ever-changing and broadening range of typefaces available for purchase by printers. Distinguished serif types like Baskerville, Bodoni, Garamond, Caslon, Goudy, and other favorites that still appear in our digital font lists today, are shown here in all of their original glory, juxtaposed with sans-serif crowd-pleasers like Bernhard Fashion and Agency Gothic. Exciting and useful ornamental faces also make their debut in this collection, including the graceful Bernhard Tango, the sensational Broadway, a glamorous Parisian series, and the smart Tower face that indulges 1930s art deco. Vanity and calligraphic initials to fit every opening paragraph or monogram can be found in the back of the book, oversized to show off exquisite detail. To the 1934 buyer, this catalogue was an indispensable resource; today, it is a trip back in time to learn what makes a successful typeface, simultaneously acting as a timeless shopping catalog, as many of the typefaces within are now available for standard word processors.

WE ENCOURAGE YOU to read the original preface to this book, reprinted for your interest. Describing the recent decade at the American Typefounders Company, the preface offers a summary of industry demands, like script fonts and bold-facing, and innovations, like angle-bodied type and recessed capitals (note the conclusion of the preface, "Progress In Type Founding"). This preface of the latest printing technologies was indicative of a company philosophy, not a quaint introduction to fill space; ATF concerned itself with selling its typefaces as well as informing burgeoning design. ATF's mission was clear: to better an industry that served the betterment of all.

TODAY, ATF is all but dissolved. In 1993, an auction was held to sell all remaining type, matrices and presses. In the printing world, just four companies still manufacture metal type; hand-setting type is reserved only for a few small fine presses, university sponsored book arts programs, curious hobbyists, and third world countries. The legacy of ATF lives now at Columbia University's typographic museum and library, transferred there in 1936 from the original ATF factory.

REVIVING THIS 1934 CATALOGUE was a labor of love. The work we do as publishers is dependent upon the work of so many manufacturers who came before us, not the least of which was The American Typefounders Company. Without such pioneers, movable type may have experienced stagnation at a crucial moment in the advancement of literacy and design, crippling both disciplines. Instead, a standard of perpetual reinvention was set, and today, our personal computers are the typesetters, our ink-jet and laser printers are the presses, and the desire for new and revitalized typefaces grows stronger every day.

Laura Mikowychok

BOOK OF AMERICAN Types

STANDARD FACES

4880 Lower Valley Road, Atglen, Pennsylvania 19310

Published by Schiffer Publishing Ltd.
4880 Lower Valley Road
Atglen, PA 19310
Phone: (610) 593-1777; Fax: (610) 593-2002
E-mail: Info@schifferbooks.com

For the largest selection of fine reference books on this and related subjects, please visit our web site at
www.schifferbooks.com
We are always looking for people to write books on new and related subjects. If you have an idea for a book please contact us at the above address.

This book may be purchased from the publisher.
Include $3.95 for shipping.
Please try your bookstore first.
You may write for a free catalog.

In Europe, Schiffer books are distributed by
Bushwood Books
6 Marksbury Ave.
Kew Gardens
Surrey TW9 4JF England
Phone: 44 (0) 20 8392-8585; Fax: 44 (0) 20 8392-9876
E-mail: info@bushwoodbooks.co.uk
Website: www.bushwoodbooks.co.uk
Free postage in the U.K., Europe; air mail at cost.

Copyright © 2007 by Schiffer Publishing, Ltd.
Library of Congress Control Number: 2007927179

All rights reserved. No part of this work may be reproduced or used in any form or by any means—graphic, electronic, or mechanical, including photocopying or information storage and retrieval systems—without written permission from the publisher.
The scanning, uploading and distribution of this book or any part thereof via the Internet or via any other means without the permission of the publisher is illegal and punishable by law. Please purchase only authorized editions and do not participate in or encourage the electronic piracy of copyrighted materials.
"Schiffer," "Schiffer Publishing Ltd. & Design," and the "Design of pen and ink well" are registered trademarks of Schiffer Publishing Ltd.

Designed by Sue
Type set in Humanist 521 BT

ISBN: 978-0-7643-2770-4
Printed in China

INDEX

	PAGE
Adonis	123
Agency Gothic	164
Agency Gothic Open	165
Alternate Gothic No. 1	168
Alternate Gothic No. 2	169
Alternate Gothic No. 3	170
American Backslant	9
American Text	156
Announcement Roman	126
Announcement Italic	127
Antique Shaded	144
Bank Gothic Bold	140
Bank Gothic Light	140
Bank Gothic Medium	140
Bank Gothic Condensed Bold	141
Bank Gothic Condensed Light	141
Bank Gothic Condensed Medium	141
Baskerville Roman	93, 192–196
Baskerville Italic	93, 192–196
Benton	9
Bernhard Booklet	48, 193–196
Bernhard Booklet Italic	49, 193–196
Bernhard Fashion	50
Bernhard Gothic Extra Heavy	47
Bernhard Gothic Heavy	46
Bernhard Gothic Light	44, 192–197
Bernhard Gothic Light Italic	45, 192–197
Bernhard Gothic Medium	42
Bernhard Gothic Medium Italic	43
Bernhard Tango	9
Blair	142
Bodoni	18, 192–197
Bodoni Italic	19, 192–197
Bodoni Bold	22
Bodoni Bold Italic	23
Bodoni Book	20, 192–196
Bodoni Book Italic	21, 192–196
Bodoni Open	17
Body Type	192–197
Bookman Oldstyle	94, 192–197
Bookman Italic	95, 192–197
Boul Mich	160
Bradley Ultra Modern Initials	206
Brandon	131
Broadway	158
Broadway Condensed	159
Broadway Monogram Initials	200
Bulletin Typewriter	190
Bulmer Roman	60, 192–196
Bulmer Italic	61, 192–196
Calligraph Initials	203
Camelot Oldstyle	123
Canterbury	59
Card Light Litho	131
Caslon Bold	70
Caslon Bold Italic	71
Caslon Bold Condensed	72
Caslon No. 540	64, 192–196
Caslon Italic No. 540	65, 192–196
Caslon Italic Swash Characters	66
Caslon Oldstyle No. 471	62, 192–196
Caslon Oldstyle Italic No. 471	63, 192–196
Caslon Oldstyle No. 472	62
Caslon Openface	67
Caslon Quaint Characters	63
Century Bold	90
Century Bold Italic	91
Century Bold Condensed	92
Century Catalogue	85, 192–196
Century Catalogue Italic	85, 192–196
Century Expanded	88, 192–197
Century Expanded Italic	89, 192–197
Century Oldstyle	82, 192–197
Century Oldstyle Italic	83, 192–197
Century Oldstyle Bold	84
Century Schoolbook	86, 192–197
Century Schoolbook Italic	86, 192–197
Century Schoolbook Bold	87
Cheltenham Oldstyle	104
Cheltenham Italic	105
Cheltenham Bold	108
Cheltenham Bold Italic	109
Cheltenham Bold Condensed	110
Cheltenham Bold Extended	112
Cheltenham Bold Extra Condensed	111
Cheltenham Medium	106
Cheltenham Medium Italic	107
Cheltenham Wide	113
Civilite	128
Cloister Black	155
Cloister Oldstyle	76, 192–197
Cloister Initials	206
Cloister Italic	77, 192–197
Cloister Bold	80
Cloister Bold Italic	81
Cloister Lightface	78, 192–196
Cloister Lightface Italic	79, 192–196
Cochin	100
Cochin Italic	100
Comstock	143
Condensed Title Gothic No. 11	171
Cooper	114
Cooper Italic	115

	PAGE
Cooper Black	116
Cooper Black Italic	117
Cooper Hilite	118
Copperplate Gothic Bold	139
Copperplate Gothic Condensed Heavy	137
Copperplate Gothic Condensed Light	137
Copperplate Gothic Heavy	136
Copperplate Gothic Heavy Extended	138
Copperplate Gothic Italic	139
Copperplate Gothic Light	136
Copperplate Gothic Light Extended	138
Della Robbia	124
Diamond Combination Monograms	198
Eagle Bold	163
Elite Monogram Initials	199
Engravers Bodoni	130
Engravers Bold	129
Engravers Old English	154
Engravers Roman	129
Engravers Shaded	143
Engravers Text	150
Extra Condensed Title Gothic No. 12	172
Fifth Avenue Initial Frames	200
Fifth Avenue Monogram Initials	200
Franklin Gothic	174
Franklin Gothic Italic	175
Franklin Gothic Condensed	176
Franklin Gothic Extra Condensed	177
Freehand	153
Gallia	121
Garamond	28, 192–196
Garamond Italic	29, 192–196
Garamond Bold	30
Garamond Bold Italic	31
Garamond Open	27
Georgian Initials	202
Gothic Nos. 520–526	182
Gothic No. 544	180
Gothic No. 545	181
Gothic No. 578	179
Gothic Condensed No. 521	183
Gothic Condensed No. 524	182
Gothic Condensed No. 529	184
Gothic No. 11, Condensed Title	171
Gothic Condensed Title No. 117	178
Gothic No. 12, Extra Condensed Title	172
Gothic, Lightline	189
Gothic, Lightline Title	189
Goudy Oldstyle	32, 192–197
Goudy Italic	33, 192–197
Goudy Bold	36
Goudy Bold Italic	37
Goudy Catalogue	34, 192–197
Goudy Catalogue Italic	35, 192–197
Goudy Cursive	40
Goudy Handtooled	38
Goudy Handtooled Italic	39
Goudytype	41
Gravure	101
Greeting Monotone	153
Hobo	157
Hollywood	161
Hollywood Combination Initials	200
Initials	66, 67, 103, 201–206
Bradley Ultra Modern Initials	206
Calligraph Initials	203
Caslon Italic Swash Characters	66
Cloister Initials	206
Georgian Initials	202
Liberty Initials	201
Raleigh Initials	103
Ransom Shaded Initials	67
Stationers Initials	202
University Initials	203
Vanity Initials	204, 205
Vogue Initials	201
Invitation	133
Invitation Shaded	133
Jumbo Typewriter	190
Keynote	51
Liberty	125
Liberty Initials	201
Lightline Gothic	189
Lightline Title Gothic	189
Litho Roman	132
Modern Roman No. 64	192–196
Modern Roman No. 64 Italic	192–196
Monograms	198–200
Broadway Monogram Initials	200
Diamond Combination Monograms	198
Elite Monogram Initials	199
Fifth Avenue Initial Frames	200
Fifth Avenue Monogram Initials	200

	PAGE
Monograms—Continued	
Hollywood Combination Initials	200
Newport Monograms	199
Princess Combination Monograms	199
Virkotype Combination Monograms	198
Virkotype Frames	198
Virkotype Tint Blocks	198
New Caslon	68
New Caslon Italic	69
Newport	167
Newport Monograms	199
News Gothic	186
News Gothic Condensed	187
News Gothic Extra Condensed	188
Nicolas Cochin	98
Nicolas Cochin Italic	99
Nubian	120
Othello	9
Paramount	73
Parisian	122
Park Avenue	16
Parsons	119
Pericles	11
Piranesi	12, 193–196
Piranesi Italic	13, 193–196
Piranesi Bold	14
Piranesi Bold Italic	15
Poster Gothic	185
Princess Combination Monograms	199
Railroad Gothic	173
Raleigh Cursive	102
Raleigh Gothic Condensed	166
Raleigh Initials	103
Ransom Shaded Initials	67
Rivoli	74
Rivoli Italic	75
Roman No. 510	192–196
Roman No. 510 Italic	192–196
Roman No. 524	192
Roman No. 524 Italic	192
Roman No. 527	192
Roman No. 527 Italic	192
Romany	10
Rosetti	162
Royal Script	145
Scotch Roman	96, 192–197
Scotch Roman Italic	97, 192–197
Schoolbook Oldstyle	87, 192–197
Shadow	9
Shaw Text	152
Stationers Initials	202
Steelplate Gothic Shaded	142
Stymie Bold	56
Stymie Bold Italic	57
Stymie Elongated Characters	58
Stymie Light	54, 192–197
Stymie Light Italic	55, 192–197
Stymie Medium	52
Stymie Medium Italic	53
Thermo	135
Tower	9
Typewriter Faces	190, 191
American Typewriter	191
Bulletin Typewriter	190
Elite Oliver Typewriter	191
Elite Underwood Typewriter	191
Jumbo Typewriter	190
New Model Elite Remington Typewriter	191
New Model Remington Typewriter	191
New Model Underwood Typewriter	191
Remington Typewriter No. 2	191
Reproducing Typewriter	191
Ribbonface Typewriter	191
Silk Remington Typewriter	191
Standard Typewriter	191
Underwood Typewriter	191
Typo Roman	134
Typo Roman Shaded	134
Typo Script	146
Typo Script Extended	146
Typo Shaded	148
Typo Text	149
Typo Upright	147
Typo Upright Bold	147
Ultra Bodoni	24
Ultra Bodoni Italic	25
Ultra Bodoni Extra Condensed	26
University Initials	203
Vanity Initials	204, 205
Virkotype Combination Monograms	198
Virkotype Frames	198
Virkotype Tint Blocks	198
Vogue Initials	201
Waldorf Text	149
Wedding Text	151

American Type Founders
Sales Corporation

Location of Selling Branches

BOSTON, MASS. . . . . 270 Congress Street
NEW YORK CITY . . . . 104 East Twenty-fifth Street
PHILADELPHIA, PA. . . Thirteenth and Cherry Streets
BALTIMORE, MD. . . . . . 109 South Hanover Street
BUFFALO, N.Y. . . . . . . 327 Washington Street
PITTSBURGH, PA. . . . . 405 Penn Avenue
CLEVELAND, OHIO . . . . 1231 Superior Avenue
CINCINNATI, OHIO . . . . . . 646 Main Street
ATLANTA, GA. . . . . . 192 Central Avenue, S. W.
CHICAGO, ILL. . . . . . . 519 West Monroe Street
DETROIT, MICH. . . . . . 557 West Larned Street
WASHINGTON, D.C. . . . 1224 H Street, N. W.
ST. LOUIS, MO. . . . . . Ninth and Walnut Streets
MILWAUKEE, WIS. . . . 607 North Second Street
MINNEAPOLIS, MINN. . . 421 Fourth Street, South
KANSAS CITY, MO. . . . . . 932 Wyandotte Street
DENVER, COLO. . . . . 1351 Stout Street
PORTLAND, ORE. . . . 115 S. W. Fourth Avenue
SAN FRANCISCO, CAL. . . . . 500 Howard Street
VANCOUVER, B.C. . . . . . 571 Hamilton Street
SEATTLE, WASH. . . Western Avenue and Columbia
DALLAS, TEXAS . . . . . 600 South Akard Street
LOS ANGELES, CAL. . 222 South Los Angeles Street

The Price of This Book is Two Dollars

PREFACE

During the last decade there has been a period of experimental effort in typography the influence of which at times has carried us a long way from the traditional past. Older rigid notions of classifications limiting a type face to certain definite kinds of use have been largely discarded. Script types that once were confined to stationery and society printing are now appearing even in newspaper advertisements in daring association with bold-face letters.

This period of search for a new style of expression in type has been one of intense activity in type founding. New series have been added to those shown in our former catalogues and the range of many of the others increased by the addition of one or more new sizes. This has meant the cutting of many thousands of matrices, increasing the total number of series that have been currently offered to more than six hundred.

With the increasing demand for new designs and the shifting of interest from many older ones, it has been necessary to reappraise our entire line to keep the number of type faces within reasonable manufacturing limits. Many of the older standard series continue to show steady sales attesting to the soundness of their design and their usefulness in general printing. There are many others of less common need which have a place that nothing else will fill. Their inherent beauty requires their retention on the basis of intrinsic merit alone. Something over two hundred designs have been selected and are shown on the pages of this catalogue. In this group are ideal faces for every practical use in modern printing.

Where thousands of items are involved, the carrying of adequate stocks presents a complex problem to any manufacturer. Every effort will be made to keep at each of our countrywide Branches adequate stocks of the designs shown on the following pages. Older faces not shown in this book will continue to be available but possibly will require slightly longer time for delivery as stocks of them at Branches when exhausted may not be renewed.

No type specimen book can ever be complete in the strictest sense. As the printing proceeds, new designs enter the early stages of preparation. Alphabets from leading artists and from our own pre-eminent staff of designers are being continually studied in the effort to anticipate style trends. Designing of new type faces has a strong promotional value for the printer as well as the type founder because the enormous use of printed matter of every kind requires variety of style. If a printer of today is to retain his clients he must be able to develop typographically the ideas of the artist and layout man.

Decorative material will be treated in a later book. This catalogue shows only type faces and very little effort has been made to show the use of the type in display. This book is intended as an exhibit of type styles rather than as a suggestion of how to use them. Supplementary specimens will be issued from time to time showing individual types and suitable combinations. This will permit greater latitude in layout and kinds of display than if they were confined to the limitations of a book page. Change is inherent in progress and every effort will be made to have these separate specimens reflect the most recent trends while at all times maintaining the highest typographic standards.

PROGRESS IN TYPE FOUNDING

IN THE last few years three distinct improvements have become standard practice. Large sizes of practically all new faces are now cast on two sizes of body. In 144 point, for instance, all characters that extend below the line are being made on 144 point and the others on 120 point. This makes possible close setting of lines of caps and materially reduces the weight and therefore the price of the font. Sizes made this way are designated as 144/120.

ANGLE BODY

THE TROUBLESOME question of kerns has been solved by the introduction of Angle Body Italics. By this greatly improved method sizes 24 point and larger are cast on a sloping body practically eliminating the overhangs that break frequently when the form is being stereotyped or while it is on the press. Angle Body is as easy to set as type cast in regular molds. It is the modern way of making italic type.

RECESSED CHARACTERS

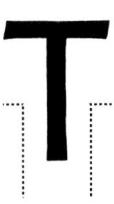

ONE OR MORE of the capital letters A, F, L, P, T, V, W and Y cast with body recessed are now included in fonts of the larger sizes of many recent designs. These letters will fit closely together without the unsightly white spaces that otherwise would be unavoidable and will work easily with the regular type without any special spacing. Casting the type with recesses makes unnecessary the expensive "cutting in" of type in the composing room and is a feature that has been much appreciated by the printers.

New Type Faces in Preparation

As this book is being completed a group of New Type Faces of great interest is in preparation. In the limited space below we give a few lines to show the varied character of these designs. Specimens to be issued later will exhibit them completely and in all sizes

TOWER—36 Point

Tall and compact, Tower gives to printing the modern touch of vertical lines which adapts it to many uses. It makes possible the saying of a great deal clearly and smartly in a small space. The lack of hair lines insures durability and the design combines in pleasing form the qualities of the sans serif and the square serif letters now so greatly in demand.

Bernhard Tango

Lucian Bernhard, who designed for us this pleasing type face, has drawn it with a flowing grace rarely equalled in a cursive letter. Wisely used, it will carry a message of refinement and quality by the sure force of its own beauty. A large number of sizes will be available together with a special set of Swash Capitals cast on larger bodies which will adapt this face to extensive use in modern display.

Othello

Many type designs of today that have been received with wide acclaim as something new under the sun are scarcely more than adaptations from those of previous generations. In the "First Collective Specimen Book" of the American Type Founders Company, issued in 1895, may be traced the parentage of many of the "new" square serif and sans serif letters. Shorn of superfluous ornamentation to make it conform to the tastes of today, Othello is named for and modeled on a stalwart letter shown in our catalogue of forty years ago. Many distinguished users of type who have seen preliminary proofs believe Othello fills a need for heavy mass effects. It is full of color and easy to read.

American Backslant

Following the natural slope of handwriting, habit seems to have tied letter design permanently to a right-hand slope for italics. Very striking novelties in design may be secured by reversing the direction of the lines. American Backslant is offered as an aid to variety in modern type display. This interesting face makes possible new effects without resort to the eccentricity in layout so frequently disastrous to legibility. The unfamiliar slope of the lettering arrests the eye and compels immediate attention.

Benton

Like the beauty of old lace, the attractiveness of a type page depends upon a combination of many separate designs, each one beautiful in itself but without individual oddities to detract from the mass effect. Benton is the result of a long study of the best of the classical types. It retains many of the notable characteristics of both the Oldstyle and the Modern and produces a page which is readable and brilliant without being dazzling. This paragraph is 10 Point Benton.

SHADOW

Tonal effects secured by the use of outline types are necessary to the working out of certain design problems that are common in present-day printing. The ATF "Shadow," with its suggestion of a Gothic letter against a heavy background, is eminently fitted for this purpose. It has the three dimensional appearance so much in demand.

Romany Series

72 Point 3A 5a

Delightfully Explored

60 Point 3A 5a

Novelty Snapshot Contest Surprised Judges

48 Point 4A 8a

Analyzed Reports Delight Mayor

36 Point 5A 10a

Specialty Dancer Presented Foreign Style Magnificently

24 Point 7A 14a

Metropolitan Society Impress Independent Campaign Arranges Program

Additional sizes: 12, 14 and 18 Point are in preparation

Characters in Complete Font

A A B C D E
F G H I J K
L M N O P Q
R S T U V W
X Y Z & $ 1 2
3 4 5 6 7 8 9 0
a b c d e f g h
i j k l m n o p q
r s t u v w x y z
. , - ` ' : ; ! ?

Pericles Series

60 Point 3 A

PERFUMES $123456 7890

48 Point 4 A

NEW DESIGN

36 Point 6 A

MODERN & RICH
★$1234567890★

24 Point 9 A

RIVERSIDE PARK STUDIOS
ADVERTISING, ETC.

18 Point 12 A

NUMBER ONE NORMANDY DRIVE
„GARDEN SPOT OF ERIE"

Recessed Characters, where made, included in fonts 24 Point and larger

A F L P T V W Y

TYPE PERICLES

DESIGNED BY

ROBERT FOSTER

MCMXXXIV

The
American Type Founders
present the new classic type which
combines the purity of the Greek with
the virility of the modern

Pericles used with 10 Point Bernhard Gothic Medium

CHARACTERS IN COMPLETE FONT

A B C D E F G H I J K L M N O P Q R R S T U V
W X Y Z & $ 1 2 3 4 5 6 7 8 9 0 . , = ' „ " : ; ! ? · ς ★

Piranesi Series

72 Point 3A 4a
Delightfully Explained

60 Point 4A 6a
Exhibited Colorful Lingerie

48 Point 5A 8a
Intelligently Displays Composition

42 Point 5A 9a
Opened Modern Apartment Buildings

36 Point 6A 11a
Most Exclusive Homes Exquisitely Decorated

30 Point 7A 14a
QUIET PLACE
Serene Neighbors

24 Point 10A 20a
RAREST DESIGN
Beautiful monograms
and brochures shown

18 Point 15A 30a
INTRODUCES MODEL
Prominent European stylist
desired pleasing compliment

Characters in Complete Font

A B C D E F G H
I J K L M N O P
Q R S T U V W
X Y Z & $ 1 2 3
4 5 6 7 8 9 0
a b c d e f g h i
j k l m n o p q r
s t u v w x y z &
. , - ' ' : ; ! ?

The following characters, from 24 Point to 72 Point, are cast recessed

A F L P T V W Y

---

14 Point 22A 44a
QUAINTEST DESCRIPTION
Celebrated university teacher held
big audience of youths spellbound

12 Point 25A 50a
EXTOLS SOUTHERN CUSTOMS
Northern paper manufacturer arrived to
attend convention and golf tournaments

10 Point 28A 56a
PICTURESQUE HIGHLAND LAKES
Invigorating atmosphere and natural beauty
enjoyed by summer vacationists and tourists

8 Point 30A 60a
BECOMING FRENCH COSTUME ADMIRED
Distinguished woman wore exquisitely tailored creation
at the recent opening charity dance and entertainment

★ *Piranesi Italic*

48 Point 5A 13a

Modernistic Style Delighted Teachers
Bright Industrial Outlook

42 Point 6A 15a

Radical Effects Featured Jewelry Display
Noteworthy Daily Supplement

36 Point 6A 15a

Hieroglyphics Confounded Babylonish Expedition
Archaeologist Jubilantly Continued

30 Point 7A 18a

Balmy Atmosphere
Exquisite Laces

24 Point 9A 23a

Society Holds Banquet
Optimistic Governor
Picturesque Landscape

18 Point 15A 38a

Renders Interesting Rhapsody
Most Charming Setting
Displayed Beautiful Lingerie

Characters in Complete Font

A B C D E F G
H I J K L M N
O P Q R S T U
V W X Y Z & $
1 2 3 4 5 6 7 8 9 0
a b c d e f g h i j
k l m n o p q r s t
u v w x y z ct st
. , - ' ' : ; ! ?

Plain Capitals are fonted separately and furnished only when specially ordered

A B C D E F G
H I J K L M N
O P Q R S T U
V W X Y Z &

The following characters, from 24 Point to 72 Point, are cast recessed

A F L P T V W Y

★ 24 to 48 Point cast on Angle Body

14 Point 21A 52a

Beautiful Oriental Flowers Blooming
Enjoys Rhythmic Syncopation
Exquisite Chamber Music Rendered

12 Point 24A 60a

Lawyer Banqueted Cosmopolitan Sportsman
Thrilling Story Amazed Listeners
Noted Professor Introduced English Envoy

10 Point 27A 68a

Splendid Display Makes Countryside Attractive
Magnificent Japanese Cherry Trees
Extraordinary Typographic Specimens Displayed
Exceptionally Delightful Spring Celebration

8 Point 30A 75a

Sport Camps Attract Many Young People Every Summer
Enjoyed Holidays Amid Loftiest Mountains
Surrounded by Wonderful Lakes and Numerous Brooks
Outdoor Activities Bring Healthful Enjoyment

:[13]:

Piranesi Bold

72 Point 3A 4a

FINER Designs 29

60 Point 4A 5a

80 Splendid ORDERS

48 Point 4A 7a

LEASED New Building 45

42 Point 4A 7a

31 Displayed Finest LINGERIE

36 Point 4A 9a

MODERN Refrigerators Installed 76

30 Point 5A 10a

FINE GEMS
Elegant Jewel

24 Point 7A 13a

NICE DESIGN
Splendid Gowns

18 Point 11A 21a

PLEASING SCENE
Exquisite Atmosphere

14 Point 14A 28a

QUAINT RESIDENCES
Picturesque Italian Garden

Characters in Complete Font

A B C D E F G H I J
K L M N O P Q R S
T U V W X Y Z &
$ 1 2 3 4 5 6 7 8 9 0
a b c d e f g h i j k l
m n o p q r s t u v w
x y z . , - ' ' : ; ! ?

The following characters, from 24 Point to 72 Point, are cast recessed

A F L P T V W Y

Lining Figures furnished in separate fonts or will be supplied in the regular fonts instead of Old-style Figures when so specified on the order

$ 1 2 3 4 5 6 7 8 9 0

12 Point 17A 34a

INTERESTING PREVIEWS
Noted college professor held big
audience of students spellbound

10 Point 19A 38a

PRAISED NOVEL MACHINES
Eastern shoe manufacturer attended
convention and electrical expositions

8 Point 22A 44a

PICTURESQUE MOUNTAIN HOMES
Marvelous atmosphere and the natural beauty
of this rugged and peaceful valley were greatly
enjoyed by summer vacationists and campers

6 Point 25A 50a

BECOMING FRENCH COSTUME ADMIRED
Eminent woman displayed exquisitely tailored creation
and was admired by the large crowd that attended the
very recent gigantic theatrical dance and entertainment

Piranesi Bold Italic

The Elegance of Burnished Silver

To the finely wrought characters of Piranesi Bold there has been added an Italic with a series of Beautiful Swash Capitals reminiscent of the engraved letters of the 18th Century. Used with other types or alone it has a delicacy and brilliance that speaks of the chaste and polished elegance of fine silver. Piranesi Bold Italic will be made in thirteen sizes

★ 42 Point 4A 7a

Splendid Modern Design Exhibited Wonderful Color Arrangement

★ 36 Point 4A 8a

Delightful Singing Noted Thespian

★ 30 Point 4A 9a

Fine Oriental Tapestry Exquisitely Draped

★ 24 Point 5A 13a

Beautiful Lingerie Display Foreign Gown Colorful

18 Point 9A 22a

Extraordinary Celebrities Congregated Advanced Program Given

CHARACTERS IN COMPLETE FONT

A B C D E F G H I
J K L M N O P Q R
S T U V W X Y Z &
$ 1 2 3 4 5 6 7 8 9 0
a b c d e f g h i j k l m
n o p q r s t u v w x
y z ct st . , - ' ' : ; ! ?

Plain Capitals are fonted separately and furnished only when specially ordered

A B C D E F G H I
J K L M N O P Q R
S T U V W X Y Z &

★ 24 to 72 Point cast on Angle Body

Park Avenue

72 Point — 3A 6a

Gentlefolks

Point — 4A 7a

Beauty Shop

48 Point — 5A 10a

College Diplomas

42 Point — 6A 11a

Magnificent Gown

36 Point — 6A 11a

Wonderful Reception

CHARACTERS IN COMPLETE FONT

A B C D E F G H
I J K L M N O P Q
R S T U V W X Y
Z & $ 1 2 3 4 5 6 7 8 9 0
a b c d e f g h i j k l m n o p q r s
t u v w x y z rs er es . , - ' ' : ; ! ?

Sizes 24 Point and larger cast on Angle Body

Hezlan

Tailors
TO
Gentlemen

HEZLAN *has become an accepted standard by which good clothing is judged. Call and see us.*

BUSINESS SUITS:
Ready for wear . . $85

EIGHTH and MARKET STREETS

PARK AVENUE BERNHARD BOOKLET 10 POINT OLD ENGLISH BORDER NO. 44

30 Point — 7A 13a

Smart Fabrics
Beautiful Spring Gown

24 Point — 9A 18a

Landscapes Beautiful
Fragrant Narcissus Perfume

18 Point — 11A 23a

Sixteenth Annual Exhibit
Very Distinguished Portrait Painter

14 Point — 15A 32a

Enthusiastic Admirers Greatly Pleased
Mid-Season Promenade of Artists' Models

12 Point — 18A 36a

American Type Designs Bring Results
Good Typography Will Stimulate Your Business

:[16]:

Bodoni Open

48 Point 4A 7a

Girl Bought ANTIQUES

36 Point 5A 10a

ERECTS MODERN BUILDING
Many Refinements Incorporated

30 Point 6A 10a

PURCHASE DESIRABLE RECORDS
Bank Syndicate Employs New Method

24 Point 6A 13a

PHOTOGRAPHED MARVELOUS SCENERY
Returning Bold Adventurer Being Entertained

18 Point 10A 20a

HARMONIOUS DRAPERIES
Decorates Interior Beautifully

14 Point 15A 30a

RECEIVED BUILDING CONTRACTS
Japanese Dancer Opened New Theatre

12 Point 16A 32a

PICTURESQUE GRECIAN LANDSCAPES
Where one might imagine that mythological
kingdoms still existed and wood gods lived

10 Point 18A 36a

MANY PRINTERS ATTENDED ART EXHIBIT
Featuring many colorful modernistic specimens
which visiting rug manufacturer greatly admired

Characters in Complete Font

A B C D E F G H I
J K L M N O P Q R
S T U V W X Y Z &
$ 1 2 3 4 5 6 7 8 9 0
a b c d e f g h i j k
l m n o p q r s t u v
w x y z ff fi fl ffi ffl
. , - ' ' : ; ! ?

Bodoni Series

72 Point — 3 A 4 a
Sight

60 Point — 3 A 5 a
Maple

48 Point — 5 A 8 a
HEAPS
IS King

42 Point — 5 A 8 a
MONTH
July One

36 Point — 5 A 10 a
NUMBER
Third Rig

30 Point — 6 A 11 a
MOULDED
Letter Style

24 Point — 7 A 14 a
FINE HOUSE
Submit Design

---

18 Point — 11 A 22 a

USED TRACK
REPAIR finished
in time for race

14 Point — 16 A 31 a

REMARKS MADE
DEMANDS statement
about large concern

12 Point — 18 A 35 a

SECURE PRINTING
GETTING qualifications
considered reasonable
under good conditions

10 Point — 21 A 40 a

QUESTION METHODS
HAPPY childhood pranks
amused sedate professor
while visiting at nursery

8 Point — 23 A 46 a

EXHIBIT GREAT SUCCESS
LAVISH business arrangement
in western city amazed visitor
from the slumbering lakeside

6 Point — 28 A 52 a

PRINTERS GETTING BIG PROFITS
THOSE BUSINESS men who cannot secure
the elusive dollars nowadays are certain
some morning to awake and realize that
the outlook is rocky and very uncertain
unless they catch up with the crowd and
realize that efficiency means prosperity

Distinctly Feminine

WINTER AND SUMMER
STYLE CREATIONS DISPLAYED IN
LARGE VARIETY

∴

MADAME DUPONT
3519 Fifth Avenue

6 POINT TEAGUE BORDER NO. 616

Characters in Complete Font

A B C D E F G H I J K L M
N O P Q R S T U V W X Y Z
& $ 1 2 3 4 5 6 7 8 9 0 a b c
d e f g h i j k l m n o p q r s t u v
w x y z ff fi fl ffi ffl " " . , - ' ' : ; ! ?

SMALL CAPS from 6 to 18 Point, and Oldstyle Figures 1234567890
from 6 to 18 Point, are put up in separate fonts and
furnished only when specially ordered

BEAUTY

IN ADVERTISING
AND IN THE
THING ADVERTISED
IS A MOST
POTENTIAL AGENT
IN SECURING
RESULTS

READE PRINTING
COMPANY
Metropolitan Building
Chicago, Ill.

ITALIAN BAND

Bodoni Types
Have a singularly alert,
forceful look, and never
fail to add life and color
to the printed page

3 POINT BROCHURE BORDER NO. 15

THE
MODERN
Phonograph

FROM time immemorial
music has been the great
giver of delight. Nations
were born in the glory of
music. Dreams of kings
have been shattered and
kingdoms uprooted, yet
music has sprung from
the ruins and flourished.
Such is the fine spirit of
music which came to us
through ages, and which
the Modern Phonograph
reproduces so feelingly.

Bodoni Italic

Form
THE FINE FRUIT OF EVOLUTION

• Form is more than a convention, more than a precept, more than a practice; it is the mold in which ideas are most perfectly cast; it is not only a source of delight to the reader or the beholder, but it is invaluable discipline to the thinker, to the poet, to the painter, to the sculptor; it compels him to see, think, and express himself clearly.

ARTHUR JEROME EDDY

---

10 Point — 21 A 41 a
EXQUISITE SHOWING
Beautiful sculpture being commended by numerous art connoisseurs of repute

8 Point — 22 A 45 a
DISTINGUISHED HUNTER
Renowned professors arrange for an indefinite sojourn with explorer in uninhabited lands

6 Point — 28 A 55 a
GIVES INTERESTING EXHIBITION
Educational supervisor expressing great personal satisfaction with latest display of ornamental porcelain that proved of intense interest to home builders as well as craftsmen. Many unique and artistic specimens received favorable comment

18 Point — 11 A 22 a
HIDE DESIGN
Successful clerk wins promotion

14 Point — 16 A 31 a
RESTORES BOND
Prominent financier builds country home

12 Point — 18 A 33 a
EXPERT DIRECTOR
Musical society renews membership campaign under energetic leader

---

Characters in Complete Font

ABCDEFGHIJKLMN
OPQRSTUVWXYZ&$
1234567890abcdefghi
jklmnopqrstuvvwx
y z ff fi fl ffi ffl " " . , - ' ' : ; ! ?

Youth is the golden season of foolishness for which the wise would barter all their wisdom, the rich all their wealth, and call it a bargain, knowing the value of youth

VANITY INITIAL

---

72 Point — 3 A 4 a
Dark

60 Point — 3 A 5 a
Staple

48 Point — 4 A 8 a
Beyond

42 Point — 5 A 9 a
NORTH
Graceful

36 Point — 5 A 9 a
REBUKE
Huge Disc

30 Point — 6 A 11 a
BRIDGING
Kept Hotels

24 Point — 7 A 13 a
NOBLE BIRD
Each Numeral

Bodoni Book

48 Point   5 A 9 a
RESUMING
Bring Orders

42 Point   5 A 10 a
HARMONIZE
Simple Reason

36 Point   5 A 10 a
Nicely Decorated

30 Point   6 A 12 a
INTRODUCING
Graphical Sketch

24 Point   8 A 16 a
LARGE INDUSTRY
Neighbor Enterprises

18 Point   12 A 24 a
REPRODUCE MACHINE
ELIMINATES Unusual Defect

14 Point   17 A 33 a
BRIGHTER GREEN COLORING
HANDSOME Masterpieces Exhibited

GIAMBATTISTA BODONI

WHOSE WORKS SHED LUSTRE ON THE TYPOGRAPHIC ARTS

John Baptist Bodoni, whose works shed lustre on the typographic arts, was born in Italy in 1740, at Saluzzo, Piedmont, a town near the Alps, and learned the printing art in the small plant of his father in that same town. At eighteen he entered the printing house maintained in Rome by the Catholic church. It was here that the foundation of his later fame was laid.

12 Point   19 A 38 a
COMPOSITION OF DISCOURSE
ENGLISH must follow high standard of correct usage that is observed in the writings of the greatest authors

10 Point   22 A 42 a
THE MODERN SHORT SENTENCE
SENTENCE construction as our ancestors knew this term is not cause for unmixed satisfaction among present-time writers

8 Point   24 A 47 a
KEEPING OFFICE RECORD FACILITIES
MOST managers will find that keeping available record facilities means reducing the overhead expenses and the general increase of efficiency

6 Point   27 A 52 a
INDUSTRIAL DISEASE PREVENTION ENCOURAGED
THE FUNCTION and duty of employers to exercise not ordinary but extraordinary care to prevent occupational diseases is no longer an arguable or debatable question. Adequate means are available whereby the spread of disease can be prevented

---

Characters in Complete Font ABCDEFGHIJKLMNOPQRSTUVWXYZ&$1234567890
abcdefghijklmnopqrstuvwxyzfffiflffiffl""".,-'':;!?[]() Characters [] () not furnished with 24, 30, 36, 42 and 48 Point sizes. SMALL CAPS from 6 to 18 Point are put up in separate fonts and furnished only when specially ordered

Bodoni Book Italic

THE MODEL RADIO

A demonstration of the MODEL *at Oliver's Music Store... All this Easter week.*

THE MODEL RADIO COMPANY

G. ADAMS
2679 Lakeside Road
CHICAGO

36 Point · 6 A 9 a
BURDENSOME
Replace Original

30 Point · 6 A 12 a
DISENCUMBERED
Magnificent Country

24 Point · 8 A 15 a
SCIENTIFIC METHOD
Bright young prospectors introduced unique system

18 Point · 12 A 24 a
INTERESTED COURIER
Spent many delightful days visiting several uninhabited places whilst seeking health

14 Point · 16 A 33 a
WONDERING ASTRONOMERS
Observations reporting exceptional planetary activities cause populace many anxious moments during day

12 Point · 19 A 39 a
BUILDER CONSERVING GROUND
Delightfully attractive bungalows with spacious basement quarters. Contractors enthusiastic concerning housing people

10 Point · 22 A 43 a
NORTHERN SCENERY INSPIRING
Beautiful fields and enticing mountain trails become wonderfully attractive to sportsmen and vacationists during late summer and early fall. Nature provides numerous recreations during this season

8 Point · 24 A 46 a
INTERESTING DISCOVERY RECORDED
Pleasing as the origins of our alphabet are in their details, they are not any more fascinating or interesting than the incidents by which these results have been gained. The patient working out of the meaning of various rock inscriptions has occupied the attention of notable scholars

6 Point · 30 A 56 a
EDUCATION INCREASING MECHANICAL EFFICIENCY
Technical education has proved a propelling force in the march of progress in all parts of the world. It teaches modern business methods in a scientific manner, creates a spirit of self-reliance, and ensures a standard of proficiency that is to-day absolutely essential to the individual ambitious to become an efficient and skilled craftsman, and who expects to be really successful in life

KELLY AUTOMATICS

Kellys are the acknowledged "pacemakers of the pressroom," good for three shifts a day, week in and week out—taking the run-of-the-hook. Kellys give large production, accurate register and satisfactory profit-margin per dollar turnover. Kellys are swift, sure, practically continuous in operation and always dependable. The Kelly is "the press of no regrets," as thousands of printers in busy pressrooms the world over are demonstrating by daily experience.

AMERICAN TYPE FOUNDERS SALES CORPORATION

6 POINT AMERICAN BORDER NO. 616

Characters in Complete Font

A B C D E F G H I J K L M N O P Q R S T U V W X Y Z & $ 1 2 3 4 5 6 7 8 9 0
a b c d e f g h i j k l m n o p q r s t u v v w x y z ff fi fl ffi ffl " " . , - ' ' : ; ! ?

Bodoni Bold

144/120 Point — 3 A 4 a

Gill

120/96 Point — 3 A 4 a

Halt

96/84 Point — 3 A 4 a

Brisk

84/72 Point — 3 A 4 a

Single

72 Point — 3 A 4 a

Explain

60 Point — 3 A 5 a

Resource

48 Point — 4 A 8 a

Replied

42 Point — 4 A 8 a

Inquirer

36 Point — 5 A 8 a

MORTISE
Regulated

30 Point — 6 A 10 a

CONCERTS
Novel Music

24 Point — 6 A 12 a

INSTRUCTED
Large Deposits

18 Point — 10 A 20 a

FIND TRADE
Expert Advice

14 Point — 15 A 30 a

LOST INTEREST
Continues practice
of ignoring orders

12 Point — 17 A 32 a

SOLVES PROBLEM
Discuss new schemes
for promoting clerks

10 Point — 19 A 36 a

PRINTER INVENTIVE
Ambitious students will
display modern designs

8 Point — 21 A 41 a

AN INVALUABLE SERIES
Bodoni is adaptable to every
class of work one may select

6 Point — 25 A 49 a

TASTE IN SETTING COVER PAGE
Much of the real advertising value of
any book, pamphlet or brochure lies
in the type and quality of stock used

Characters in Complete Font

A B C D E F G H I
J K L M N O P Q R S
T U V W X Y Z & $
1 2 3 4 5 6 7 8 9 0
a b c d e f g h i j k
l m n o p q r s t u v
w x y z ff fi fl ffi ffl
. , - ' ' " " : ; ! ?

Bodoni Bold Italic

10 Point   18 A   35 a
DEFINED SENTENCE
Oakland supreme court judge delivered oration at leading country club

8 Point   19 A   38 a
INSURES AUTOMOBILES
Noted youthful underwriter inaugurates modern system for securing office efficiency

6 Point   24 A   48 a
PRODUCING MOTION PICTURES
Several manufacturing concerns take advantage of new advertising novelty by having motion picture films made showing methods of producing goods made by them. This plan creates civic pride and is also a business stimulant

---

FIRST PUBLIC
MUSICALE
GIVEN BY PUPILS OF
Hampden School
BALTIMORE

THE AUDITORIUM
Thursday Evening, May First
AT EIGHT-THIRTY

---

18 Point   10 A   19 a
ENTERPRISE
Maine scientist received medal

14 Point   15 A   29 a
HUGE BUILDING
Beautiful entrance lends enchantment

12 Point   16 A   31 a
FOREIGN ARTISTS
Danish military band rendered remarkable descriptive overtures

---

Characters in Complete Font

A B C D E F G H I J K L M N O P Q R S T U V W X Y Z & $ 1 2 3 4 5 6 7 8 9 0 a b c d e f g h i j k l m n o p q r s t u v w x y z ff fi fl ffi ffl " " . , - ' ' : ; ! ?

The Bodoni Family

BEAUTIFUL PRINTING is an educator, the same as is any art. *The thoughts of an author take on added values by reason of it.* The mind is always receptive in proportion as it is helped to comprehend the real meaning of the writer. Nothing will assist more than an effective page of nicely printed type in enabling readers to arrive at that meaning quickly and easily, and for this purpose the *members of the Bodoni Type Family are not surpassed for power and beauty.*

AMERICAN TYPE FOUNDERS SALES CORPORATION

---

72 Point   3 A   4 a
Nigh

60 Point   3 A   5 a
Effort

48 Point   4 A   6 a
MINDS

Striped

42 Point   4 A   8 a
HOMES

Diligent

36 Point   5 A   8 a
BOUNCE

Rejection

30 Point   6 A   12 a
NUMBERS

Proficiency

24 Point   6 A   12 a
HISTRIONIC

Fine Mansion

Ultra Bodoni

120/96 Point ★ 3A 4a
I Got

96/84 Point ★ 3A 4a
Sit IN

84/72 Point ★ 3A 4a
HE led

72 Point 3A 4a
Hit FIN

60 Point 3A 5a
INK slab

48 Point 3A 6a
First SALE

42 Point 3A 6a
BIG displays

★ 120, 96 and 84 Point, excepting the lowercase descenders and the cap Q and $, are cast on one size smaller body

36 Point 4A 7a
Right PEN

30 Point 5A 9a
MAGICIANS
Improve Act

24 Point 6A 11a
FINE TROPHY
Original Model

18 Point 9A 18a
NEW GOLF COURSE
Splendid Recreation

14 Point 13A 26a
LARGE BANK DEPOSITS
Checking Account Opened

12 Point 15A 30a
IMPROVE RADIO STATION
Arrange Splendid Programs

10 Point 19A 37a
PROCURED FINANCIAL BACKING
Merchant Receiving Liberal Credit

8 Point 20A 38a
ANTIQUATED MACHINERY REPLACED
Progressive Printer Reduced Expenses

6 Point 22A 40a
DILIGENT WORKMAN EARNED PROMOTION
Superintendent Recognized Executive Ability

Characters in Complete Font

A B C D E F G H I J K
L M N O P Q R S T U V
W X Y Z & $ 1 2 3 4 5
6 7 8 9 0 a b c d e f g h
i j k l m n o p q r s t u
v w x y z . , - ' ' : ; ! ?

Characters below are cast recessed in sizes from 30 to 120 Point
A F L P T V W Y

Ultra Bodoni Italic

14 Point 12 A 24 a
TELEVISION
Offers newest
transcription

12 Point 14 A 28 a
ENCOURAGES
Bright printer
exercised care

10 Point 17 A 34 a
NOVEL PICTURE
Austrian scholars
attend art exhibit

8 Point 19 A 38 a
FORTUNE HUNTER
Every business open
to future merchants

6 Point 20 A 40 a
STUDENT REWARDED
Creating original ideas
brings rapid promotion

36 Point 5 A 8 a
MIST
Eagle

30 Point 5 A 9 a
RINGS
Curfew

24 Point 6 A 10 a
EDITOR
Printing

18 Point 9 A 18 a
ORGANIZE
Community

72 Point 3 A 4 a
FAIR
Sting

60 Point 3 A 5 a
HONE
Dispel

48 Point 4 A 6 a
NAMES
Eagerly

42 Point 4 A 7 a
REFUND
Lost Ship

Characters in Complete Font

A B C D E F G H I J K
L M N O P Q R S T U
V W X Y Z &
$ 1 2 3 4 5 6 7 8 9 0
a b c d e f g h i j k l m
n o p q r s t u v w x y z
. , - ' ' : ; ! ?

Characters shown below are cast recessed in sizes from 30 to 72 Point

A F L P T V W Y

Complete angle body fonts, in sizes 24 to 72 Point, will come to you in parcels as follows:
Caps A to Z & — Lowercase a to z — Figures 1 to 0 $ £ — Points . , - ' ' : ; ! ?
6 to 18 Point sizes of Ultra Bodoni Italic are cast only on the regular straight body

Ultra Bodoni Extra Condensed

36 Point — 4A 8a

GREAT RIDER
Improve Style

30 Point — 6A 10a

EARLIER POEMS
Players Rejected

24 Point — 7A 15a

HONORED STUDENT
Receives High Honor

18 Point — 11A 22a

INCOME TAX REDEMPTION
Characteristic Experiments
Highest Grade Quality Foods

12 and 14 Point sizes in preparation

Characters in Complete Font

A B C D E F G
H I J K L M N
O P Q R S T U
V W X Y Z & $
1 2 3 4 5 6 7 8 9 0
a b c d e f g h i
j k l m n o p q r
s t u v w x y z
. , - ' ' : ; ! ?

72 Point — 3A 4a

8 NUMBER
Nice Circus

60 Point — 3A 5a

LONELY GIRL
Forms Bank 2

48 Point — 4A 5a

MODERN MINER
Respected Major

42 Point — 4A 6a

EXPLORED RIVERS
Nomadic Craftsmen
Beautiful Sculpture

Garamond Open

72 Point 4A 6a
BIG Specialty

60 Point 5A 7a
Dignified MAN

48 Point 6A 10a
BEST Clothing Sold

42 Point 6A 11a
Plays Excellent MUSIC

36 Point 7A 12a
OPEN Fine Haberdashery

30 Point 8A 14a
Exquisitely Designed GOWNS

24 Point 9A 19a
SUPERIOR Manufacturing Companies

18 Point 15A 29a
Delightful Performance Pleases Large AUDIENCE

Characters in Complete Font

A B C D E F G H I J K L M N O P Q R S
T U V W X Y Z & $ 1 2 3 4 5 6 7 8 9 0
a b c d e f g h i j k l m n o p q r s t u v w x y z
. , - ' ' : ; ! ?

Myriad cut velvets are now on exhibition in a large variety of the newest patterns & colors. They offer uncommon artistic advantages as well as durable qualities

GIFTS
FOR EVERY OCCASION
ARTICLES OF PROVEN MERIT
FRANK M. BRIGHTON
STATIONER

Plays

CLELAND BORDERS AND ORNAMENTS

Garamond Series

THESE ARTISTS WILL APPEAR

THE complete list of concert artists of the highest musical standing whose names are printed here will appear under our personal direction during the coming season. To those who are familiar with the exacting standards of this office and with its reputation in the past no further introduction than the mention of these renowned names will be necessary. Broxton concerts never disappoint

PLAYS

THOSE interested in the drama, classic and contemporary, are sure to find our stock of plays and works on dramatic literature and technique in all its branches unrivalled by that of any establishment in the city. We have specialized in books of this kind for many years and we offer our knowledge in this department to any who care to avail themselves of this service

ADAMS BOOK SHOP
136 HARCOURT STREET

CLELAND BORDER AND ORNAMENTS

---

72 Point   4 A   6 a
Marks

60 Point   5 A   7 a
Sighted

48 Point   6 A   10 a
Eruption

42 Point   6 A   11 a
MODELS Delighted

36 Point   7 A   12 a
INSPIRED Huge Clock

---

30 Point   8 A   14 a
RESIGNS
Helps Girl

24 Point   9 A   19 a
ROMANCE
Gay songbird returns home

18 Point   15 A   29 a
MONUMENTS
BEGUN memorial dedicated to hero

16 Point   17 A   34 a
ENTERPRISING
FRENCH musicians banqueted by club

14 Point   22 A   42 a
BRIGHT PERSONS
NUMBER among your virtues piety and truth

---

12 Point   24 A   47 a
INTRODUCING ENGLISH STYLE
SEVERAL importing establishments will show latest designs in silks and satins by foreign textile mills

10 Point   26 A   53 a
DILIGENCE WITH TRUTH IS GAINED
ROADS seldom are too wearisome or lengthy for one who advances

8 Point   26 A   53 a
BROAD INFLUENCE OF CORDIAL CHATS
REAL enjoyment is never derived from books until ideas thus obtained have been ventilated in sound conversation with others

6 Point   30 A   60 a
GREAT DANGER MAKES MEN MORE INFLEXIBLE
STRONG courage increases the chances of success oftentimes by creating opportunities and availing itself of them. It gives the strength and power to see and overcome hidden dangers

---

Characters in Complete Font

A B C D E F G H I J K L M N O P Q R S T U
V W X Y Z & $ 1 2 3 4 5 6 7 8 9 0 a b c d e f g h i j
k l m n o p q r s t u v w x y z ct st ff fi fl ffi ffl . , - ' ' : ; ! ?

SMALL CAPS from 6 to 18 Point are put up separately and furnished only when specially ordered
The following characters are fonted separately and furnished only when specially ordered

Garamond Word Terminals   Garamond Oldstyle Figures
Made in sizes 6 to 72 Point inclusive   Made in sizes 6 to 72 Point inclusive

a e m n t $ 1 2 3 4 5 6 7 8 9 0

Garamond Auxiliaries—Made in sizes 6 to 18 Point inclusive

ẹ @ % ℀ ℔ ℞ * § † ( ) [ ] ‖ [ ] ‡ - — —
1   2   3   4   5   6   7   8   9   10   11   12   13   14   15   16   17   18   19   20

¢ « » ⌢ ⌣
21   22   23   24   25

Braces are cast smaller than regular font bodies

Garamond Italic

12 Point — 24 A 48 a
SECURE DESIGN
FOR MAGAZINE
*Display of new styles
in typography proved
interesting exhibit at
recent shows. Student
exhibition very clever*

10 Point — 27 A 54 a
COLONIAL PERIOD
TIME OF PROGRESS
*Faithful workers should
evince a continual desire
to surpass their previous
efforts each eventful day*

8 Point — 30 A 60 a
FINER FRENCH TYPE
CAST BY GARAMOND
*The very neat work turned
out by printers centuries ago
astonishes people to-day and
especially if we consider the
equipment at their disposal*

6 Point — 32 A 63 a
CLEVER ORGANIZATION
SPECIALIZING METHODS
*Experience has greatly extended
and immensely broadened ideas
governing the management and
development of business. During
this productive period many fine
records of efficiency were reported*

24 Point — 10 A 19 a
DIGESTION
*Fine samples of
imported frocks
attract maiden*

18 Point — 16 A 28 a
MISCONSTRUE
*Conscientious effort
stamps the work of
true craftsmanship*

16 Point — 17 A 34 a
GOVERNMENTS
*Eastern organization
distributing religious
tracts through station*

14 Point — 22 A 44 a
NOBLE PRIVILEGE
*Pleasingly designed type
faces favorably influence
the cause of fine printing*

48 Point — 6 A 10 a
FORCED
Displayed

42 Point — 7 A 12 a
HOMING
New Basket

36 Point — 7 A 12 a
METHODS
Unfrequented

30 Point — 9 A 16 a
ECONOMIZE
*Color in printing
is very attractive*

HORS D'OEUVRES

CONSOMME ROYALE
au croutons

BROOK TROUT
Celery   Sauté Meuniere   Olives

RIS DE VEAU
Montebello
Petit Poids à l'etuvée

SELLE D'AGNEAU
Colbert

COEURS DE LAITU

COUPE GARAMOND
Petit Fours

CAFE

CLELAND ORNAMENTS

Characters in Complete Font

*A B C D E F G H I J K L M N O P Q R S T U V W X
Y Z & $ 1 2 3 4 5 6 7 8 9 0 a b c d e f g h i j k l m n o p q r s t
u v w x y z . , - ' ' : ; ! ?*

These characters are supplied with all regular italic fonts but not made on Angle Body
ff fi fl ffi ffl as is us ct fr ll sp St tt

The following characters are fonted separately and furnished only when specially ordered. They are not made on Angle Body.

Garamond Italic Swash Letters. Made from 6 to 48 Point.
A B C D E G L M N P R T Y &

Garamond Italic Word Terminals	Garamond Italic Quaint Characters	Garamond Italic Oldstyle Figures
a e m n t The	*ſſ ſſi ſl ſh ſi ſl ſp ſs ſt gy*	*1234567890$*
Made from 6 to 48 Point	Made from 6 to 24 Point only	Made from 6 to 48 Point

---

SPOTS

A SPOT OF COLOR
HERE AND THERE
WILL DOUBLE THE
VALUE OF PRINT-
ING · MANY NEW
AND BEAUTIFUL
ORNAMENTS ARE
DISPLAYED FOR
THE FIRST TIME IN
THIS CATALOGUE

6 POINT CLELAND BORDER NO. 631

IMPORTANT NOTICE

*Garamond Italic, 24 to 48 Point, is cast on
Angle Body without overhangs as well as on
regular body. Angle Body fonts are packed
in parcels as follows: Caps A to Z & — Lowercase a to z — Figures 1 to 0 $ £ — Points
. , - ' ' : ; ! ? — A liberal supply of Angle Body
Spaces furnished with fonts, and extra fonts
of spaces are obtainable.*

Garamond Bold

120 Point   3 A   4 a

Lyric

96 Point   3 A   4 a

Night

❧TYPOGRAPHY SENDS
KNOWLEDGE ABROAD
AS HEAVEN SENDS THE
RAIN · ONE FRUCTIFIES
THE SOIL, THE OTHER
MAN'S INTELLIGENCE

3 POINT TEAGUE BORDER NO. 322

84 Point   3 A   4 a

Staples

36 Point   6 A   11 a

Scriptural

16 Point   15 A   30 a

FINE AMBITION
Exhibits Machinery

30 Point   8 A   14 a

HISTORIC
Enthusiasm

14 Point   20 A   40 a

GREAT COUNTRY
Marvelous Landscape

12 Point   22 A   44 a

EXCELLENT GOWNS
Displayed Latest Model

72 Point   4 A   6 a

Gradual

24 Point   8 A   17 a

NEIGHBORS
Local Problem

10 Point   23 A   47 a

WEEKLY CONFERENCE
Housewives Outlined Plan

8 Point   26 A   50 a

AID SCIENTIFIC RESEARCH
Newest Devices and Inventions

18 Point   13 A   26 a

UNDERSTUDIES
Rapidly Improved

6 Point   28 A   54 a

PROGRESS IN PUBLIC SCHOOLS
Employing Many Printing Instructors

60 Point   5 A   7 a

Delighted

Characters in Complete Font

A B C D E F G H I J K L M N O P Q
R S T U V W X Y Z & $ 1 2 3 4 5 6
7 8 9 0 a b c d e f g h i j k l m n o p q
r s t u v w x y z ff fi fl ffi ffl . , - ' ' : ; ! ?

Oldstyle Figures
Made in sizes from 6 to 72 Point only. Fonted separately and furnished only when specially ordered

1 2 3 4 5 6 7 8 9 0 $

48 Point   5 A   9 a

Reimbursed

42 Point   6 A   10 a

Natural Form

:[30]:

Garamond Bold Italic

Characters in Complete Font

A B C D E F G H I J K L M N
O P Q R S T U V W X Y Z & $
1 2 3 4 5 6 7 8 9 0 a b c d e f g h i
j k l m n o p q r s t u v w x y z
. , - ' ' : ; ! ? { }

Swash Characters are included in all fonts 6 to 48 Point inclusive on regular body but are not included with Angle Body. They are also put up and sold in separate fonts in sizes 6 to 72 Point for both regular and Angle Body

A B C D E G L M N P R T Y & The
a e k m n t v w ff fi fl ffi ffl
as is us ct st ll sp tt fr gy ke

Garamond Bold Italic Lining Figures
Lining Figures furnished in separate fonts, or will be supplied in the regular fonts instead of Oldstyle Figures when so specified on the order

1 2 3 4 5 6 7 8 9 0 $

IMPORTANT NOTICE
Garamond Bold Italic, sizes 24 to 72 Point, cast on Angle Body without overhangs as well as on regular body. Angle Body fonts are packed in parcels as follows: Caps A to Z & – Lowercase a to z – Figures 1 to 0 $ £ – Points . , - ' ' : ; ! ? { } – Extra fonts of Angle Body Spaces are obtainable

---

72 Point 4A 6a
MINED
Brightest

60 Point 5A 7a
CHINESE
Mysterious

48 Point 6A 10a
HUNDRED
Special Night

42 Point 8A 12a
REGIMENTS
Dutch Tapestry

36 Point 8A 13a
EXPERIENCES
Unique Sensation

30 Point 8A 14a
ORDERED PRINTING
Newest Specimen 1234678

12 Point 23A 44a
NORTHERN CAMPS
Summer campers locate very fine fishing stream

10 Point 26A 50a
BEAUTIFUL SCENERY
Pretty mountain lakes and rivers afford great pleasure

8 Point 28A 56a
GOOD PLEASURE RESORT
Every summer many thousands visit this ideal vacation region

6 Point 30A 60a
MOST REFINED ATMOSPHERE
Countless lakes and rushing streams are the haunts of rural walking clubs

24 Point 10A 17a
MODERNIZE
Historic Record

18 Point 15A 28a
BLEAK GROTTO
Sublime Atmosphere

16 Point 16A 29a
INSPIRING DEEDS
Charming Decoration

14 Point 21A 37a
PICTURESQUE GLENS
Ohio Lakes Attract Many

Goudy Oldstyle

72 Point — 4A 6a
RICH
Spirits

60 Point — 5A 7a
MODE
Highest

48 Point — 5A 9a
NOTICE
Bright lad
leads class

42 Point — 5A 10a
DANCED
Celebrated
big holiday

36 Point — 6A 10a
HOME
Quaint

30 Point — 7A 14a
FOUND
Musician
delighted

24 Point — 8A 16a
NOTICES
Unfinished
framework

18 Point — 12A 23a
MECHANIC
GIVES experts
usual warning

14 Point — 17A 34a
EXPERIMENTS
BRIGHT magician spent much time unraveling tricks

12 Point — 21A 40a
GRAND PICTURE
RECENT photographs inspire many leading theatrical promoters

10 Point — 24A 48a
PERFECT SPECIMEN
SIMPLE design exhibited considered very artistic for modern typography

8 Point — 27A 54a
CUT-COST EQUIPMENT
MODERN cabinets containing leads and quads reduce labor costs considerably. Efficiency material creates large profits

6 Point — 29A 58a
STIMULATING PRODUCTION
PROGRESSIVE printers recognize the fact that economy lies in equipping their plants with modern materials and machinery. Now is the time, as every minute lost swells the pay roll

---

Characters in Complete Font

ABCDEFGHIJKLM
NOPQRSTUVWX
YZ & $ 1234567890
abcdefghijklmnopq
rstuvwxyz ff fi fl ffi ffl ct
¶ ℬ . , - ' : ; ! ?

SMALL CAPS from 6 to 18 Point, and Oldstyle Figures 1234567890 in all sizes, are put up in separate fonts and furnished only when specially ordered

---

1234567890

60 Point Figures set solid

:[32]:

The HENDERSON GALLERIES

63 Ardsley Court
NEW YORK

Exhibition & Sale

OF A COLLECTION OF

Old English Antiques

FROM THE

GENERAL WOLFE MANSION

Roxbury, Mass.

THIS fine collection is offered for sale at the order of Mr. John Blunt of London. It consists of the complete furnishings of the mansion including wood carvings, paintings, sculpture, vases, wrought iron and many heirlooms and highly prized rare books.

Sale starts
Friday, May 8th
at three o'clock, under the direction of
Mr. Edwin Blake

Goudy Italic

★72 Point   3A 5a
Enlist

★60 Point   4A 7a
Restful

★48 Point   5A 9a
Singular

★42 Point   6A 10a
CREAM
Graphites

Characters in Complete Font

A B C D E F
G G H I J J K
L M N O P Q
R S T T U V
W X Y Y Z
& $ 1 2 3 4 5 6
7 8 9 0 a b c d e
f g h i j k l m n o
p q r s t u v w x
y z ff fi fl ffi ffl
Qu ct . , - ' ' : ; ! ?

★New Sizes

---

36 Point   6A 11a
PRINTERS
Harpsichord

30 Point   7A 14a
MECHANIC
English Subject

24 Point   9A 18a
INTRODUCED
Quaint Inhabitant

18 Point   14A 28a
MODERN SYSTEM
Large Mercantile Firm

14 Point   19A 36a
EXCURSION STEAMER
Delights Numerous Children

12 Point   24A 46a
BEAUTIFUL COMPOSITION
Hartford Sculptor Awarded Medal

10 Point   26A 52a
PRINTING LEADING MANKIND
Michigan College Students Enlightened
Bright Scholars Learning Graphic Arts

8 Point   29A 58a
ENFORCES FIRE PREVENTION RULES
Drastic Regulations Ordered by Advisory Board
Brilliant Artist Receives Highest School Award
Sculptor Beginning Statue Destined For Library

6 Point   33A 65a
AMERICAN TYPE STYLES INCREASE BUSINESS
National Advertisers Demand Latest Typographic Designs
Magnificent Craftsmanship Delighted Cultured Audience
Interesting Specimens Inspired Printers Attending Exhibits

Goudy Catalogue

PATENT APPLIED FOR

72 Point — 3 A 5 a

Her KIN

60 Point — 3 A 5 a

NEW Cars

48 Point — 5 A 8 a

Quick MOVE

42 Point — 5 A 9 a

KINGS
Blandly

36 Point — 6 A 10 a

HERON
Madrigal

30 Point — 6 A 12 a

NUMBER
Rhapsodist

24 Point — 8 A 16 a

UNIFORMS
Philanthropy

18 Point — 13 A 24 a

BACKBONE
Monthly sales are expanding

14 Point — 17 A 34 a

LAST EDITION
The best books of fiction seldom fail to have good sales

12 Point — 20 A 39 a

PRODUCTS SOLD
Men are interested in all matters pertaining to their own business

TO THE RISING PROFESSIONAL MAN

NOW THAT YOUR EFFORTS SEEM TO BE CARRYING YOU FORWARD—THAT YOU ARE GETTING TO THE POSITION THAT WILL MEAN SUCCESS, YOU SHOULD KNOW HOW IMPORTANT IT IS FOR YOU TO CONSERVE AS MUCH AS POSSIBLE OF YOUR ENERGY. IF IT IS NEEDLESSLY SPENT IN CARS AND TRAINS, YOU WOULD DO WELL TO LOOK AT APARTMENTS WE HAVE VACANT IN GRACE COURT WEST TWELFTH STREET IN THE HEART OF THE BUSINESS DISTRICT OF NEW YORK

10 Point — 23 A 44 a

SELECTED CLERK
Expensive handmade papers are much used at the present time for the finest sort of work

8 Point — 26 A 51 a

EXCITING QUESTION
Newsprint is consumed in enormous amounts by the city newspapers especially for the Sunday editions of several bulky supplements

6 Point — 30 A 60 a

COMPLICATED MACHINES
The wood pulp used for making newsprint contains the original impurities present in the wood; that is why our newspapers turn quite yellow and become brittle

Characters in Complete Font

ABCDEFGHIJKLM
NOPQRSTUVWX
YZ&$1234567890ab
cdefghijklmnopqrst
uvwxyzffffiflffiffl.,-':;!?

VANITY BEAUTY SALON

Ralston Road, near Sandringham Park

A shop of rare charm and distinction that caters only to women of discriminating taste and refined judgment

Telephone for an Appointment

Now under the exclusive control of Mme. Bonelle

12 POINT TEAGUE BORDER NO. 1205 ROTERS ILLUSTRATOR NO. 10846

Goudy Catalogue Italic

PATENT APPLIED FOR

10 Point — 24 A 48 a
SENSIBLE ACTION
Only few are qualified
to shine in society; but
it is possible for almost
all men to be agreeable

18 Point — 13 A 24 a
FRANCHISE
Grand opening
for trade school

72 Point — 3 A 5 a
Right End

8 Point — 26 A 51 a
PROFIT BY MISTAKES
Experience is a safe light to
walk by and he is not a rash
man who expects to succeed
in future by the same means
that helped him in days past

14 Point — 16 A 32 a
HARMONIOUS
Enjoyable musical
selections heard by
means of the radio

60 Point — 3 A 5 a
Society Girls

6 Point — 30 A 60 a
MEDICAL COURSES LIKED
Reading is to our minds the same
as exercise is to our bodies. By the
one, health is greatly invigorated
and preserved; by the other, virtue
which is the health of the mind is
kept alive and tenderly cherished

12 Point — 22 A 42 a
CENTER MARGIN
Rare manuscripts and
books often yield ideas
that are very practical

48 Point — 5 A 9 a
One Certificate

Characters in Complete Font

A B C D E F G H I J
K L M N O P Q R
S T U V W X Y Z &
1 2 3 4 5 6 7 8 9 0 $
a b c d e f g h i j k l m n
o p q r s t u v w x y z
ff fi fl ffi ffl ct . , - ' ' : ; ! ?

DURING DECEMBER

AN EXHIBITION
~OF~
PAINTINGS

WATER COLORS
ETCHINGS AND DRAWINGS OF
INTERIORS

ROMANO STUDIO

---

42 Point — 6 A 10 a
HOME
Unfilial

36 Point — 6 A 11 a
EDITOR
Breakfast

30 Point — 7 A 14 a
DUBIOUS
Melancholy

24 Point — 8 A 16 a
UNSPOKEN
Phantom Ship

Special consideration has been given to register, durability, rigidity of impression, easy running qualities, speed and distribution, in KELLY AUTOMATIC PRESS construction. No effort is spared to produce a high-grade dependable printing unit to meet conditions as they are found in the up-to-date, progressive printing office.

Goudy Bold

★120 Point — 3 A 4 a
HE is

★96 Point — 3 A 4 a
Dry IT

★84 Point — 3 A 4 a
NO hat

72 Point — 3 A 4 a
Dial

60 Point — 3 A 5 a
Sight

48 Point — 4 A 8 a
Baked

42 Point — 5 A 9 a
Ringlet

36 Point — 5 A 10 a
Epitaphs

30 Point — 6 A 12 a
PRINTS Booklet

24 Point — 8 A 14 a
Brought SPECIMEN

18 Point — 12 A 23 a
NEIGHBOR
Help another
general cause

14 Point — 17 A 32 a
DESIGN BOND
Exhibit beautiful
document before
critical audiences

12 Point — 20 A 38 a
HIGH POSITIONS
Commission desired
doctors having large
influential following

10 Point — 23 A 44 a
EXPERTS DECIDE
Gathering in lyceum
creates development
regarding imports of
foreign merchandise

8 Point — 25 A 48 a
MAKES FINAL PLANS
Passenger resumes travel
after long and wearisome
months spent in locating
wonderful marble quarry
for building corporations

6 Point — 29 A 57 a
THRONGED MAIN STREET
Downpour of rain disastrously
interferes with joyous carnival
and celebration that had drawn
immense crowds. After waiting
considerable time the majority
went to their respective homes

Characters in Complete Font

ABCDEF
GHIJKL
MNOPQ
RSTUV
WXYZ&
$123456
7890abc
defghijkl
mnopqrs
tuvwxyz
ff fi fl ffi ffl
. , - ' ' : ; ! ?

★New Sizes

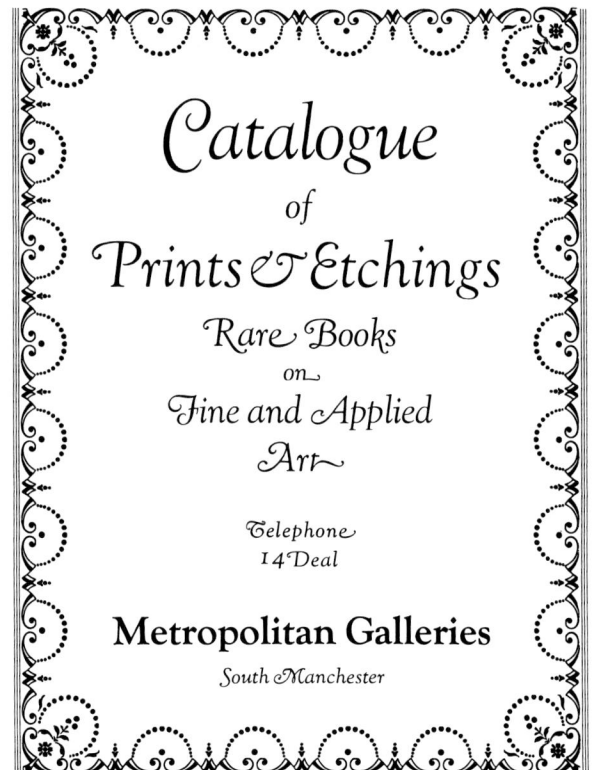

Catalogue
of
Prints & Etchings
Rare Books
on
Fine and Applied
Art

Telephone
14 Deal

Metropolitan Galleries
South Manchester

TEAGUE BORDERS

Goudy Bold Italic

NON-KERNING

10 Point — 23 A 45 a
TENTH LECTURE
Most knowing judges
continue granting the
youth letters praising
comprehensive theme

8 Point — 26 A 52 a
ENTHUSE BUILDERS
Prosperous manufacturer
recently notified employes
who contemplate erecting
houses immediately of his
indiscriminate assistance

6 Point — 29 A 58 a
FINEST ENTRANCE GATE
The thought commonly coupled
with a gate is its intention as a
barrier stopping the entrance of
unwelcomed guests, yet in these
days a flowery garden entrance
may attract rather than restrict

18 Point — 12 A 23 a
CONQUERS
Several tender
vines matured

14 Point — 17 A 34 a
NICE SERVICE
Prominent mayor
from remote town
craves ceremonies

12 Point — 21 A 41 a
ENJOY OUTINGS
Kindergarten lecture
receives compliments
from grateful patron

72 Point
Big RUN

60 Point — 3 A 5 a
DIGS Hole

48 Point — 5 A 8 a
Find UNCLE

❦ 37 ❦

42 Point — 5 A 9 a
CHIDE
Helpful

36 Point — 6 A 10 a
DINERS
Engulfed

30 Point — 7 A 12 a
FURNISH
Neat Styles

24 Point — 3 A 16 a
MUNCHED
Printer aided
deaf students

AMERICAN
CUT-COST SYSTEM
OF PRINTING PLANT
EQUIPMENT

◆◇◆

Time-Saving and Space-Saving

American Cut-Cost Equipments are made in
both steel and wood

18 POINT OLD ENGLISH BORDER NO. 40

Characters in Complete Font

ABCDEFGGHIJKLMNOPQRSTU
VWXYZ&$1234567890abcdefghi
jklmnopqrstuvwxyz ff fi fl ffi ffl ct .,-'':;!?

Goudy Handtooled

PATENT APPLIED FOR

★120 Point — 3 A 4 a

IS flat

★96 Point — 3 A 4 a

Set UP

★84 Point — 3 A 4 a

BIG file

72 Point — 3 A 4 a

Dial

60 Point — 3 A 5 a

Sight

48 Point — 4 A 8 a

Epoch

42 Point — 5 A 9 a

Hybrid

36 Point — 5 A 10 a

Epitaphs

30 Point — 6 A 12 a

RECIPE
Nymphs
soon fled

24 Point — 8 A 14 a

HOCKEY
Ice skating
quite early

18 Point — 12 A 23 a

NEIGHBOR
Helpful hints
about buying

GOUDY TYPE FACES

A Showing of Popular Goudy Types

CONFIDENCE

FOR YEARS WE HAVE
HELD THE COMPLETE
CONFIDENCE OF OUR
PATRONS AND HAVE
HELPED THEM SOLVE
PRINTING PROBLEMS
THAT ARE ACCEPTED
AS PART OF OUR JOB

ART PRESS

North Hampton
Maine

14 Point — 17 A 32 a

BURLESQUE
European light
opera with fine
music featured
first showing of
imported plays

12 Point — 20 A 38 a

INDEPENDENT
Remote little isles
given opportunity
to obtain freedom
from foreign king

10 Point — 23 A 44 a

MEN GRADUATE
Students from many
states complete their
courses and graduate
from popular college

Characters in Complete Font

A B C D E F
G H I J K L
M N O P Q
R S T U V
W X Y Z &
$ 1 2 3 4 5 6 7
8 9 0 a b c d e
f g h i j k l m
n o p q r s t u
v w x y z ff fi fl
ffi ffl . , - ' : ; ! ?

★New Sizes

Goudy Handtooled Italic

PATENT APPLIED FOR

14 Point — 17 A 34 a
MODERNIZE
*Improved ways
of manufacture
being employed*

12 Point — 21 A 41 a
SUBSCRIPTION
*Notable magazine
increasing number
of pages because of
additional interest*

10 Point — 23 A 45 a
HUNTING HORSE
*Southern equestrians
display unusual skill
in handling imported
steeds in circus arena*

30 Point — 7 A 12 a
BRAND
Naughty

24 Point — 8 A 16 a
GNOMES
*Responded
after lunch*

18 Point — 12 A 23 a
DECEMBER
*Quaint dance
was approved*

72 Point — 3 A 4 a
HOUSE
Big Shop

60 Point — 3 A 5 a
REFINES
Insure Life

48 Point — 5 A 8 a
MINE
Judges

42 Point — 5 A 9 a
KINGS
Spirited

36 Point — 6 A 10 a
DRONE
Northern

Characters in Complete Font

A B C D E F
G H I J K L
M N O P Q
R S T U V W
X Y Z & $
1 2 3 4 5 6 7 8 9 0
a b c d e f g h
i j k l m n o p q
r s t u v w x y
z ff fi fl ffi ffl ct
. , - ' ' : ; ! ?

GOUDY HANDTOOLED
ITALIC
REGULARLY USED
IN DISPLAY
EFFECTIVELY IDENTIFIES
& CALLS ATTENTION
TO THE
MESSAGE OF THE
ADVERTISER

ABCDEFGHIJKLMNOPQRST
UVWXYZ
abcdefghijklmnopqrstuvwxyz
$1234567890

Goudy Cursive

★72 Point   3A 5a

Intelligent Question

★60 Point   4A 7a

Symphonic Orchestras

★48 Point   5A 9a

Locate Mysterious Explorer

★42 Point   6A 10a

Foreign Business Shows Growth

36 Point   6A 11a

Methodical

30 Point   7A 14a

Quaint Etching

24 Point   9A 18a

Anniversary Sales

18 Point   14A 28a

Splendid Achievement

14 Point   19A 36a

Marvelous Jewels Displayed

12 Point   24A 46a

Gigantic Opportunities Everywhere

10 Point   26A 52a

Distinguished Orator Scores Pessimists

8 Point   29A 58a

Beautiful Gardens Blossoming With Flowers

6 Point   33A 65a

Prominent Merchants Advocate Universal Cooperation

Characters in Complete Font

A A B C D E F G H I J J
K K L M N N N O P Q R R
S T U U W X Y Z QU Qu
Th & $ 1 2 3 4 5 6 7 8 9 0
a b c d e f g g h i j k k l
m m n n o p q r s t u
v v w x y z ff fi fl ffi ffl
qu ct st ſs . , - ' ' : ; ! ? ~ ~ ~

The capital letters shown below are cast in special molds which provide a lug or projecting body that forms a partial mortise for the overhanging part of the letter and makes the overhang as strong as the body itself. The introduction of these lugs on the type necessitates the casting of lower-case vowels on a smaller body than that of the capitals, in order that the lines may be easily justified. These letters are furnished with all fonts from 18 to 72 Point

K N N R Z a e i o u

Character QU not made in 42, 48, 60 and 72 Point sizes

★ New Sizes

Goudytype Series

72 Point 3A 4a
GEMS
Richly

60 Point 3A 5a
MUSIC
Original

48 Point 4A 7a
FICTION
New Story

42 Point 5A 8a
EXHIBITS
Modernistic
type designs

36 Point 5A 9a
HIDES
Expired

30 Point 6A 10a
MOTOR
Specialize

24 Point 7A 13a
POSITIVE
Right Kind

18 Point 10A 20a
CONGENIAL
Lodge member
inspired guests

14 Point 15A 31a
FINE CITIZENS
Splendid tribute to
aged public official

12 Point 17A 35a
GRAND SHOWING
Big municipal pageant
thrills large gatherings

10 Point 20A 40a
GROWING SUBURBS
Local contracting concern
erecting marble structures
of early Swiss architecture

8 Point 22A 45a
PICTURESQUE SCENERY
Our many national parks offer
visitors views of much interest
and unusual beauty and charm

6 Point 25A 52a
ADVERTISERS PLEASE NOTICE
This new design should interest those
who desire a fresh, out-of-the-ordinary
touch in their printing and advertising

Characters in Complete Font

A A B B C D D E F
G H H I J K L M M
N N O P P Q R R S
T T U V W X Y Y Z &
$ 1 2 3 4 5 6 7 8 9 0
a b c d e f g h i j k l m
n o p q r s t u v w x y z
ff fi fl ffi ffl ct . , - ' ' : ; ! ?

Bernhard Gothic Medium

Copyright, 1929, by Lucian Bernhard
Manufactured under Special License

★144/120 Point — 3A 4a

IF Set

★120/96 Point — 3A 4a

Ink ON

★96/84 Point — 3A 4a

Kite

★84/72 Point — 3A 4a

Melt

72 Point — 3A 4a

Slope

60 Point — 3A 5a

Drakes

★ All characters, excepting descenders, cast on the smaller size body.

48 Point — 4A 6a

Speaker

42 Point — 4A 7a

Resigning

36 Point — 5A 9a

GROWER
Buys Home

30 Point — 6A 12a

MERINGUE
Quieted Boys

24 Point — 8A 16a

FINE DESIGN
Helped Student

18 Point — 12A 24a

INTERESTING TOPIC
enjoyable speaker quoted
some contemporary poets

14 Point — 20A 40a

PRAISES MODERN TREND
distinguished advertising expert
eloquently defended modernism

12 Point — 24A 48a

USING TRADITIONAL METHOD
finest pottery and fabrics are produced
successfully upon old looms and wheels

10 Point — 26A 52a

PRODUCING SUPERFINE PRINTING
enterprising publishing house with splendid
facilities was awarded some large contracts

8 Point — 28A 56a

ADVERTISING TECHNIQUE SHOWS CHANGE
economical business methods demand that publishers
produce magazines with intelligently arranged formats

6 Point — 32A 64a

THINKING STRAIGHT BECOMES MOST NECESSARY
exacting conditions that nowadays confront executives require
that the technique of advertising and marketing be understood

Characters in Complete Font

A B C D E F G H I J
K L M N O P Q R S T
U V W X Y Z & $ $
1 2 3 4 5 6 7 8 9 0
a b c d e f g h i j k l m
n o p q r s t u v w x y z
. , - ' ' : ; ! ? · ❖

Character $ not made in 6, 8 and 10 Point
Characters Th th not made for 84, 96, 120 and 144 Point
The following characters, from 30 to 144 Point, are cast recessed
A F L P T V W Y

Special Characters fonted separately and furnished on order only
E K S Th th a e k r s u z

Lining Figures furnished in separate fonts or will be supplied in the regular fonts instead of Oldstyle Figures when so specified on the order

$ 1 2 3 4 5 6 7 8 9 0

Bernhard Gothic Medium Italic

Copyright, 1930, by Lucian Bernhard
Manufactured under Special License.

72 Point 3A 4a

BIG night

60 Point 3A 5a

holiday JOY

48 Point 4A 7a

FINE shipmate

42 Point 4A 8a

tempting MENU

36 Point 5A 10a

OLDEST Neighbors

30 Point 6A 12a

Stenographers REPORT

24 Point 8A 15a

PRINTED furniture catalogue

IMPORTANT NOTICE

Bernhard Gothic Medium Italic, sizes 24 to 72 Point, is cast on Angle Body without overhangs. Angle Body fonts are packed in parcels as follows: Caps A to Z &— Lowercase a to z—Figures 1 to 0 $ £— Points . , - ' ' : ; ! ?—A liberal supply of Angle Body Spaces furnished with fonts and extra fonts of spaces are obtainable

18 Point 12A 22a

HISTORIC MANSION
tastefully furnished rooms

14 Point 19A 37a

STRIKE OPTIMISTIC NOTE
latest bulletins indicate progress

12 Point 22A 43a

DELIGHTFUL MUSIC ENJOYED
engage excellent symphony orchestra

10 Point 25A 48a

HANDSOME SPECIMEN EXHIBITED
interesting display includes several models

8 Point 26A 52a

UNEXCELLED CRAFTSMANSHIP IN DEMAND
preference for printing of the best grade is justified
from the standpoint of good business administration

6 Point 30A 60a

PROGRESSIVE HOUSES DEMAND GOOD PRINTING
every intelligent person knows that appearance counts largely
these days and that men are more often judged by their clothes

6 to 18 Point sizes of Bernhard Gothic Medium Italic
are cast only on the regular body

Characters in Complete Font

A B C D E F G H I J
K L M N O P Q R S T
U V W X Y Z & $ $
1 2 3 4 5 6 7 8 9 0
a b c d e f g h i j k l m
n o p q r s t u v w x y z
. , - ' ' : ; ! ?

Character *$* not made in 6, 8 and 10 Point
Characters *" "* are furnished with sizes from 18 to 72 Point
The following characters, from 24 to 72 Point, are cast recessed

A F L P T V W Y

Special Characters fonted separately and furnished on order only

A B D E E F H K P R S
Th a e k r u

:[43]:

Bernhard Gothic Light

Copyright, 1930, by Lucian Bernhard
Manufactured under Special License

★120/96 Point 3A 4a
BIG bell

★96/84 Point 3A 4a
Sold TAR

★84/72 Point 3A 4a
KIND chef

72 Point 3A 4a
Solid ROAD

60 Point 3A 5a
BRAVE soldiers

48 Point 4A 6a
Hopeful WARDEN

42 Point 4A 7a
GRACEFUL student

36 Point 5A 9a
Majestical EXPOSITION

★All characters, excepting descenders, cast on the smaller size body

30 Point 6A 12a
DISTRIBUTION
foreign diplomat

24 Point 8A 16a
MUSIC STUDIOS
three pupils enrolled

18 Point 12A 24a
EXQUISITE PERFUMES
delicately scented boudoir

14 Point 20A 40a
FINE SOUVENIR PROGRAM
interesting typography displayed

12 Point 24A 48a
GREAT IMPROVEMENT REPORTED
large advertising campaigns in progress

10 Point 26A 52a
FOREIGN MOTION PICTURE SHOWN
internationally known star plays leading role

8 Point 28A 56a
INTREPID FLYER REACHES HIGHEST ALTITUDE
daring aviator and his mechanic perform thrilling stunt

6 Point 32A 64a
MODERN TYPE DESIGN THE BASIS OF FINE PRINTING
successful printers must react quickly to advances in typography

Characters in Complete Font

A B C D E F G H I J K L M
N O P Q R S T U V W X Y
Z & $ $ 1 2 3 4 5 6 7 8 9 0
a b c d e f g h i j k l m n
o p q r s t u v w x y z
. , - ' ' : ; ! ? · ❖

Character $ not made in 6, 8 and 10 Point

Recessed Characters cast in sizes from 30 to 120 Point
A F L P T V W Y

Special Characters made from 6 to 72 Point; furnished on order only
E K S a e k r s u z

Lining Figures furnished in separate fonts or will be supplied in the regular fonts instead of Oldstyle Figures when so specified on the order

$ 1 2 3 4 5 6 7 8 9 0

Bernhard Gothic Light Italic
Copyright, 1930, by Lucian Bernhard
Manufactured under Special License

72 Point 3A 4a

RISK rights

60 Point 3A 5a

daintily ICED

48 Point 4A 7a

FINER longhand

42 Point 4A 8a

hackneyed SONG

36 Point 5A 10a

INHERENT CHARM
enjoying holiday dance

30 Point 6A 12a

EXTENDED HORIZON
banquet speakers optimistic

24 Point 8A 15a

HEARD UNIQUE LEGEND
fascinating mythological kingdom

IMPORTANT NOTICE

Bernhard Gothic Light Italic, in sizes 24 to 72 Point, is cast on Angle Body without overhangs. All Angle Body fonts are packed in parcels as follows: Caps A to Z &— Lowercase a to z—Figures 1 to 0 $ £—Points . , - ' ' : ; ! ?—A liberal supply of Angle Body Spaces is furnished with each font and extra fonts of spaces are obtainable

18 Point 12A 22a

EXQUISITE SUBJECTS
seven magnificent imported
paintings exhibited recently

14 Point 19A 37a

VOGUE NEARING ZENITH
the insatiable urge for something
new brings frequent style change

12 Point 22A 43a

BEAUTIFUL CINEMA MAGAZINE
employing recently discovered process
for reproducing pictures in natural color

10 Point 25A 48a

ETCHINGS HAVE AESTHETIC CHARM
perfect technique and splendid craftsmanship
dominate these remarkably beautiful displays

8 Point 26A 52a

INTERPRETING SYMPHONIC COMPOSITIONS
metropolitan conductor handled augmented orchestra
and deserves credit for exceptionally fine performance

6 Point 30A 60a

MODERN ADVERTISING INTRIGUES US INTO BUYING
Creative typography demands something more than mere technical
knowledge; it calls for ideals, imagination, the longing to excel;
it cultivates a viewpoint that is eagerly and ardently modernistic

6 to 18 Point sizes of Bernhard Gothic Light Italic
are cast only on the regular body

• • •

Characters in Complete Font

A B C D E F G H I J
K L M N O P Q R S T
U V W X Y Z & $ $
1 2 3 4 5 6 7 8 9 0
a b c d e f g h i j k l m
n o p q r s t u v w x y z
. , - ' ' : ; ! ?

Character *$* not made in 6, 8 and 10 Point

The following characters, from 24 to 72 Point, are cast recessed

A F L P T V W Y

Special Characters fonted separately and furnished on order only

B D E E F H K P R S a e k r s u

Bernhard Gothic Heavy

Copyright, 1930, by Lucian Bernhard
Manufactured under Special License

★120/96 Point 3A 4a
BE art

★96/84 Point 3A 4a
big AID

★84/72 Point 3A 4a
ICE cold

72 Point 3A 4a
drake BIG

60 Point 3A 5a
NICE folder

48 Point 4A 6a
perfect VERSE

42 Point 4A 7a
MINOR terminal

36 Point 5A 9a
educated ANIMALS

30 Point 6A 12a
BUYS equipment

24 Point 8A 16a
QUAINT HEARTH
thirty beautiful rugs

18 Point 12A 24a
PICTURESQUE SCENES
charming landscape lauded

14 Point 20A 40a
EXHIBIT CLEVER SPECIMENS
intelligent typographic craftsmen

12 Point 24A 48a
NINTH AUTOMOTIVE EXPOSITION
electrical supply manufacturer attended

10 Point 26A 52a
BUYS MODERN PRINTING EQUIPMENTS
suburban printer received large consignment

8 Point 28A 56a
FOREIGN TOURISTS VISITED HISTORIC SHRINE
metropolitan industrialist entertained large gatherings

Characters in Complete Font

A B C D E F G H I J
K L M N O P Q R S
T U V W X Y Z & $
1 2 3 4 5 6 7 8 9 0
a b c d e f g h i j
k l m n o p q r s t
u v w x y z . , - ' '
" "   : ; ! ? . ❖ $

Character $ not made in 8 and 10 Point
The following characters, from 30 to 120 Point, are cast recessed
A F L P T V W Y

Special Characters made from 8 to 72 Point and furnished only on order
E K a k r s u

★All characters, excepting descenders, cast on the smaller size body

:[46]:

Bernhard Gothic Extra Heavy

Copyright, 1931, by Lucian Bernhard
Manufactured under Special License

★72/60 Point 3A 4a

NUMBER
rich codes

60 Point 3A 5a

MINERALS
silver cache

48 Point 4A 6a

FINER GLOBE
best statement

42 Point 4A 7a

NICEST HOMES
dignified student

36 Point 5A 9a

RESULTS MARKED
beautiful debutante

★All characters excepting descenders cast on 60 point body

CHARACTERS IN COMPLETE FONT

ABCDEEFGHI
JKKLMNOPQ
RSTUVWXYZ
& $ 1234567
890aabcdef
ghijklmnopqr
sstuvwxyz.,-
' ' " " :;!?❖.

The following characters from 30 to 72 cast recessed
A F L P T V W Y

30 Point 6A 12a

RESOURCES
big shipment

24 Point 8A 16a

FRENCH SILKS
lighter material

18 Point 12A 24a

CHARMING MUSIC
delights royal tourist

14 Point 20A 40a

FASHIONABLE LINGERIE
exquisite colorful creations

12 Point 24A 48a

MODERN PRINTING PLANTS
have approved quicker methods
and favor automatic machinery

Bernhard Booklet

72 Point　3A 4a

MODEL Recognized

60 Point　3A 6a

Enterprising URCHINS

48 Point　5A 10a

COUNSEL Reporting Eagerly

42 Point　5A 11a

Exquisite Display ANTICIPATED

36 Point　6A 11a

HUNDREDTH Quarterly Development

30 Point　7A 13a

DISPORTING
Guiding Players

24 Point　8A 17a

FINE THEATRE
Splendid Musicale

18 Point　14A 28a

CONTRACT BRIDGE
Lawyer Plays Fine Game

Figures
1 2 3 4 5 6 7 8 9 0 $

Characters

A B C D E F G
H I J K L M N
O P Q R S T U
V W X Y Z &
a b c d e f g
h i j k l m n
o p q r s t u
v w x y z ¢ §
. , - ' ' " " : ; ! ?

These characters " " not made in
8 and 10 Point sizes

14 Point　19A 38a

IMPROVEMENTS SHOWN
Merchant Places Larger Order

12 Point　22A 44a

BEAUTIFUL SURROUNDINGS
Remodels Exquisite Country Home

10 Point　26A 52a

IMPORTS GENUINE BROADCLOTH
Superbly Designed Silk Gowns Displayed

8 Point　28A 58a

SUMMER VACATIONISTS CRUISING LAKE
English Geologist Climbs Lofty Mountain Height

These characters are cast recessed in sizes 24 to 72 Point

A F L P T V W Y

Bernhard Booklet Italic

72 Point 3A 4a

FOUND Playwright

60 Point 3A 6a

Great Linguist SPEAKS

48 Point 5A 10a

REVIEW Delightful Musicales

42 Point 5A 11a

New European Opera INSPIRING

36 Point 6A 11a

MODERN Apartment Building For Sale

30 Point 7A 13a

PROSCRIBED
Gets Scholarship

24 Point 8A 17a

JOVIAL WRITER
Finest Opportunities

18 Point 14A 28a

PLEASING SCENERY
Admires Beautiful Flowers

Figures
1 2 3 4 5 6 7 8 9 0 $

Characters
A B C D E F G
H I J K L M N
O P Q R S T U
V W X Y Z & Th
a b c d e f g
h i j k l m n
o p q r s t u
v w x y z . ,
' ' " " : ; ! ?

These characters " " not made in
8 and 10 Point size

Sizes 24 to 72 Point cast on Angle Body

14 Point 19A 38a

MODERN IMPROVEMENT
Displayed Old Period Furniture

12 Point 22A 44a

CHARMING ENVIRONMENTS
Desires Ideal Atmospheric Condition

10 Point 26A 52a

PLEASING TYPOGRAPHIC DESIGN
French Craftsman Reviews Many Displays

8 Point 28A 58a

THE CENTURY OF PROGRESS EXPOSITION
Prominent Thespian Gave Exceptional Performances

These characters are cast recessed in sizes 24 to 72 Point

A F L P T V W Y

Bernhard Fashion

Copyright, 1929, by Lucian Bernhard
Manufactured under Special License

72 Point 3A 4a

BID High

60 Point 3A 6a

Purple INK

48 Point 5A 9a

BEST Original

42 Point 5A 10a

CHARMING
Beautiful Specimen

36 Point 6A 11a

FRAGRANCE
Hyacinthe Perfumery

30 Point 7A 13a

DAINTY GOWNS
Elegant Display Admired

24 Point 8A 16a

COVER DESIGN
Reproduces Fine Printing

18 Point 12A 24a

AUTOMOBILE SOLD
Owner Drives Excellent Bargain
Rebuilt Cars Giving Satisfaction

14 Point 18A 35a

ENJOYS PERFORMANCE
Delightful Musicale by Splendid Musicians
Beautiful Souvenir Programs Distributed

12 Point 22A 43a

MODERN FINISHING SCHOOL
An Educational Institution of Highest Character
Scholarship Recently Awarded by Philanthropist

CHARACTERS IN COMPLETE FONT

A A A B C D E E
E F G H I J K L M
N N O P Q R S S T
U V W W X Y Z &
$ $ 1 2 3 4 5 6 7 8 9 0
a b c d e f g h i j k l m
n o p q r s t u v w x y z
. , - ' ` : ; ! ? « »

Keynote Series

96 Point — 3A 5a
Splendid Girl

72 Point — 3A 6a
Majestic Royalty

60 Point — 3A 9a
Printed Artistic Gem
Original Silk Design

48 Point — 4A 11a
Lightning Speeds
Thirsty Mechanic

36 Point — 4A 13a
Beautiful Letter Form
Delights Aged Printer

24 Point — 7A 20a
Quality Will Increase Demand
Normal Craft Conditions Follow
Military Ball Brilliant Success

Characters in Complete Font

A B C D E F G H I J
K L M N O P Q R
S T U V W X Y Z &
$ 1 2 3 4 5 6 7 8 9 0 a b c
d e f g h i j k l m n o p q r s
t u v w x y z ff er es is or os
Th th . , - ' ' : ; ! ?

Keynote is made in six useful sizes from 24 point to 96 point

The Miamian

WORLD'S FINEST AND FASTEST

Train from New York to Miami

DANCE AND PLAY BRIDGE IN DE LUXE CARS

No Snow Down in Miami

WHEN ARE YOU LEAVING?

Harlequins, Typographic Dots, Cubist Moderniques and Brass Rule   8 Point Wave Bands No. 801

Stymie Medium

★144/120 Point — 3A 6a

Bald

★120/96 Point — 3A 6a

Night

★96/84 Point — 3A 6a

Job

★84/72 Point — 3A 4a

Girl

★72/60 Point — 4A 5a

Rain

★66/60 Point — 4A 6a

Spite

48 Point — 4A 7a

Spirit

42 Point — 5A 8a

Maple

36 Point — 5A 10a

IS Light

30 Point — 6A 12a

Dye RED

24 Point — 7A 14a

GREATEST Perspective

18 Point — 10A 20a

COMPOSING Popular Lyrics

---

18 Point No. 2 — 12A 24a

INDUSTRIAL PROSPECTS
Business Revival Predicted

14 Point — 15A 30a

CONSTANT PERFORMANCE
Arranging Delightful Program

12 Point — 18A 35a

MAGNIFICENT STAGE COSTUME
Audience Admires Exquisite Gowns

10 Point — 25A 45a

INDUSTRIOUS WORKERS PROMOTED
Supervisor Advances Diligent Mechanic

10 Point No. 2 — 25A 45a

MORE DISTINCTIVE PRINTING REQUIRED
Beautiful Showing Attracts Unusual Attention

8 Point — 27A 55a

SUBURBAN HOME OWNERS CONSIDER CHARGE
Honest Public Officials Courted Widest Investigation

6 Point — 30A 60a

PROMINENT BANKER ISSUES ENCOURAGING STATEMENT
Late Financial Reports Indicate Steadily Increasing Prosperity

★All characters, excepting descenders, cast on the smaller size body

---

Characters in Complete Font

A B C D E F G
H I J K L M N
O P Q R S T U
V W X Y Z & $
1 2 3 4 5 6 7 8 9 0
a b c d e f g h i
j k l m n o p q r
s t u v w x y z
. , - ' ' : ; ! ? (

Superior **$** furnished with all fonts from 24 to 144 Point

Characters **A F L P T V W Y** cast recessed from 24 to 144 Point

Special Characters **A A a f r t y** made in all sizes and sold separately

Stymie Medium Italic

72 Point 3 A 5 a
BE Rigid

60 Point 4 A 6 a
Nice PAY

48 Point 4 A 7 a
RICH Styles

42 Point 5 A 8 a
Quietly BUILT

36 Point 5 A 10 a
MANY THANKS
Lovely Reception

30 Point 6 A 12 a
CHARMING SONGS
Gratify Royal Couple

24 Point 7 A 14 a
WONDERFUL CONTEST
Sportsmen Enjoyed Game

---

18 Point 12 A 24 a
COLORFUL LINGERIE
Many Exquisite Shades

18 Point No. 2 12 A 24 a
IMPORTS LOCOMOTIVE
Heaviest Models Required

14 Point 15 A 30 a
MECHANICAL OPERATION
Improved Equipment Ordered

12 Point 18 A 35 a
DISPLAYED EXCLUSIVE DESIGN
Sold Beautifully Embellished Books

10 Point 25 A 45 a
CRAFTSMEN VISIT ART EXHIBITION
English Merchant Receives Gold Medal

10 Point No. 2 25 A 45 a
PRESIDENT GREETS FOREIGN DELEGATE
English Statesman Rejoins Waiting Colleague

8 Point 27 A 55 a
MERCHANT MAKES GENEROUS CONTRIBUTION
Eminent Philanthropist Celebrates Golden Wedding

6 Point 27 A 55 a
STOVE MANUFACTURERS HOLD ANNUAL CONVENTION
Membership Plans Extensive Business Advertising Campaigns

IMPORTANT NOTICE

Stymie Medium Italic, in sizes 24 to 72 Point, is cast on Angle Body without overhangs. All Angle Body fonts are packed in parcels as follows: Caps A to Z &—Lowercase a to z—Figures 1 to 0 $ £—Points ., - ' ' : ; ! ? (—A liberal supply of Angle Body Spaces is furnished with each font and extra fonts of spaces are obtainable

---

Characters in Complete Font

A B C D E F G H I J
K L M N O P Q R S
T U V W X Y Z & $
1 2 3 4 5 6 7 8 9 0
a b c d e f g h i j k
l m n o p q r r s t u v
w x y z . , - ' ' : ; ! ? (

The following characters are cast recessed from 24 to 72 Point

A F L P T V W Y

Superior **$** furnished with all fonts from 18 to 72 Point
Characters " " furnished with all fonts from 6 to 18 Point

Stymie Light

★144/120 Point   3 A 6 a

IF set

★120/96 Point   3 A 6 a

Hits IT

★96/84 Point   3 A 6 a

Sky

48 Point   4 A 7 a

Mates

42 Point   5 A 8 a

Politics

★84/72 Point   3 A 4 a

Holt

36 Point   5 A 10 a

Quilting

30 Point   6 A 12 a

SHOWER
New Birds

★72/60 Point   4 A 5 a

Stalk

24 Point   7 A 14 a

ROADSTER
Saw Bargain

60 Point   4 A 6 a

Mirth

18 Point   10 A 22 a

REMARKABLE
Brake Adjusted

---

18 Point No. 2   12 A 24 a

HELPING TYPOGRAPHERS
New Creation Aided Industry

14 Point   15 A 30 a

PICTURESQUE LANDSCAPES
Foreign Artists Highly Enthused

12 Point   20 A 40 a

GOOD TYPE FACES ARE ESSENTIAL
Advertisers Approve Modern Designs

10 Point   25 A 50 a

RURAL COMMUNITIES HOLD MEETING
Many Recommendations Were Introduced

10 Point No. 2   25 A 50 a

EXCLUSIVE MANSIONS BEING AUCTIONED
Prominent Financier Made Most Attractive Offer

8 Point   25 A 50 a

METROPOLITAN STUDENTS RECEIVE CREDENTIALS
Distinguished French Professor Makes Lengthy Speech

6 Point   27 A 55 a

TYPOGRAPHIC CRAFTSMEN REVIEW MODERNISTIC PRINTING
Celebrated authorities highly commended the various specimens
that were displayed at the recent printing and painting exposition

★ All characters, excepting descenders, cast on the smaller size body

---

Characters in Complete Font

A A A B C D E F
G H I J K L M N
O P Q R R S T U
V W X Y Z & $ 1 2
3 4 5 6 7 8 9 0
a a b c d e f f g h
i j k l m n o p q
r s t u v w x y z
. , - ' ' : ; ! ? (* § « »

The following characters are cast recessed from 24 to 144 Point

A F L P T V W Y

Superior $ furnished with all fonts from 24 to 144 Point

Stymie Light Italic

18 Point 12A 24a
EUROPEAN PERFUMES
Imports Nearing Normal

18 Point No. 2 12A 24a
EXPORTED AUTOMOBILE
Buying Improvement Noted

14 Point 15A 30a
CHARMING WINTER SPORTS
Promotes Healthful Recreation

12 Point 18A 35a
RECEPTION TENDERED PRESIDENT
Notable Personages Attend Function

10 Point 25A 45a
MAGNIFICENT SYMPHONIC RECITALS
Soothing Melody Provides Entertainment

10 Point No. 2 25A 45a
MILLIONAIRE CONTRIBUTES ABUNDANTLY
Several Institutions Sharing Charitable Legacy

8 Point 27A 55a
BEAUTIFUL DEBUTANTES PLACIDLY SOJOURNING
Popular Winter Resorts Enjoying Marvelous Weather

6 Point 27A 55a
FURNITURE MANUFACTURERS HOLD YEARLY CONVENTION
Membership Planning Extensive Business Advertising Campaign

• • • •

Characters in Complete Font

A B C D E F G H I J
K L M N O P Q R S
T U V W X Y Z & $
1 2 3 4 5 6 7 8 9 0
a b c d e f f g h i j k l
m n o p q r s t u v w x y z
. , - ' ' : ; ! ? (« »

The following characters are cast recessed from 24 to 72 Point

A F L P T V W Y

Superior $ furnished with all fonts from 24 Point to 72 Point
Characters '' '' furnished with all fonts from 6 to 18 Point

---

72 Point 3A 5a
IS Bright

60 Point 4A 6a
Gold RIM

48 Point 4A 7a
HER Special

42 Point 5A 8a
Elegant LINEN

36 Point 5A 10a
MODERN Doctors

30 Point 6A 12a
Beautiful SPECIMENS

24 Point 7A 14a
EXHIBITED SCULPTURES
Received Highest Mention

IMPORTANT NOTICE

Stymie Light Italic, in sizes 24 to 72 Point, is cast on Angle Body without overhangs. All Angle Body fonts are packed in parcels as follows: Caps A to Z &—Lowercase A to Z—Figures 1 to 0 $ £—Points . , - ' : ; ! ? (« » —A liberal supply of Angle Body Spaces is furnished with each font and extra fonts of spaces are obtainable

Stymie Bold

★144/120 Point — 3A 5a

Half

★120/96 Point — 3A 5a

Stork

★96/84 Point — 3A 5a

Iris

★84/72 Point — 3A 4a

Old

★72/60 Point — 4A 5a

Bets

60 Point — 4A 6a

Sage

48 Point — 4A 7a

Duty

42 Point — 5A 8a

Joiner

36 Point — 5A 10a

Laughs

30 Point — 6A 12a

Imported

24 Point — 7A 14a

GREATER
Equipment

18 Point — 10A 20a

DEMANDED
Right Quality

---

18 Point No. 2 — 11A 22a

PROSPEROUS BROKER
Extends Unlimited Credit

14 Point — 15A 30a

INTRODUCE MODERNISM
American Merchants Pleased

12 Point — 18A 35a

PRODUCES STRIKING DESIGNS
Unusually Attractive Display Effect

10 Point — 25A 45a

RECOMMEND HAND COMPOSITOR
Excellent Typography Earns Admiration

8 Point — 27A 55a

PRINTING PLANTS INSTALLED IN SCHOOLS
Distinguished Educators Approve Printing Course

6 Point — 30A 60a

ENTHUSIASTIC SPORTSMEN ENTERTAIN ATHLETE
Wonderful Reception Tendered Promising Football Player

★ All characters, excepting descenders, cast on the smaller size body

---

Characters in Complete Font

A B C D E F G
H I J K L M N O
P Q R R S T U V
W X Y Z & $ $
1 2 3 4 5 6 7 8 9 0
a b c d e f g h i
j k l m n o p q r
s t u v w x y z
. , - ' ' : ; ! ?

Superior $ furnished with all sizes from 12 to 144 Point
Characters **A F L P T V W Y** cast recessed from 24 to 144 Point

Condensed Figures **1 2 3 4 5 6 7 8 9 0 $** for Stymie Bold made from 6 to 84 Point and sold separately

Special Characters **A A a f r t y** made in all sizes and sold separately

Stymie Bold Italic

18 Point No. 2   9A 19a
INCREASED BUSINESS
Old Stockholders Pleased

14 Point   12A 24a
GYMNASTIC EXHIBITION
Promoted Healthful Exercise

12 Point   15A 30a
RELIABLE INSURANCE BROKER
Offers Agent Splendid Inducement

10 Point   16A 32a
AUTOMOBILE SALES INCREASING
Great Advertising Campaigns Planned

8 Point   19A 38a
MOTHERS ATTEND BENEFIT PERFORMANCE
Excellent Musical Program Follows Entertainment

6 Point   20A 40a
MODERN ADVERTISEMENT ATTRACTS ATTENTION
American Faces and Decorative Material Used Exclusively

Characters in Complete Font

A B C D E F G
H I J K L M N
O P Q R S T U
V W X Y Z & $
1 2 3 4 5 6 7 8 9 0
a b c d e f
g h i j k l m
n o p q r s
t u v w x y z
. , - ' ' : ; ! ?

Superior **$** furnished
with all sizes from 24 to 72 Point

Characters **A F L P T V W Y** cast recessed
from 24 to 72 Point

---

72 Point   3A 4a
BE Safe

60 Point   3A 5a
Nice FIT

48 Point   3A 5a
SING Lyric

42 Point   4A 6a
Employ MEN

36 Point   4A 6a
LOAN Required

30 Point   4A 8a
Magnificent HOME

24 Point   5A 10a
PATENTS INVENTION
Several Claims Allowed

18 Point   8A 17a
BANK DEPOSITS INCREASE
Financial Reports Encouraging

Sizes 24 to 72 Point cast on Angle Body

Stymie Elongated Ascenders and Descenders

Elongated Characters for Stymie Types can be had in Bold, Medium and Light. Sold in sets or single characters for all sizes from 18 Point to 144 Point.

For 36 Point Stymie Light

For 36 Point Stymie Medium

For 36 Point Stymie Bold

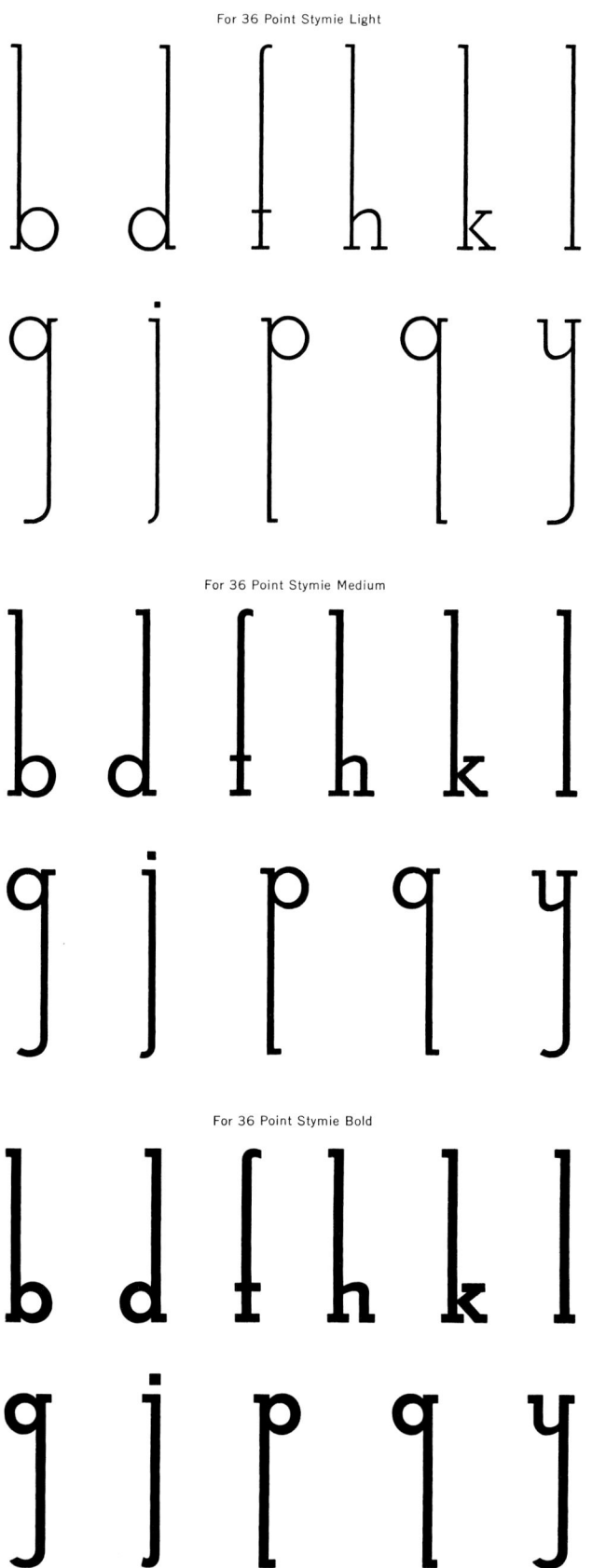

RADIO OR AUTOMOBILE
RECHARGED
IMMEDIATELY

battery

• The Keystone Battery Service have just installed in their modern service station one of the latest methods of recharging batteries

keystone battery service

Keystone Highway, Pennsylvania

GUARANTEED   NEW EXTRA HEAVY DUTY

Mileage
TIRES

New Process Eight-Ply Cord

Mileage Tires are of exceptional beauty and strength . . . built of super-twist, long-staple cotton and of the finest quality rubber

AFFILIATED RUBBER COMPANY

Canterbury Series

48 Point 7A 13a

MODERN AUTOMOBILES

Lovely New Hampshire Countryside

42 Point 8A 14a

EUROPEAN NIGHTINGALE

Bewitching Old Melody Enthralls Listener

36 Point 8A 16a

ENVIRONMENTS

Beautiful Announcements

30 Point 10A 19a

PLEASING PROGRAM

Rendered by English Musician

24 Point 11A 23a

HONORARY MEMBERSHIP

Buffalo Club Rewards Six Members

18 Point 18A 36a

COMMUNITY BENEFIT MUSICALE

Operatic Arias Enliven Christmas Entertainment

14 Point 25A 50a

SUCCESS DEPENDS ON AMBITION

Manager Approves Granting Numerous Bonuses

12 Point 27A 54a

PALATIAL METROPOLITAN RESIDENCES

Handsome City Homes Situated Along Riverside Drive

Characters in Complete Font

A A B B C C D E
E F G H H I J K
L L M M N N N O
P Q R S T T U U
V W W X Y Z & $
1 2 3 4 5 6 7 8 9 0
a b c d e f g h i j k l
m n o p q r s t u v w x
y z ff fi fl ffi ffl . , - ' ' : ; ! ?

:[59]:

Bulmer Roman

48 Point 6A 10a

REFRESHED
Splendid Plays

42 Point 6A 11a

QUIET FIELDS
Delightful Grove

36 Point 6A 11a

MUSIC STUDIOS
Proper Atmosphere

30 Point 8A 14a

ROMANTIC OPERA
Unique Camping Place

24 Point 9A 17a

WHISPERING ZEPHYRS
Especially interesting island

18 Point 13A 26a

VISITING NORTHERN WOODS
Motorists from distant cities traverse

---

14 Point 19A 39a

UNIQUE SUBURBAN MANSIONS
Many prominent men have had their homes built in this interesting region

12 Point 22A 45a

SERVES DELICIOUS BROOK TROUT
These speckled beauties are excellent fare for sportsmen and they are keenly relished when prepared and served at the lake shore

10 Point 25A 49a

SPLENDID OPPORTUNITIES IN WINTER
Tobogganing, snowshoeing and numerous other healthful winter sports lure several hundreds of outdoor enthusiasts to this beautiful lake region

8 Point 26A 52a

OUTDOOR RECREATIONS PROVED POPULAR
Golf and tennis are very enjoyable amid such beautiful surroundings and zestful atmosphere, while motoring along the marvelous highways and exploring the forest trails brings inconceivable pleasure to the vacationists

6 Point 28A 58a

JUNE CAMPERS HAVE COMPREHENSIVE SCHEDULES
Every season thousands of red-blooded sportsmen spend their summer vacation very pleasantly and profitably camping in this most remarkable mountainous section and the vast lakes, where hunting, fishing and boating may be enjoyed to its fullest extent

Characters

A B C D E F G H I
J K L M N O P Q R
S T U V W X Y Z &
$ 1 2 3 4 5 6 7 8 9 0
a b c d e f g h i j k
l m n o p q r s t u v
w x y z ff fi fl ffi ffl
. , - ' ' : ; ! ?

Small Caps from 6 to 18 Point are put up in separate fonts and furnished only when specially ordered

Bulmer Italic

14 Point 23A 44a

HONOR MEMBERS WHO SAILED
Many scholars departed aboard steamer
bound for uninhabited Eastern Islands

12 Point 23A 48a

RELATES HAZARDOUS EXPERIENCE
Prominent foreign geologist entertained the
ambitious university students with the most
remarkable tales of adventure and intrigue

10 Point 26A 53a

THE ENTIRE CITY WELCOMES AVIATORS
Fervidly enthusiastic multitudes vociferously cheer
the foreign contingent of aviators upon completion
of their great record breaking transcontinental trip

8 Point 28A 54a

DILIGENCE AND PERSEVERANCE OF INSECTS
At the next opportunity when you make a journey through
the woodlands and meadows during the early warm spring
days of the year, just take a little time to observe some of the
fascinating and intensive activities of the common bee or ant

6 Point 31A 60a

MAN HARDLY COMPREHENDS WONDERS OF UNIVERSE
Practically every other day prominent scientists and astrologists with
the help of wonderfully powerful and carefully adjusted telescopes
and cameras discover the existence of still another new planet and
we are only beginning to understand how big this universe really is

Characters

A B C D E F G H I J
J K L M N O P Q R S
T U V W X Y Z & $
1 2 3 4 5 6 7 8 9 0
a b c d e f g h i j k l
m n o p q r s t u v
w x y z ff fi fl ffi ffl
. , - ' ' : ; ! ?

48 Point 6A 10a

MONSTROUS
Sailors Healthy

42 Point 6A 12a

FINER STOCKS
Diligent Cavalier

36 Point 6A 12a

BOUGHT HOUSE
Repair Conservatory

30 Point 8A 16a

EARNEST MARINER
Mechanic Complimented

24 Point 9A 20a

NUMBERING MACHINES
Complete Exhibition Inspected

18 Point 15A 31a

UNEXPLORED ARCTIC REGION
Daring Navigators Flying Northward

Cast on Original Line

Caslon Oldstyle No. 471

72 Point — 3 A 3 a

Best Act

60 Point — 3 A 4 a

Rich Girls

48 Point — 4 A 6 a

KINGDOMS
Bravest Knight

42 Point — 4 A 6 a

HEARD
Dialogue

36 Point — 5 A 7 a

MEN SING
Help Choir

30 Point — 6 A 10 a

NAME USED
Right Subject

---

24 Point — 7 A 14 a

RED INK
Displaying

22 Point — 8 A 16 a

NICE MEN
Live Stylish

18 Point — 10 A 25 a

EXPEDIENT
PLENTY of type
increases profit

14 Point — 14 A 40 a

RENEW DOME
WORN letters cause
of expensive delays

---

12 Point — 15 A 45 a

FINE QUALITY
CASLON adds dignity
to beautiful printing

10 Point — 18 A 55 a

PILGRIM ROMANCE
IDEALIZING historical events
becomes ridiculous if some
narrative is unsubstantiated

8 Point — 20 A 60 a

HISTORIC MELODRAMA
COMPOSERS sometimes take tunes
lacking in worth and glorify them
into symphonies; so the alchemy
of genius has transformed this play

6 Point — 22 A 65 a

SONGS PRODUCE HAPPINESS
CHILDHOOD was spent in chasing
golden butterflies; then came those
youthful days of dreams. Happiness
came with the realization of power

9 and 11 Point carried in stock only at the Foundry

Characters in Complete Font

A B C D E F G
H I J K L M N
O P Q R S T U
V W X Y Z & $
1 2 3 4 5 6 7 8 9 0
a b c d e f g h i j
k l m n o p q r s
t u v w x y z ff fi
fl ffi ffl ct ( ) [ ]
. , - ' : ; ! ?

Characters ( ) [ ] made only in sizes from 6 to 48 Point

SMALL CAPS from 6 to 36 Point are put up in separate fonts
and furnished only when specially ordered

Caslon Quaint Characters shown on opposite page

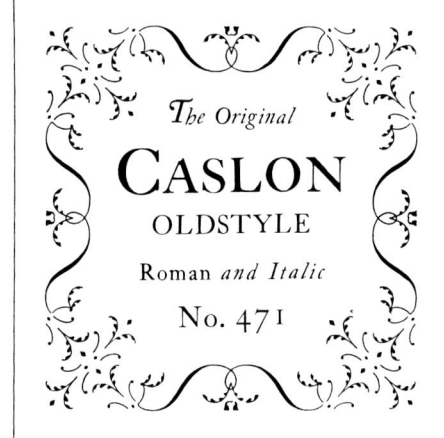

The Original
CASLON
OLDSTYLE
Roman and Italic
No. 471

THIS type face is cast also on the AMERICAN POINT LINE. The difference is entirely in the shortening of several of the descenders. Its catalogue name is CASLON NO. 540 and Caslon Italic No. 540. The sizes are from 6 to 120 point in the roman and from 6 to 96 point in the italic

---

Caslon Oldstyle No. 472

Caslon Oldstyle No. 472 is made in 18, 22 and 24 point only. The face is precisely the same as the Caslon Oldstyle No. 471, but cast from different matrices with a closer fit as shown in the examples at the right. Sold in weight fonts only.

Caslon Oldstyle No. 471

The sharp elements of
this type face insures a
legible job of printing

Caslon Oldstyle No. 472

The sharp elements of
this type face insures a
legible job of printing

:[62]:

Caslon Oldstyle Italic No. 471   Cast on Original Line

12 Point   14 A 42 a
ODD SPECIMEN
Leaflet printed in the
early day found intact
and presented to firm

10 Point   16 A 48 a
ANTIQUE PICTURE
Brought beautiful painting
depicting hostile meeting on
frontier with savage Indian

8 Point   18 A 55 a
HONORS FOR PURITANS
To break with the past, entrusting
their lives to the wilds, required
a spirit of adventure, challenging
the great admiration of the world

6 Point   18 A 55 a
COLONIZING AT PLYMOUTH
Pilgrim men and women from across
the ocean, fired with determination to
secure freedom, landed upon the stern
and forbidding New England shores

22 Point   7 A 16 a
NOTIONS
Folks acquire
strange habits
from learning

18 Point   9 A 25 a
COLONISTS
Sturdy mariner
returning north
with sweetheart

14 Point   12 A 36 a
CONSIDERED
European professors
showed appreciation
throughout exercises

9 and 11 Point carried in stock only at the Foundry

48 Point   3 A 5 a
BEST MUSIC
Entertain Society

42 Point   4 A 6 a
PROUD GIRLS
Diplomatic Chorus

36 Point   4 A 6 a
RICH LEADER
Determine Multitude

Wedding
Gifts

For the wedding season many
articles of beauty and utility
are offered. Sterling silver dinner
sets and choice pieces of exquisite
design are shown in great variety.

This trade-mark identifies
Hamilton & Sandford Craftsmanship

H&S

Characters in Complete Font

A B C D E F G H
I J J K L M N O P
Q R S T T U V
W X Y Z & $
1 2 3 4 5 6 7 8 9 0
a b c d e f g h h i j k
l m n o p q r s t u v
w x y z ff fi fl ffi ffl ct
. , - ' : ; ! ?

Swash Characters shown on page 66

30 Point   5 A 10 a
MINISTER
English prelate
journeying east

24 Point   6 A 14 a
EXHIBITION
New masterpieces
recently discovered

CASLON QUAINT CHARACTERS

These characters were in general use in William Caslon's time, and have been preserved in their original form. They are not furnished with regular fonts but are sold separately in packages containing either Roman or *Italic*.

f ff ffi ffl fb fh fi fk fl ft ct   *ſ ſſ ſſi ſſl ſb ſh ſi ſk ſl ft ct*

For the Roman Series of Caslon Oldstyle No. 471 all characters shown above are available in sizes from 6 to 36 Point. The 42, 48 and 60 Point contain the long s and ct only (ſ ct).

For Caslon Oldstyle Italic No. 471 the 11 characters shown above are available for all sizes from 6 to 30 Point. Only the long s, sk and ct (ſ ſk ct) are made for the 36 Point size and only the long s and ct (ſ ct) are made for the 42 and 48 Point sizes.

:[63]:

Caslon No. 540

120 Point 3A 4a
Spilt

96 Point 3A 4a
Bond

84 Point 3A 4a
Night

72 Point 3A 4a
Squash

60 Point 3A 4a
Displays

48 Point 3A 6a
Rectangle

42 Point 3A 7a
Mythology

Characters in Complete Font

A B C D E F G H I
J K L M N O P Q R
S T U V W X Y Z &
$ 1 2 3 4 5 6 7 8 9 0
a b c d e f g h i j k l m n
o p q r s t u v w x y z ff
fi fl ffi ffl ct . , - ' : ; ! ? ( ) [ ]

Characters ( ) [ ] made only in sizes from 6 to 42 Point

SMALL CAPS from 6 Point to 18 Point inclusive and Quaint Characters ſ ſb ſh ſi ſk ſl ſt ff ffi ffl ct from 6 to 30 Point inclusive are fonted separately and are furnished only when specially ordered. Only the Quaint Characters ſ and ct are fonted in the 36 and 42 Point sizes

11 Point carried in stock only at the Foundry

36 Point 3A 7a
GUILD
Highest

30 Point 4A 10a
ZEPHYR
Complete

24 Point 5A 12a
ENGAGED
Quadrangles

20 Point 7A 14a
KINGDOMS
Antique Carpet

18 Point 9A 19a
INQUIRED
Philanthropic

14 Point 12A 27a
MONUMENTS
Beautiful Scenery

12 Point 13A 32a
QUAINT HOMES
Picturesque Gardens

10 Point 16A 44a
IMPROVED CENTRE
Newly Arranged Lighting

8 Point 18A 45a
ORIGINAL CONCEPTION
European designer brings many fantastic modern motor designs

6 Point 22A 63a
NATIONAL PRINTING EXHIBITION
Remarkable display attracts very important group of Latin American newspaper editors

:[64]:

Caslon Italic No. 540

Characters in Complete Font

A B C D E F G H I J J
K L M N O P Q Q R S
T T U V W X Y Z &
$ 1 2 3 4 5 6 7 8 9 0
a b c d e f g h h i j k l m
n o p q r s t u v w x z ff
fi fl ffi ffl & . , - ' : ; ! ? ( )

To Users of Caslon Oldstyle Italic No. 471
The five largest sizes of the Caslon Italic No. 540 with Swash Characters are the equivalent of 60, 72, 84, 96 and 120 Point Caslon Oldstyle Italic No. 471

11 Point carried in stock only at Foundry

14 Point 12A 28a
EQUESTRIAN
Shady bridle paths
intersect this region

12 Point 14A 33a
MODEL HOUSES
Dainty summer flowers
bedecked the landscape

10 Point 18A 43a
RUSTIC NEIGHBORS
Beautiful suburban residences
are located on the hillside and
are homes well worth owning

8 Point 19A 46a
CHARMING ENGLISH CITY
Narrow streets and quaint inns
create an atmosphere of peculiar
charm which delights strangers

6 Point 21A 68a
PICTURESQUE UNIVERSITY TOWERS
Venerable elms surround the campus carpeted
with velvety lawns and bordered by brilliant
colored beds of geraniums, asters and peonies

30 Point 4A 9a
BUGLE
Quantities

24 Point 5A 12a
PRECEDE
Enjoys Books

20 Point 7A 14a
FLOUNDER
Manager bought
new fishing boat

18 Point 8A 19a
SELECTIONS
Conductor renders
new interpretation

96 Point 3A 4a
Night

84 Point 3A 4a
Stylish

72 Point 3A 4a
Healthy

60 Point 3A 5a
Multiples

48 Point 3A 6a
Bibliograph

42 Point 4A 7a
Candy Dealer

36 Point 4A 8a
INSTINCTS
New Kingdom

:[65]:

Caslon Oldstyle Italic No. 471 Swash Characters

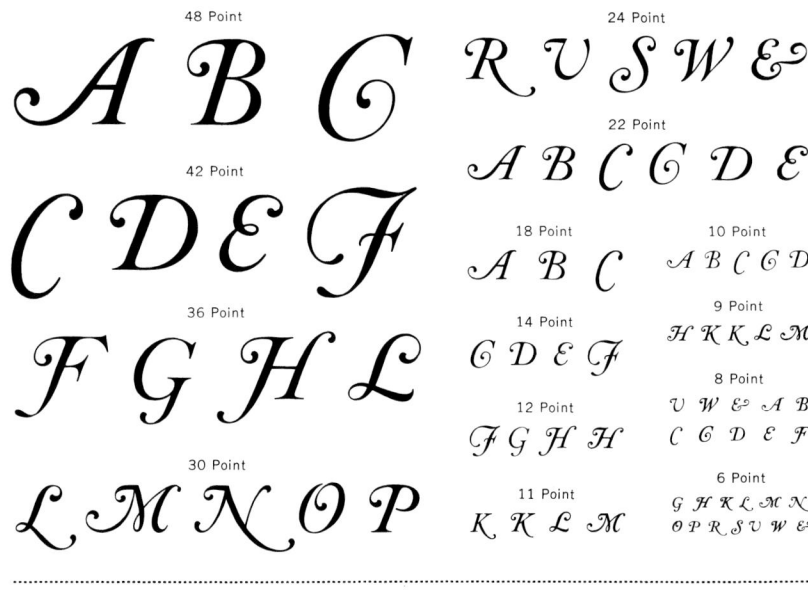

Each size contains all characters shown in this Font

Sizes 6 to 14 point and 22 point do not contain the characters a e o u

Caslon Italic No. 540 Swash Characters

Caslon Italic No. 540 Swash Characters are cast in special molds that provide a mortise so that lowercase letters can be fitted inside the overhanging parts without use of kerns. Lowercase letters included in the fonts are cast on bodies of proper size to fit the mortises in these capitals.

Font No. 1. Made in seven sizes, 36, 42, 48, 60, 72, 84 and 96 point. Fonts of each size include all the characters shown in the 36 point example.

Font No. 2. Made for the same sizes as Font No. 1, but in each case the capitals are cast on the next larger body to avoid overhangs. Fonts of each size include all the characters shown in the 36 point example, and the three largest sizes also include some additional lowercase letters.

Examples

Rie
Noh
We Lad

Font No. 2—*for 36 point*

C F
G H
K L
N k
R S
a e o u

Capitals in this font are cast on 42 point body
Lowercase cast on bodies to work with capitals

Font No. 1—*for 36 point*

A B C
D E I
M O P
U V W
& v w E
a e o u

Capitals in this font are cast on 36 point body. Lowercase cast on bodies to work with capitals

Caslon Openface

48 Point — 3 A 5 a
1 Bright Girl

42 Point — 3 A 5 a
Display Hats 2

36 Point — 3 A 5 a
39 Real Bargain

30 Point — 5 A 8 a
Sale 50 New Modes

24 Point — 6 A 10 a
Submitted Novel Designs

18 Point — 9 A 18 a
IMPORTED TAPESTRIES
Majestic Creation Receives Prize

14 Point — 15 A 28 a
MERCHANTS
Stationery Bought

10 Point — 18 A 36 a
REGAINS PRESTIGE
Official explained conduct
satisfactorily for electorate

12 Point — 15 A 30 a
NICE PRINTING
Delightful Photograph

8 Point — 20 A 40 a
INSTRUCTIVE SERMON
Distinguished audience applauds
young speaker delivering address

Characters in Complete Font

A B C D E F G H I
J K L M N O P Q R
S T U V W X Y Z &
$ 1 2 3 4 5 6 7 8 9 0
a b c d e f g h i j k l m n o
p q r s t u v w x y z ff fl ffl
. , - ' : ; ! ?

Overhanging characters A V W Y furnished in all sizes of Caslon Openface

Ransom Shaded Initials
(Clearcut Shaded Capitals)

Characters in Complete Font

A B
C D
E F
G H
I J
K L
M N O P Q
R S T U V
W Y & ! ?

12 Point — 10 A
A B C D E F

14 Point — 8 A
A B C D E

18 Point — 6 A
A B C D

24 Point — 5 A
A B C D

30 Point — 4 A
A B C

36 Point — 4 A
A B C

48 Point — 3 A
A B C

Ransom Shaded Initials
are cast without
overhangs

Usable in
combination with
Caslon
Oldstyle 471

New Caslon

84 Point — 3A 4a
Races 5

72 Point — 3A 4a
8 Soldier

60 Point — 3A 4a
Inexplicit

48 Point — 3A 6a
74 BOUND
Elegant Cap

42 Point — 4A 6a
DOMESTIC
Regular Stock

36 Point — 4A 7a
BOYS CHOSE
Selected Quality

30 Point — 5A 9a
DRUM
Identify

24 Point — 5A 12a
ROUND
Magnetic

18 Point — 8A 17a
BURDENS
Depreciated

14 Point — 12A 24a
HISTRIONIC
Exemplification

12 Point — 15A 30a
PICTURESQUE
Beautiful waterfall pleased sojourners

10 Point — 17A 34a
HUGE BUILDING
Springfield real estate brokers transact deals

8 Point — 21A 42a
REVIEWED REGIMENT
French military commander inspecting northern garrison

6 Point — 23A 47a
SPECIAL MOTION PICTURE
Leading Cleveland cinema theatres show brilliant collegiate production

5 Point — 21A 42a
ORGANIZING MUSICAL SOCIETY
Prominent saxophone and clarinet soloist renders selection. Enthusiastic directors furnishing incentive for youthful violinist

1. No matter what you make today, and how healthy you are, there is no way of telling what urgent need may arise *Save!*

2. Let your savings earn for you. A dollar is a very efficient worker if intelligently used and not foolishly hoarded *Save!*

FOUR REASONS

Characters in Complete Font

A B C D E F G H I
J K L M N O P Q R
S T U V W X Y Z &
$ 1 2 3 4 5 6 7 8 9 0
a b c d e f f g h i j k
l m n o p q r s t u v
w x y z . , - ' : ; ! ?

The following characters are furnished with all fonts from 5 Point to 18 Point inclusive

ff fi fl ffi ffl

Fractions and Auxiliaries are made for New Caslon

New Caslon Italic

8 Point   17A 51a
SLUMBERING HAMLETS
Eventually time mellowed and increased beauty of countryside where courageous pioneers had maintained their modest homes notwithstanding dire privation

6 Point   20A 60a
BEAUTIFUL DESERT GARDENS
Beneath the scorching desert sky grow many distinctively characteristic and unusual species of profusely blooming cacti that display marvelous adaption to environment and interest botanists because of their peculiar bristled and barbed construction and gay blossoms

5 Point   17A 52a
UNOBTRUSIVE HOME FURNISHINGS
Craftsman furniture and home furnishings are suggestive of forest and woodland atmosphere and restful greens and woodsy browns became deservedly popular. Probably the reason some houses have been too elaborately ornamented is because variety and color are unconsciously sought and ultimately quickens the color spirit

14 Point   11A 30a
MONOTONES
Sepia landscapes invariably create sound impression

12 Point   13A 38a
CONSTRUCTION
Officials will appoint special committees to furnish new building and arrange opening

10 Point   15A 44a
QUAINT CUSTOMS
Navajo Indians display unexpected cleverness in building houses weirdly symbolizing their myths

3   *A knowledge that you are thrifty and prudent insures employment and enables you to face senility without alarm*   *Save!*

4   *The basis on which the world gets ahead and betters its condition in manifold ways is aptly expressed in one word*   *Save!*

Save

Characters in Complete Font

A B C D E F G
H I J K L M N
O P Q R S T U
V W X Y Z & $
1 2 3 4 5 6 7 8 9 0
a b c d e f g h i
j k l m n o p q r s
t u v w x y z ff fi
fl ffi ffl . , - ' : ; ! ?

48 Point   3A 6a
FINISHED
High Score 5

42 Point   4A 7a
MUSICIANS
8 Rare Novelty

36 Point   4A 9a
COVER STOCK
Important Rules 3

30 Point   4A 11a
ENLARGE STORE
Splendid Achievement

24 Point   5A 14a
BUILDS CHARACTER
Great Opportunity Offered

18 Point   8A 22a
PROGRESSIVE MERCHANT
Inaugurating Publicity Campaign

Caslon Bold

96 Point — 3 A 4 a

Bug 2

84 Point — 3 A 4 a

3 Rays

72 Point — 3 A 4 a

Hoping

60 Point — 3 A 4 a

Designed

48 Point — 3 A 5 a

Magnificent

42 Point — 3 A 6 a

Newest Mode

36 Point — 3 A 6 a

QUICK MINOR
Special Delivery

---

30 Point — 4 A 9 a

GRIPS
Fragile

24 Point — 5 A 11 a

DESIRE
Royalist

18 Point — 8 A 17 a

INSURED
Perplexing

14 Point — 12 A 23 a

QUESTIONS
Magnificence

---

12 Point — 16 A 30 a

FINE SERMON
Energetic pastor
much stimulated

10 Point — 16 A 32 a

HISTORIC SHIPS
Our representative
prevented disposal

8 Point — 19 A 38 a

SHREWD MANAGER
Northeastern merchant
particular disciplinarian

6 Point — 22 A 43 a

EASTERN RAIL SERVICE
Improvements contemplated
assure nice accommodations

5 Point — 21 A 40 a

GRACEFUL DESERT GARDENS
Royal caravans reached wonderful
oasis before their meagre supplies
and water were entirely exhausted

CASLON
BOLD

Characters in Complete Font

A B C D E F G
H I J K L M N
O P Q R S T U
V W X Y Z & $
a b c d e f g h i
j k l m n o p q r
s t u v w x y z
ct st . , - ' : ; ! ?

Two-third Set   En Set
1234567890   1234567890

Both en set and two-third set figures are made up to and including 12 Point; above 12 Point the wide figures only are made and each size is made uniform set. Up to 12 Point inclusive, regular job and weight fonts contain en set figures only; above 12 Point, all fonts contain the wide uniform set figures. Both kinds furnished separately in five-pound fonts.

9 and 54 Point carried in stock only at Foundry

Caslon Bold Italic

10 Point — 16 A 30 a
ECONOMIZING
Production outlay
honestly curtailed
before organizing

8 Point — 18 A 36 a
CHOICE ORCHARD
Northwestern farmers
predict enormous crop
from monthly spraying

6 Point — 21 A 40 a
MINIMIZE RESOURCES
Several housewives making
organized plans to conserve
by forming purchasing guild
among chary acquaintances

5 Point — 19 A 38 a
INTERIOR EFFECTS PLEASE
Bringing indoors a suggestion of
gay formal gardens and sparkling
water by sympathetic treatment of
the innumerable colors assembled

18 Point — 8 A 14 a
MASTER
Noted and
thoughtful

14 Point — 12 A 20 a
DECORATE
Gardener has
special flower
at convention

12 Point — 15 A 28 a
ENTHUSIASM
Quiet performer
modestly roused
loftier sentiment

CASLON
~ *BOLD ITALIC* ~

Characters in Complete Font

A B C D E F G
H I J K L M N
O P Q R S T U
V W X Y Z & $
1 2 3 4 5 6 7 8 9 0
a b c d e f g h i
j k l m n o p q r
s t u v w x
y z rs . , - ' : ; ! ?

The following characters are furnished with all fonts
from 5 Point to 24 Point inclusive

ff fi fl ffi ffl

9 and 54 Point carried in stock only at Foundry

60 Point — 3 A 4 a
BISQUE
Special 8

48 Point — 3 A 5 a
RUSHING
9 Big Sale 5

42 Point — 3 A 5 a
MUNITION
30 New Silks

36 Point — 3 A 5 a
RUG DESIGN
Oriental Motifs

30 Point — 4 A 8 a
FINE PRINTING
Cleverest Educator

24 Point — 5 A 9 a
FOREIGN BROKERS
Diplomats Enthusiastic

Caslon Bold Condensed

120 Point — 3 A 4 a

He Bid

96 Point — 3 A 4 a

Nice Act

Characters in Complete Font

A B C D E F G H
I J K L M N O P
Q R S T U V W
X Y Z & $ 1 2 3
4 5 6 7 8 9 0
a b c d e f g h i
j k l m n o p q r
s t u v w x y z
ct st . , - ' : ; ! ?

54 Point carried in stock only at Foundry

84 Point — 3 A 4 a

Red Ink

72 Point — 3 A 4 a

Car Lines

60 Point — 3 A 4 a

Hard Metal

48 Point — 3 A 6 a

DETERMINE
Artistic Prints

42 Point — 4 A 7 a

MARK
Ductile

36 Point — 4 A 7 a

HOMES
Existing

30 Point — 6 A 10 a

BRANCH
Majestical

24 Point — 7 A 15 a

KEROSENE
Useful Brush

18 Point — 12 A 23 a

MAGNITUDE
Historic Chest

14 Point — 15 A 30 a

NEIGHBORING
Perfect Harmony

12 Point — 19 A 38 a

BANK DIRECTORS
Reluctant Depositor

10 Point — 21 A 43 a

NEW METHODS USED
Publicity agent securing
certain profitable results

8 Point — 24 A 48 a

GEOGRAPHIC MAGAZINES
Distinguished explorers write
mighty interesting description

6 Point — 26 A 52 a

OBTAINED HANDSOME PICTURE
Fearless photographer displays great
acrobatic skill in securing numerous
views from position on high building

:[72]:

Paramount Series

72 Point   3A 4a

England

60 Point   4A 5a

BRIDGE

friendship

48 Point   4A 6a

PERFUME

lovely women

dine together

42 Point   4A 7a

MOUNTED

brighter shades

used effectively

36 Point   5A 7a

DINNER

fine service

30 Point   6A 10a

ENSURED

bright lawyer

24 Point   8A 17a

CREDITORS

gain confidence

in foreign trade

18 Point   12A 26a

STRING MUSIC

symphony orchestra

gives weekly concert

14 Point   20A 40a

UNIQUE RINGS
remarkable sapphire
of extraordinary size

12 Point   22A 44a

SUBURBAN HOME
famous carpet merchants
modernize old buildings

10 Point   23A 47a

BEAUTIFUL EXHIBIT
futuristic oil paintings and
antique furniture displayed
in prominent show windows

8 Point   26A 52a

JUDGE UPHELD DECISION
concerning large foreign shipments
of all goods. The proposed general
revision of the tariff should restore
confidence and stimulate business

6 Point   30A 60a

UNIVERSAL TRUST COMPANY
If you draw up a will you can state your
own terms for the division of the estate
you built up throughout your life. If you
do not make a will you simply delegate
the State to distribute all your property

Characters in Complete Font

A B C D E F G H I J
K L M N O P Q R
S T U V W X Y Z &
$ 1 2 3 4 5 6 7 8 9 0
a b c d e f g h i j k l m
n o p q r s t u v w x y z
. , - ' ' : ; ! ?

:[73]:

Rivoli Series

48 Point 4A 6a

MODERN
Elaborate Displays

42 Point 4A 7a

ORIGINAL
Belgian Architecture

36 Point 5A 7a

PRODUCING
Delightful Entertainment
Best Orchestra

30 Point 6A 10a

SPLENDID SHOP
Remarkable Millinery Exhibit
Unusual Designs

24 Point 9A 19a

AMERICAN CARS
Exceptionally Beautiful Arrangement
Elegant Upholstery

18 Point 12A 26a

VIOLET PERFUME
Obtained at Exclusive Shops Only
Distinctively Individual

14 Point 22A 42a

MODERNISTIC DESIGN
Beautifully Carved Bust Greatly Admired
Several Masterpieces Sold

12 Point 24A 47a

DELIGHTFUL MUSICALE
Entertainment and Dance by University Graduates
Beautiful Music Thrills Dancers

10 Point 26A 53a

ADMIRABLE RESOLUTION
Employers Offer Liberal Bonuses to Conscientious Men
Greater Opportunity for Beginners

Characters in Complete Font

A B C D E F
G H I J K L
M N O P Q
R S T U V W
X Y Z & $
1 2 3 4 5 6 7 8 9 0
a b c d e f g h i
j k l m n o p q r
s t u v w x y z
. , = ' ' : ; ! ?

Rivoli Italic

18 Point 12A 26a
CHAMBER MUSIC
Quartette Sings Christmas Carols

14 Point 22A 42a
PICTURESQUE SCENE
Upland Landscape Attracted Thousands

12 Point 24A 47a
BELGIAN ARCHITECT
Designed Modernistic Residential Skyscrapers

10 Point 26A 53a
ADMIRABLE RESOLUTION
Employers Offer Large Bonuses to Conscientious Men
Greater Opportunity for Beginners

Characters in Complete Font

A A B B C C D D
E E F G G H H I J
J K K L L M M N
O P Q R R S S T
U V W X Y Z &
$ 1 2 3 4 5 6 7 8 9 0
a b c d e f g h i j
k l m n o p q r s
t u v w x y z ct
. , = ' ' : ; ! ? ( )

48 Point 4A 6a
LINGERS
Modern Designs

42 Point 4A 7a
PERFUME
Spanish Atmosphere

36 Point 5A 7a
EMPORIUM
Beautiful Masterpieces

30 Point 6A 10a
AUTOMOBILE
Manufacturer Displays Car

24 Point 9A 19a
EXHIBITS JEWELS
Remarkably Beautiful Collections

Complete angle body fonts, in sizes 24 to 48 point, will come to you in parcels as follows:
Caps A to Z &–Lowercase a to z–Figures 1 to 0 $–Points . , = '' : ; ! ? ( ). A liberal supply of Angle Body Spaces is furnished with each font
and extra fonts of spaces are obtainable. 10 to 18 point sizes of Rivoli Italic are cast only on the regular straight bodies

Cloister Oldstyle

72 Point — 4 A 6 a
Flight

60 Point — 5 A 7 a
Husky

48 Point — 6 A 10 a
IS Quiet

42 Point — 7 A 12 a
Red INK

36 Point — 8 A 13 a
IMPORTS
Eighth Boat

30 Point — 9 A 14 a
SYMBOLIC
Describe Race

24 Point — 10 A 18 a
FINE ARTIST
Complete Border

18 Point — 16 A 30 a
REJOINS OUTFIT
SELLING Fine Houses

---

16 Point — 18 A 36 a
MODERN SHOP
NEWEST devices for
making wire bought

14 Point — 22 A 42 a
BANKER RETIRES
ERECTED biggest stores
for this business section

12 Point — 24 A 47 a
STORE TO EXPAND
VERY LARGE influx of the
volume of business shown
by company in statements

Characters in Complete Font

ABCDEF
GHIJKL
MNOPQ
RRSTTU
VWXYZ
&$123456
7890abcde
fghijklmn
opqrstuvw
xyzffffifflffiffl
Qu & ( ) [ ]
.,-'' "" :;!?

SMALL CAPS
from 6 to 18 Point, and
Lining Figures 1234567890
in all sizes, are put up in
separate fonts and
furnished only
when specially ordered

THE BEST OF EVERYTHING FOR THE PRINTER
AMERICAN TYPE
Borders and Brass Rule
KELLY PRESSES
Revolutionized the Pressroom
CUT-COST EQUIPMENT
For Efficient Composing Rooms
PEERLESS FEEDERS

---

10 Point — 25 A 50 a
PECULIAR ATTITUDE
ENTHUSIASTIC conclave held
by printers from many states
concerning modern methods

8 Point — 28 A 56 a
ARRANGE SPRING TRIPS
PASSENGER lines anticipate a very
busy season due to the many new
markets opened in foreign lands

6 Point — 32 A 60 a
AUDIENCE ENJOYS NEW PLAY
DELIGHTED crowd cheered players at the
opening performance last night of one of
the best plays ever seen in this city. From
all the comments heard it seems destined
for a long and prosperous run and will be
enjoyed by the thousands who may see it

~~~ The ~~~
CLOISTERS

CLOISTER OLDSTYLE ❦ CLOISTER ITALIC ❦ CLOISTER BOLD ❦ CLOISTER BOLD ITALIC ❦ CLOISTER BOLD CONDENSED ❦ THE CLOISTER INITIALS

CLOISTER OLDSTYLE, the first series of the Cloister family, was designed along lines similar to the type face designed and cast in Venice by NICOLAS JENSON, and first used by that excellent printer in the Eusebius of 1470. To the first series were added other members of the Cloister family as shown in this catalogue. All are cast on Art Line

NICOLAS JENSON produced the finest books that were printed in the first half century of printing. Born in France in 1420, he commenced printing in Venice, Italy, in 1470, and in his first year produced four important editions, and more than one hundred and fifty during the remaining ten years of his life. Most of these books were composed entirely in his roman types, which competent authorities agree have never been surpassed for their beauty. All of his books are printed in either quarto or folio, and one of their chief characteristics is simplicity

CLOISTER INITIALS

Cloister Italic

10 Point — 28 A 56 a
SHOWING AT MUSEUM
Great crowds flock to see picture painted in many beautiful colors by a distinguished foreign worker

8 Point — 30 A 60 a
NEW ISLANDS DISCOVERED
Astronomer reports finding of several new celestial bodies which had baffled scholarly professors all over the world

6 Point — 33 A 65 a
PLEASING COMBINATION TRIED
Securing harmonious results in your printed matter calls for the proper selection of paper, ink and type coupled with neat and careful workmanship from beginning to end. Only in this way can the good will of a customer be secured and counted among a printer's assets

American Line
TYPE
The Best in Style Variety and Design

American faces, both in fashion and finish, lead the world, and it is the policy of this Company to produce new ornaments and borders which are designed to ensure perfect harmony

American Type Founders Sales Corporation

16 Point — 19 A 38 a
GIRL PROMOTED
Stenographer awarded position as private aide

14 Point — 23 A 46 a
LEADING WORKER
Sells building to manager of big furniture company

12 Point — 26 A 52 a
JOINT PROPOSITION
Merchants settle final details for risk conference to be held next week in neighboring city

Characters in Complete Font
AaBbCc
DdEeFg
GhIiJjKl
MmNn
OoPpQrR
SsTtUuV
WXYyZ
&$1234567
890abcdefg
hijkklmnop
qrstuvvww
xyzffffiflffiffl
Qu & st () []
. , - ' " " .,;:!?

Lining Figures 1234567890
are put up in separate fonts
and furnished only when
specially ordered

72 Point — 4 A 6 a
Bipeds

60 Point — 5 A 8 a
Register

48 Point — 6 A 12 a
PIN Stick

42 Point — 7 A 13 a
Huge ELK

36 Point — 8 A 16 a
KITCHEN
Busy Student

30 Point — 9 A 17 a
PROSPERED
New Condition

24 Point — 11 A 20 a
LIGHT SHADE
Eastern Merchants

18 Point — 17 A 31 a
HOME PLEASURES
Books Supply Enjoyment

THE CLOISTER FAMILY FOR DISTINCTIVE COMPOSITION

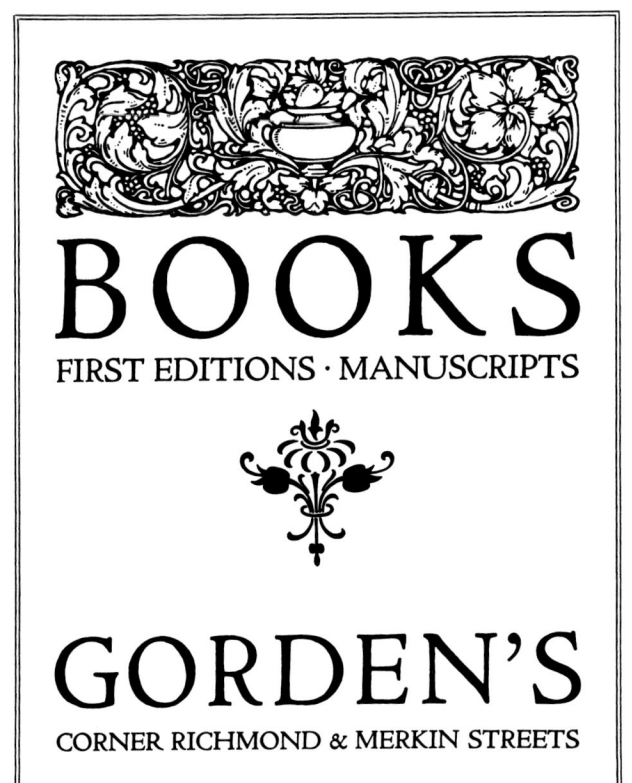

BOOKS
FIRST EDITIONS · MANUSCRIPTS

GORDEN'S
CORNER RICHMOND & MERKIN STREETS

CLOISTER ORNAMENTS

Cloister Lightface

48 Point — 6A 11a

Metaphorical Expression

42 Point — 6A 13a

New Hyacinth Cultivated

36 Point — 7A 13a

Display Excellent Qualifications

30 Point — 8A 15a

Argument Presented Diplomatically

24 Point — 10A 20a

Extraordinary Difficulties Stimulate Thought

18 Point — 15A 29a

Admirable Report
Mechanical Supervisors
Congratulated

16 Point — 16A 32a

Fine Characteristics
Distinguished Philosopher
Endows Hospital

14 Point — 22A 42a

Magnificent Spectacle
Beautiful Japanese Landscapes
Greatly Appreciated

12 Point — 24A 48a

Bicentennial Celebration
Extraordinary Monument Erected
Commemorating Event

10 Point — 26A 53a

Most Charming Personality
Governor Enthusiastically Applauded
Delivers Fine Address

8 Point — 28A 58a

Remarkably Interesting Incidents
Local Editor Publishing Autobiographies of
Most Prominent Citizens

6 Point — 31A 64a

Always Keep in Good Physical Condition
Intelligent Exercise and Careful Habits of Paramount
Importance in Preserving Health

SMALL CAPS for Cloister Lightface from 6 to 18 pt. are fonted separately and furnished only when specially ordered

---

CLOISTER OLDSTYLE and Cloister Lightface are adaptations to twentieth century use of the celebrated roman type design of Nicolas Jenson, first used by him in his printing house in Venice in 1470. Jenson's design, cut by him in one size only (approximately 16 point), has been acclaimed by many authorities as the ideal roman type design. The American Type Founders Company has conscientiously adhered to the Jenson model in the interpretations of that design now comprising the Cloister Type Family. Jenson did not use the capital letters J and U, Arabic figures or italic because none of these were at that time in use in printing. These characters had therefore to be added, as well as a squeezed form of the R (thus, HRH) for use in cap lines. Jenson did not use cap lines and for that reason

CALLIGRAPH INITIAL

AN HISTORIC
ROMAN TYPE DESIGN
OF UNSURPASSED
DISTINCTION

Characters in Complete Font

A B C D E F G H I J K L M N O P Q R R S T U V
W X Y Z & $ 1 2 3 4 5 6 7 8 9 0 a b c d e f g h i j k l m n o
p q r s t u v w x y z ff fi fl ffi ffl Qu & . , - ' ' " " : ; ! ? [ ] ( )

1 2 3 4 5 6 7 8 9 0 $ Lining Figures for Cloister Lightface in all sizes are fonted separately and furnished only when specially ordered

:[78]:

Cloister Lightface Italic

12 Point   29A   48a
An Admirable Example
Charitably Inclined Citizen Endowed
Benevolent Institutions

10 Point   31A   54a
Improving Suburban Property
More and Better Roads Most Essential to
Real Estate Development

8 Point   32A   60a
Educational Literature Distributed
Schools and Colleges Everywhere Supplied with
Latest Methods of Instruction

6 Point   37A   63a
Eighth Annual Financial Report Approved
Board of Directors Highly Complimented for Excellent
Results Obtained During Depression

18 Point   16A   32a
Honorable Mention
Unusual Executive Ability
Secured Reward

16 Point   21A   36a
Establishing Confidence
Municipal Bonds Considered
Sound Investment

14 Point   25A   44a
Progressive Merchant
American Manufacturer Offering
Distinctive Creations

48 Point   6A   12a
Municipalities
Organized

42 Point   8A   13a
Romantic Songs
Exhilarate

36 Point   9A   16a
Superior Magazine
Advertisement

30 Point   10A   18a
Diplomatic Executives
Hold Conference

24 Point   12A   21a
Bright University Graduate
Given Opportunity

---

could use a freer-flowing R, which, though more beautiful, does not adapt itself to every modern usage (thus, HRH). It was in 1914 that the American Type Founders Company announced its Cloister Oldstyle roman and italic. The intent was to restore the Jenson design in its original purity so far as modeling the letters was concerned, but a decision had to be made in the important detail of color. To adapt the design for use on smooth-surface papers, upon which the larger part of commercial printing is done, Cloister Oldstyle types were made heavier than the types cut by Jenson. Printed on smooth-surface papers, Cloister Oldstyle has the same thickness of line as the original types of Jenson appear to have when printed on the rough-surface papers that Jenson had to use, which required heavy impressions on dampened sheets, spreading the ink and creating an artificial thickness of line beyond that actually in

A ROMAN TYPE
DESIGN FIRST USED
BY NICOLAS
JENSON

Characters in Complete Font

A ᴀ B C D D E ᴇ F G G H I J Ĵ K L M M N ɴ O P P Q R R S
T ᴛ U ᴜ V ᴠ W X Y Y Z & $ 1 2 3 4 5 6 7 8 9 0 a b c d e f g h i j k k
l m n o p q r s t u v v w w x y z ff fi fl ffi ffl Qu & st . , - ' ' " " : ; ! ? ( ) [ ]

1 2 3 4 5 6 7 8 9 0 $ Lining Figures for Cloister Lightface Italic in all sizes are fonted separately and furnished only when specially ordered

Cloister Bold

72 Point — 3A 5a
Nice Motor

60 Point — 4A 7a
Same Reports

48 Point — 5A 10a
HANDSOMER
Gowns Displayed

42 Point — 6A 10a
QUAINT STORE
Strange Idol Found

36 Point — 6A 11a
HIGHER GRADE
Stronger Endurance

30 Point — 7A 13a
CHARMING WRAPS
School Swimming Races

24 Point — 9A 17a
DELIGHTFUL BARGAIN
Original Manuscript Bought

Characters in Complete Font

A B C D E F G H
I J K L M N O
P Q R R S T U
V W X Y Z & $
1 2 3 4 5 6 7 8 9 0
a b c d e f g h i
j k l m n o p q r s
t u v w x y z ff fi
fl ffi ffl Qu ct " ' "
. , - : ; ! ?

Oldstyle Figures 1234567890 are put up in separate fonts and furnished only when specially ordered

---

FROBEN & ERASMUS
The Story of a Friendship Unique in the Annals of Printing

6 POINT INTERRELATING BORDER NO. 16

---

18 Point — 13A 25a
GRAND SALE
Useful furniture
and other goods

14 Point — 18A 37a
FINEST SERVICE
Department receives
biggest consignment

12 Point — 22A 42a
BEAUTIFUL HOME
Retired cigar merchant
purchased little cottage
near highest mountains

10 Point — 23A 46a
ECONOMIC LECTURE
Newly appointed physical
instructor delights village
pupils with clever remarks

8 Point — 25A 51a
RELIABLE SUGGESTION
Good advice properly digested
guarantees success. American
products have helped printers

6 Point — 29A 56a
SPLENDID RESULT SECURED
Numerous workmen throughout the
United States are studying personal
efficiency. Improved morale satisfies
leading industrial leaders and welfare
investigators support the movement

Cloister Bold Italic

Characters in Complete Font

A A B B C C D D E
E F G G H I J J K L
M M N N O P P Q
R R S T T U V V
W X Y Y Z & $
1 2 3 4 5 6 7 8 9 0
a b c d e f g h i j k l
m n o p q r s t u v v
w w x y z ff fi fl ffi ffl
Qu ct st " " . , - ' ' : ; ! ?

JOHN FROBEN
*Presents a Communication from the Dutch
Scholar Desiderius Erasmus*

6 POINT INTERRELATING BORDER NO. 19

---

72 Point — 4A 6a

Nationally 1

60 Point — 4A 7a

6 Rough Shoes

48 Point — 6A 10a

*ASSOCIATION
of Agriculturists 2*

42 Point — 7A 10a

*FINE PRESERVES
Condiment Supreme*

36 Point — 7A 11a

*BRILLIANT ROBE
In Exquisite Displays*

30 Point — 8A 16a

*GOOD TYPOGRAPHY
Essential For Advertising*

24 Point — 9A 17a

*AMERICAN TYPE STYLES
Combine Richness of Design 4*

---

10 Point — 25A 50a
*INCREASING BUSINESS
Live printers follow modern
fashions closely and observe
the many useful type designs*

8 Point — 27A 54a
*IMPROVING CONDITIONS
Antiquated printing material is
properly replaced by something
which will attract new customers*

6 Point — 29A 58a
*ORIGINAL IDEAS RECOGNIZED
Those who excel in printing generally
possess literary skill. Leaders succeed
because they fairly appreciate the fact
that there is more for them to consider
than the turning out of a pretty design*

18 Point — 15A 30a
*MORE FRIGID
Low temperature
dispelled comfort*

14 Point — 21A 40a
*RESUMED HOMES
Simple paneling effect
strengthens outer part*

12 Point — 22A 45a
*NOTICE CONTRAST
Capable printers admire
clear, sharp results when
type used is foundry cast*

:[81]:

Century Oldstyle

72 Point — 3 A 4 a
58 Cycles

60 Point — 3 A 5 a
Raised BID

48 Point — 4 A 7 a
SON Qualifies

42 Point — 4 A 8 a
MITRE
Injector

36 Point — 5 A 8 a
HINDER
Distantly

30 Point — 5 A 10 a
BRUSHED
Liquidation

24 Point — 6 A 13 a
SOUVENIRS
Grandmother

---

18 Point — 10 A 20 a
GUARDIANS
BOATS rushed
through canal

14 Point — 14 A 26 a
EAGLE SAILED
OWNER left when
clearance arrived
from proper clerk

12 Point — 17 A 32 a
ADMIRE NATURE
MANY famous artists
now colonizing along
historic river bottom

---

10 Point — 17 A 35 a
WESTERN HOMES
TWELVE families left
pretty eastern towns
recently for Idaho to
locate disputed lands

8 Point — 21 A 42 a
ENCOURAGE SCHOLAR
SEVERAL thoughtful years
of painstaking application
generally produces versed
minds. Ambitious student
received free scholarships

6 Point — 23 A 46 a
ORGANIZED NEW SOCIETY
STUDENTS aid community club
organized recently by children
in a university town. The main
objects are to keep the campus
clean and create better feeling

9 and 11 Point carried in stock only at Foundry

Creating
Highest Business
Ideals

6 POINT TEAGUE BORDER NO. 620

Characters in Complete Font

A B C D E F G
H I J K L M N
O P Q R S T U
V W X Y Z & $
1 2 3 4 5 6 7 8 9 0
a b c d e f g h i j k
l m n o p q r s t u
v w x y z ct st ff fi
fl ffi ffl . , - ' : ; ! ?

Characters)] " " are furnished with all fonts
from 6 to 18 Point inclusive

SMALL CAPS from 6 to 18 Point are put up in separate
fonts and furnished only when specially ordered

The Euterpe
Conservatory
of Music

FRANCIS KEMPTON, *Director*

COURSES are arranged into
three sections, Interpretive,
Vocal and Instrumental. An
unexcelled faculty of noted
musicians insures high
grade instruction

43 Michigan Avenue, Detroit

VOCATIONAL CAMEO NO. 4811

Century Oldstyle Series
for Plain Talk

Century Oldstyle Italic

10 Point — 18 A 35 a
FRANK MOTIVES
Real sincerity, though not an invited guest, is free to all, and carries his welcome with him

8 Point — 20 A 42 a
UNIVERSAL DECISION
Mental pleasures never cloy; unlike those of the body, they are approved of by reflection, increased by repetition, and made stronger by enjoyment

6 Point — 23 A 45 a
HAS STRONG INFLUENCE
Beauty has been the torment and the delight of the world ever since it began. Philosophers knew of its power for they left sayings which show how great was its influence

9 and 11 Point carried in stock only at Foundry

18 Point — 9 A 20 a
DEFORMED
Many persons attended show

14 Point — 14 A 29 a
REVOLUTIONS
State officials and terminal engineer inspect new canal

12 Point — 17 A 32 a
NOBLE BURGHER
Remarkable collection of foreign gems found hidden in old chateau

72 Point — 3 A 4 a
Spirit '76

60 Point — 3 A 4 a
HIS Rights

48 Point — 4 A 8 a
Quality FINE

42 Point — 5 A 8 a
HOIST
Rapidly

36 Point — 5 A 8 a
MARCH
Heighten

30 Point — 6 A 10 a
NUMBER
Knowledge

24 Point — 6 A 12 a
UNWOUND
Queer Dialect

Care and Feeding of the Infant

SUGGESTIONS FOR THE USE OF HENKEL PURE FOOD PRODUCTS ADAPTED FOR THE LITTLE ONE

NATURE intended children to live, but the survival is not the only thing to consider. To thrive properly and to grow into perfect robust and healthy maturity an infant must have proper foods, suitable clothing and receive proper care, which includes keeping the infant as perfectly sweet, wholesome and clean as possible. It needs air as well as the warm sunshine in abundance and should not

CLOISTER ORNAMENT NO. 1822

Century Oldstyle Italic for Legibility

Norfolk Musical Association

Admit Two

6 POINT TEAGUE BORDER NO. 608

Characters in Complete Font

A B C D E F G
H I J K L M N O
P Q R S T U V
W X Y Z & $ 1 2
3 4 5 6 7 8 9 0
a b c d e f g h i j k
l m n o p q r s t u
v w x y z ct st ff fi
fl ffi ffl . , - ' : ; ! ?

:[83]:

Century Oldstyle Bold

120 Point — 3 A 4 a
Boy 6

96 Point — 3 A 4 a
8 Sales

84 Point — 3 A 4 a
Rags 1

72 Point — 3 A 4 a
2 Soups

60 Point — 3 A 4 a
High Hat

48 Point — 4 A 6 a
COUNCIL 3
Noted Band

Characters in Complete Font

A B C D E F G
H I J K L M N O
P Q R S T U V
W X Y Z & $ 1 2
3 4 5 6 7 8 9 0
a b c d e f g h i
j k l m n o p q r
s t u v w x y z
. , - ' : ; ! ?

9 and 54 Point carried in stock only at Foundry

⌐Book Marks⌐
CENTURY OLDSTYLE BOLD
HARLEQUIN SERIES 3 M 4

42 Point — 4 A 7 a
Eight

36 Point — 4 A 7 a
Spoke

30 Point — 5 A 9 a
MOIRE
Bridget

24 Point — 6 A 12 a
DEPEND
Imported

18 Point — 9 A 18 a
REBUILDS
Omniscient

14 Point — 12 A 24 a
HELIOTROPE
Plants Flowers

12 Point — 14 A 29 a
NOURISHMENT
Settlement house
has feast for kids

10 Point — 16 A 32 a
HIGH MOUNTAIN
Climbing the rocky
roads gives delight

8 Point — 19 A 38 a
GOVERNMENT BONDS
Exceptional opportunity
for investment purposes

6 Point — 21 A 42 a
BITUMINOUS COAL FIELD
Underground passages make
visiting extremely hazardous

5 Point — 20 A 40 a
BREAKS RECORD IN AVIATION
Experience gained while in France
helps aviator wonderfully making
record flights in the United States

Century Catalogue and *Century Catalogue Italic*

36 Point   6 A   10 a
NICE FIGURES 39
15 Unusual Bargains

30 Point   7 A   14 a
BROCHURE HELPED
Designed Rare Specimen

24 Point   9 A   17 a
GRAND BARGAIN SALES
Several Authentic Copies Sold

18 Point   13 A   26 a
MAGNIFICENT GARDEN HOME
Quieted Nerves Brought Contentment

14 Point   19 A   37 a
HUMBLE PEASANT FOUND TREASURE
Plough Brought Farmers Unexpected Bonanza

12 Point   22 A   43 a
ROMANTIC PRINTER ENTHUSIASTIC READER
Began life among lowly inhabitants of dismal metropolis and through intelligent reading learned rudiments of law

10 Point   24 A   48 a
GIGANTIC WORLD EXPOSITION DELIGHTS MILLIONS
Modern displays electrified audience of graphic arts connoisseurs attending magnificent advertising exhibition held in northern city

8 Point   27 A   54 a
QUANTITY PRODUCTION OF FINE PRINTING REQUIRES BRAINS
Beautiful examples of the modern trend in typography and color work are not produced like so much hash. They require intelligent planning and supervision

6 Point   30 A   60 a
MANUSCRIPT BOOKS WRITTEN AND ORNAMENTED BY ANCIENT CRAFTSMEN
Rare gems of the typographic art were produced nearly five hundred years ago, and for hundreds of years before the invention of moveable type, every book had to be written and decorated by an artist skilled in calligraphy and ornament. Is it any wonder that the first book printed far excelled later examples of typography? For printing as an art steadily declined until the last years of the nineteenth century, when William Morris started a renaissance that is reflected in work of to-day

---

Characters in Complete Font

A B C D E F G H I
J K L M N O P Q R
S T U V W X Y Z &
$ 1 2 3 4 5 6 7 8 9 0
a b c d e f g h i j k l m
n o p q r s t u v w x y z
ff fi fl ffi ffl . , - ' ' " " : ; ! ?

SMALL CAPS from 6 to 18 Point are put up separately and furnished only when specially ordered

---

Century Catalogue Italic

18 Point   13 A   26 a
PROPER METHODS
Expected Unbiased Judge

14 Point   18 A   35 a
QUESTION RENEGADES
Introduces Damaging Evidence

12 Point   23 A   44 a   8 Point   26 A   52 a
REDUCTIONS   *SEARCH BUILDING*
Perfected System   *Clever detectives found machine and equipment*

10 Point   23 A   45 a   6 Point   29 A   54 a
HIDE UNIFORM   *ENERGETIC PRINTERS*
Magnificent Design   *Prominent designers exhibit several handsome specimens*

Characters in Complete Font

A B C D E F G H I J
K L M N O P Q R S
T U V W X Y Z & $
1 2 3 4 5 6 7 8 9 0
a b c d e f g h i j k l m n
o p q r s t u v w x y z ct
ff fi fl ffi ffl . , - ' : ; ! ?

:[85]:

Century Schoolbook and *Century Schoolbook Italic*

48 Point — 5A 8a
BIG Liners 4

36 Point — 5A 10a
Splendid MUSIC

30 Point — 6A 12a
NICER Calculation 9

24 Point — 8A 14a
HEROIC COMMANDER
Courageous Sailors Cited

18 Point — 11A 22a
MANY GALLANT OFFICERS
SCOTCH Brigade Fought Bravely

16 Point — 13A 24a
MODERN SOUTHERN MANSION
IDEAL Springtime Among Blossoms

14 Point — 16A 32a
DESCRIBE INDUSTRIOUS NATIVES
UNIQUE Description of a Strange People

12 Point — 20A 40a
PROMISING TESTIMONY READILY GIVEN
QUICK Decision Sought in Recent Market Case

10 Point — 22A 44a
DELIGHTFUL SUMMERTIME EVENTS PROMISED
STEAMBOAT Outing Greatly Enjoyed by Society Children

8 Point — 26A 50a
BRONZE TABLETS AND QUAINT ORIENTAL IDOLS SECURED
HISTORICAL Treasures are Given to Scientific Museum by Explorers

6 Point — 28A 55a
MODERN DISTRIBUTION SYSTEM ADMIRED BY BRILLIANT EXECUTIVES
DISTINGUISHED Visitors Pouring Into Town for the Annual Manufacturing Exhibit

---

Characters in Complete Font

A B C D E F G H I J K L
M N O P Q R S T U V W X
Y Z & $ 1 2 3 4 5 6 7 8 9 0
a b c d e f g h i j k l m n
o p q r s t u v w x y z ff fi
fl ffi ffl . , - ' : ; ! ?

SMALL CAPS from 6 to 18 Point are put up separately and furnished only when specially ordered

9 Point Century Schoolbook *and Italic* carried in stock only at Foundry

Century Schoolbook Italic

48 Point — 5A 8a
Sight

36 Point — 6A 10a
Dutiful

30 Point — 6A 12a
Expedite

24 Point — 8A 14a
Highlands

18 Point — 11A 22a
Next Meeting

16 Point — 13A 26a
SPORTSMEN
Displayed Grit

14 Point — 16A 32a
REPRODUCED
Banking Capital

12 Point — 20A 38a
KIND MOTHER
Quarterly Booklet

10 Point — 21A 43a
NEW SELECTION
Interesting Example

8 Point — 25A 50a
PENURIOUS OWNER
Secured Competent Men

6 Point — 30A 58a
RIDICULOUS INTERVIEW
Diligent Steamship Reporters

Characters in Complete Font

*A B C D E F
G H I J K L
M N O P Q R
S T U V W X
Y Z & $ 1 2 3
4 5 6 7 8 9 0
a b c d e f g h
i j k l m n o p
q r s t u v w
x y z ff fi fl ffi
ffl . , - ' : ; ! ?*

Century Schoolbook Bold and Schoolbook Oldstyle

48 Point   4 A 7 a
LINK
River

36 Point   5 A 9 a
PURSE
Marked

30 Point   6 A 10 a
REPORT
Procured

24 Point   9 A 15 a
NUMBERS
Production

18 Point   11 A 21 a
ENDURANCE
Muscular boys
gain first prize

16 Point   12 A 22 a
NEIGHBORING
Educated youth
kindly advising

14 Point   14 A 27 a
IMPORT CIGARS
Charming oriental
aroma fills the air

---

12 Point   17 A 34 a
INCREASE PROFITS
Revival of business is
encouraging everyone

10 Point   20 A 40 a
THE GOLDEN SILENCE
Consider silently what a
man says, as words often
betray the speaker's mind

8 Point   23 A 44 a
THE ROAD TO GREATNESS
Many people say greatness is
but an eminence the ascent to
which is very steep and lofty

6 Point   26 A 52 a
A GOOD NATURED COUNTENANCE
Good nature is really more agreeable
than wit. It gives to the countenance
an air much more benign than beauty

Characters in Complete Font

A B C D E F G H I
J K L M N O P Q R
S T U V W X Y Z &
$ 1 2 3 4 5 6 7 8 9 0
a b c d e f g h i j k
l m n o p q r s t u
v w x y z ff fi fl ffi ffl
. , - ' : ; ! ?

Schoolbook Oldstyle

48 Point   5 A 8 a
Mined

36 Point   5 A 10 a
Intrudes

30 Point   6 A 12 a
Nice Bank

24 Point   9 A 15 a
MONITORS
Best Student

18 Point   12 A 23 a
QUICK WORK
RECENT Change

14 Point   17 A 32 a
FINE INTERVIEW
CURIOUS Merchants

---

12 Point   19 A 38 a
BEST AUTHORS
ENGLISH professor
writes love stories

10 Point   23 A 44 a
MIGHTY HUNTER
NOTED explorer wins
high honors in Africa

8 Point   25 A 50 a
MILITARY TACTICS
IMPRESSIVE ceremony
marked the arrival of
our victorious soldiers

6 Point   30 A 55 a
PHYSICAL AND MENTAL
HEALTHFUL recreation with
a proper diet is the best way
to prolong life and health

Characters in Complete Font

A B C D E F G H I J
K L M N O P Q R S
T U V W X Y Z & $
1 2 3 4 5 6 7 8 9 0
a b c d e f g h i j k
l m n o p q r s t u v
w x y z ff fi fl ffi ffl
. , - ' ' : ; ! ?

SMALL CAPS from 6 to 18 Point are put up in separate
fonts and furnished only when specially ordered

Century Expanded

72 Point — 3 A 4 a
BIG Rut

60 Point — 3 A 4 a
NURSE 9
High Play

48 Point — 4 A 6 a
4 BONDING
King Signed

42 Point — 4 A 7 a
CHILD MIND
Eloquent Girls

36 Point — 4 A 7 a
MANY GUILDS
Drawing Society

30 Point — 5 A 10 a
GENEROUS LEAD
Olympic games now
are pleasing writers

CENTURY EXPANDED
EASY ON EYES

24 Point — 6 A 11 a
NUMBER
Encamped

18 Point — 9 A 20 a
SQUIRMING
Indescribable

14 Point — 12 A 26 a
HEARD CHOIR
Rehearsals make
efficient vocalists

12 Point — 15 A 32 a
GENUINE STONE
SQUARE shaped relic
exhumed from ruins

10 Point — 18 A 36 a
PRINTER HONORED
MANY fellow craftsmen
worship famous master

8 Point — 20 A 40 a
PROMOTED EIGHT MEN
MANAGER promised another
promotion soon. Young men
should continually study the
science of being progressive

6 Point — 24 A 48 a
CONCERNING RUBBER TREES
INDIA rubber trees that are tapped
every other day continue to render
sap for over twenty years, and the
oldest trees produce the richest sap

5 Point — 23 A 45 a
KNOWLEDGE TAKEN BY CHANCE
ALMOST everyone you meet knows more
on some subject than you do. Turn that
side of him towards you and absorb all
you can while the opportunity is present
and endeavor to mentally remember the
most important points you have learned

4½ Point — 19 A 38 a
EDUCATING HORSES FOR THE CAVALRY
HORSES used by the United States cavalry must
be thoroughly trained in war work. The horses
not only learn to stand steady under fire, but
must know how to turn at the proper moment
when the bridle is hanging loose, how to lie
down and get up, and a score of other details

4 Point — 21 A 42 a
WHY BUBBLES ARE ROUND AND EQUAL
BUBBLES are round because the air that forms
the inside of the bubble pushes with uniform
strength against all parts of the delicate film of
water that surrounds it. The air presses evenly
against the sides of the bubble so it stays round

5½, 7, 9 and 11 Point carried in stock only at Foundry

Characters in Complete Font

A B C D E F G H I J K L
M N O P Q R S T U V W
X Y Z & $ 1 2 3 4 5 6 7 8 9 0
a b c d e f g h i j k l
m n o p q r s t u v w x
y z ff fi fl ffi ffl . , - ' : ; ! ?

Characters ( ) are furnished with sizes from 4 to 36 Point
Characters [ ] are furnished with sizes from 4 to 14 Point
SMALL CAPS from 4 to 12 Point are put up in separate fonts and
furnished only when specially ordered

Century Expanded Italic

6 Point — 23 A 45 a
CONCERNING DEPORTMENT
Politeness may be defined as a true kindness. It is more a matter of the heart than of established precedent

5 Point — 22 A 44 a
YOUR DRESS AND APPEARANCE
Personal cleanliness and neat garments are marks of self-respect, and no person should neglect these important matters

4½ Point — 19 A 38 a
READING FOR MENTAL RECREATION
Books of commonplace are the amusements of literature. It is pleasant to have at one's side a well-selected volume to which one may turn for mental recreation after unusual activities

4 Point — 22 A 44 a
ACCIDENTS DURING THE SEVENTIES
Do not think that life has been dangerous only since you began to race your tin wagon. In the exciting days of the seventies, the fast horses and grocery wagons caused the death of many

12 Point — 16 A 30 a
NICE CUSTOMER
Returning salesmen praise general trade

10 Point — 18 A 36 a
DISPUTING ORIGIN
Foreign shipments offer opportunity to study the lives of many rare birds

8 Point — 20 A 42 a
ACCURACY AND SPEED
Many business firms employ adding machines and other clever labor-saving material

5½, 7, 9, 11, 42, 48, 60 and 72 Point carried in stock only at Foundry

---

Characters in Complete Font

A B C D E F G H I J K L
M N O P Q R S T U V W
X Y Z & $ 1 2 3 4 5 6 7 8 9 0
a b c d e f g h i j k l m
n o p q r s t u v w x y z
ff fi fl ffi ffl . , - ' : ; ! ?

---

36 Point — 4 A 8 a
HEAR GUARD
Spring Clothes 10

30 Point — 5 A 10 a
BOUGHT DESIGN
29 Buy Modern Style

24 Point — 6 A 12 a
BROUGHT LINGERIE
Importers Helped Dealer

18 Point — 9 A 21 a
MYSTERIOUS RENEGADES
History full of stories about band who terrified neutral inhabitants

14 Point — 13 A 28 a
INTERESTING STORIES WRITTEN
Sea captain becomes famous novelist and learned authority on all matters nautical

---

Century Expanded Italic

THIS face is easy to read and pleasing to the eye, possessing an individuality which gives distinctiveness. It is carefully cut and accurately cast, with the kerned letters eliminated to an unusual extent for an italic. Century Expanded Italic is a member of the celebrated Century Family of type faces. Its adaptability and attractive appearance have made it an important member of this wonderfully popular family as well as a standard italic face in the world of printing

An Italic Design Without Hairlines

American Type Founders Sales Corporation

Century Expanded Italic

Easy To Read And Pleasing To The Eye

12 POINT OLD ENGLISH BORDER NO. 47   JAQUISH DASH

Century Bold

120 Point — 3A 4a

Bold 5

96 Point — 3A 4a

Red Ink

Characters in Complete Font

A B C D E F G
H I J K L M N
O P Q R S T U
V W X Y Z & $
1 2 3 4 5 6 7 8 9 0
a b c d e f g h
i j k l m n o p
q r s t u v w x
y z ff fi fl ffi ffl
. , - ' : ; ! ?

9 and 11 Point carried in stock only at Foundry

84 Point — 3A 4a

His Act

72 Point — 3A 4a

So Bad 3

60 Point — 3A 4a

Nice Land

48 Point — 4A 6a

PRODUCED
Great Leader

42 Point — 4A 7a

MIST
Right

36 Point — 4A 7a

BEND
Rights

30 Point — 5A 10a

MINER
Diptych

24 Point — 6A 12a

SHRUNK
Habituate

18 Point — 10A 18a

NEIGHBOR
Honest girls
forgot purse

14 Point — 13A 26a

DISTINGUISH
Metal salesmen
produce results

12 Point — 15A 32a

CHILD PRODIGY
Award scholarship
to youthful athlete

10 Point — 18A 36a

PROMOTE SCIENCE
Aged college professor
recipient of many gifts

8 Point — 20A 40a

MYSTERIOUS HEROINE
Identity disclosed as young
lady reveals characteristics

6 Point — 24A 48a

FOREIGN SONGBIRD ARRIVES
Country folk greet famous singer
who rendered delightful selection

:[90]:

Century Bold Italic

Characters in Complete Font

A B C D E F G
H I J K L M N
O P Q R S T U
V W X Y Z & $
1 2 3 4 5 6 7 8 9 0
a b c d e f g h
i j k l m n o p
q r s t u v w x
y z ff fi fl ffi ffl
. , - ' : ; ! ?

9 and 11 Point carried in stock only at Foundry

72 Point — 3 A 4 a

The Boy 2

60 Point — 3 A 4 a

1 Night Owl

48 Point — 4 A 6 a

Advertising 30

12 Point — 14 A 30 a

GREETS MINER
Big ovation given
speaker returning
from wage parley

10 Point — 17 A 32 a

GAINED SUPPORT
Shop magazines and
bulletins are proving
effective agencies for
strengthening credit

8 Point — 18 A 36 a

YOU WILL FIND NEW
ideas and new materials
in this catalog with which
to enhance the quality of
your print shop. The type
designs in this book show
a large number of latest
and modern faces. Every

6 Point — 22 A 44 a

EVERYTHING FOR PRINTERS
Typographic borders are still in
popular demand having acquired
it because they serve a useful and
very specific purpose. A border
or a combination of borders used
in displaying an advertisement
will distinguish it and make it
stand out from among a full page
of varied pieces of copy or as the

24 Point — 6 A 10 a

HINDER
Boy choir
applauds
song film

18 Point — 9 A 17 a

SPECIMEN
Joyful child
surprised by
schoolmates
in new home

14 Point — 14 A 27 a

MERCHANTS
Salesman used
new method to
secure smarter
business hands
in department

42 Point — 4 A 6 a

20 CENTRAL
Evening Song

36 Point — 4 A 7 a

BEAUTIFUL 10
Modest Maidens
Great Simplicity

30 Point — 5 A 9 a

NATIONAL BANK
American Republics
Interesting Bargain

:[91]:

Century Bold Condensed

72 Point — 3A 4a
Big Display 2

60 Point — 3A 5a
7 Spring Models

48 Point — 5A 8a
Reliable Bargain 19

42 Point — 5A 8a
4 DESIGN NEW ROBES
Majestical Reception

36 Point — 5A 10a
RARE IMPORTED GEMS
Delights Shrewd Jeweler

30 Point — 7A 14a
EASTER SILK HOSIERY SALE
Stylish Design Quickly Bought

24 Point — 9A 18a
HUGE MARKET LEASED BUILDING
Gigantic corporation starts activity
near picturesque eastern metropolis

Characters in Complete Font

A B C D E F G H I
J K L M N O P Q R
S T U V W X Y Z & $
1 2 3 4 5 6 7 8 9 0
a b c d e f g h i j k
l m n o p q r s t u v
w x y z ff fi fl ffi ffl
. , - ' : ; ! ?

Century Bold Condensed

18 Point — 14A 28a
HUMOROUS SONG
Broadway comedy
proving successful

14 Point — 19A 39a
NORTHERN ORCHARD
Profitable agricultural
achievement explained

12 Point — 23A 47a
RENOWNED BIOGRAPHER
Describes personality with
seldom equaled adroitness
and characteristic charity

10 Point — 25A 50a
MYSTERIOUS HAPPENING
Remarkably clever stories
describing wanderings and
adventures among strange
and uncivilized aborigines

8 Point — 31A 63a
INTERESTING SPANISH MISSION
California boasts many romantic
and picturesque old missions that
should be included in the itinerary
of every person visiting that state

6 Point — 30A 60a
BEAUTIFUL MUSICAL COMPOSITIONS
Somebody has said that practically all
the music of humankind might perish
without serious loss provided the love
songs might remain. Everybody knows
there are moments in famed love songs
unreached anywhere else in our music

Baskerville Roman

72 Point   3 A   4 a

Kid Belt

60 Point   3 A   5 a

Big Rink 7

48 Point   4 A   6 a

5 Hard Metal

36 Point   4 A   8 a

RENUMBER
Serious Knight

30 Point   5 A   9 a

MERITORIOUS
Reports Produced

24 Point   9 A   16 a

IMPORTED JEWELS
Charming Pendant Secured

18 Point No. 2   13 A   24 a

PICTURESQUE MANSION
ROMANTIC Homestead Bought

18 Point No. 1   16 A   30 a

REFURNISHING DORMITORIES
APPROVE Modernistic Color Scheme

---

14 Point   20 A   39 a

INTRODUCTION
MAIDS Enter Society

12 Point   23 A   46 a

EXQUISITE MEALS
SERVICE Unusually Fine

10 Point   27 A   55 a

RESPONSIBLE CITIZEN
PURCHASED valuable property
near greatest railroad station

8 Point   30 A   58 a

GOLD BULLION INSURED
ENORMOUS shipments of precious
metals arrived under strong guard

6 Point   37 A   75 a

PRODUCES SPLENDID TYPOGRAPHY
THE AVERAGE printer produces good work
quickly with this wonderfully adaptable face

 BASKERVILLE ROMAN
BASKERVILLE ITALIC

Baskerville Italic

18 Point No. 2   13 A   26 a

KERNING
Reorganized

18 Point No. 1   15 A   30 a

STRENGTH
Reinforcements

14 Point   20 A   40 a

HEMISPHERE
Learn Geography

12 Point   25 A   50 a

SONG ADMIRED
Delightful Rendition

10 Point   31 A   60 a

RETIRE PRESIDENT
Unprecedented Procedure

8 Point   32 A   63 a

SCIENTIFIC REGULATION
Reconstructed Railroad Terminal

6 Point   36 A   70 a

PROFIT MAKING TYPE DESIGNS
American type faces are effective business
builders and a real delight to the vision

Characters in Complete Font

A B C D E F
G H I J K L
M N O P Q R
S T U V W X
Y Z & $ 1 2 3
4 5 6 7 8 9 0
a b c d e f g
h i j k l m n
o p q r s t u
v w x y z ff fi
fl ffi ffl &
. , - ' : ; ! ?

SMALL CAPS, 6 to 18 Point,
are put up separately and furnished
only when specially
ordered

Characters in Complete Font

A A B B C D D
E E F G G H I J K
L M N N O P
Q R R S T U V
W X Y Z & $
1 2 3 4 5 6 7 8 9 0
a b c d e f g h i j k l
m n o p q r s t u v w
x y z ff fi fl ffi ffl &
. , - ' : ; ! ?

Bookman Oldstyle

72 Point — 3A 4a

Napkin 4

60 Point — 3A 4a

9 MINK
Best Coat 1

48 Point — 4A 6a

5 SMOKING
The Job Office

36 Point — 4A 6a

RANCH BAR
Signal of Quality

30 Point — 5A 9a

MODERN & CHIC
Great displays typify
exhibits at auto show

Characters in Complete Font

A B C D E F G H I
J K L M N O P Q R
S T U V W X Y Z &
$ 1 2 3 4 5 6 7 8 9 0
a b c d e f g h i j k l
m n o p q r s t u v
w x y z ff fi fl ffi ffl
. , - ' : ; ! ?

These Special Characters, except the Ornament, are put up with each font. The Ornament is furnished with the 6 to 14 Point sizes inclusive

A M R r y of & The 🍃

9 Point carried in stock only at Foundry

BOOKMAN OLDSTYLE
3 POINT TEAGUE BORDER NO. 319

24 Point — 5A 10a
SOUND
Injection

20 Point — 6A 14a
ENDEAR
Gratuitous

18 Point — 9A 18a
RESUMING
Congratulate

14 Point — 13A 26a
MONOGRAMS
Neatly Designed

12 Point — 15A 32a
SEEK FORTUNE
Explorers search for
hidden copper mines

10 Point — 18A 36a
BUYING PROPERTY
Rich merchant develops
valuable suburban farm
land adjacent to railroad

8 Point — 20A 40a
BECOME COURAGEOUS
Success comes eventually to
those who have the courage
to smile when failure is near

6 Point — 23A 47a
CREATE POPULAR DEMAND
Progressive business men speak
highly of the advantages which
may be attributed to advertising

Bookman Italic

Characters in Complete Font

A B C D E F G H I
J K L M N O P Q R
S T U V W X Y Z &
$ 1 2 3 4 5 6 7 8 9 0
a b c d e f g h i j k l
m n o p q r s t u v
w x y z ff fi fl ffi ffl
. , - ' : ; ! ?

The following Special Characters are supplied with all fonts from 6 to 14 Point inclusive. They are sold in separate fonts from 18 to 72 Point inclusive, and furnished only when specially ordered

A *M* *R* *S* *s* *y*

9 Point carried in stock only at Foundry

BOOKMAN ITALIC
6 POINT TEAGUE BORDER NO. 610

72 Point   3 A 4 a
Break 5

60 Point   3 A 4 a
2 MUSIC
Reported

48 Point   3 A 7 a
LEADER 2
Strong Mind

36 Point   4 A 7 a
PERFORMER
Quaint Acrobat

30 Point   5 A 9 a
SERIOUS GIRLS
Charming orations
win great applause

10 Point   16 A 34 a
ENFORCE ORDER
Slovenly habit caused waste of valuable time and endless confusion

8 Point   19 A 38 a
FORESEEING THINGS
Those tales of dreams that have guided men are often much exaggerated, but true

6 Point   22 A 44 a
INTEGRITY UNDOUBTED
Honest and courageous persons have very little to say regarding either their honesty or integrity

12 Point   13 A 27 a
PERFECTION BRINGS REWARD
Splendid satisfaction comes from doing work perfectly, complete in every way

24 Point   5 A 11 a
MODES
Clothing

18 Point   9 A 18 a
DIAMOND
Respectable

14 Point   11 A 23 a
BURLESQUE
Comedian Wins

Scotch Roman

48 Point — 4 A 6 a
MORTISED 2
Special Reglets

36 Point — 4 A 7 a
CLEVER GUIDE
Soldiers gather many specimens for exhibit

30 Point — 5 A 10 a
EASTERN MANSION
Large delightful grounds exhibit mysterious jungle

24 Point — 6 A 11 a
RECEIVED ORDER
Management producing reliable specifications for constructing large floats

18 Point — 9 A 18 a
SENSATIONAL REPORTS
Undoubtedly masterful sleuths accurately presented opinions of sincere legislators during action

---

Characters in Complete Font

A B C D E F
G H I J K L
M N O P Q R
S T U V W X
Y Z & $ 1 2 3
4 5 6 7 8 9 0
a b c d e f g h
i j k l m n o p
q r s t u v w
x y z . , - ' : ; ! ?

The following characters are furnished with all fonts from 6 Point to 24 Point inclusive

ff fi fl ffi ffl

11, 60 and 72 Point carried in stock only at Foundry

Scotch ROMAN

---

14 Point — 13 A 26 a
DESIRED PURPOSE ACHIEVED
Modern devices and inventions are very prominent features of the ingenuity and the energetic development of humanity

12 Point — 15 A 30 a
GUIDE HUNTER
Numerous sportsmen take advantage of the remaining deer season

8 Point — 21 A 41 a
INCREASED NEW TRADE
Several merchants have found it highly profitable to organize and are starting campaigns for more business and equal profit

10 Point — 19 A 38 a
HEALTHY CHILDREN
Plenty of exercise outdoors and sufficient sleep are fine builders of excellent health

6 Point — 22 A 45 a
CONSTRUCT MANY BUILDINGS
National statistics compiled under supervision of reliable men show a large increase during the past year in the number of buildings erected

Scotch Roman Italic

Characters in Complete Font

A B C D E F
G H I J K L
M N O P Q R
S T U V W X
Y Z & $ 1 2 3
4 5 6 7 8 9 0
a b c d e f g h
i j k l m n o p
q r s t u v w x
y z ff fi fl ffi ffl
. , - ' : ; ! ?

11 Point carried in stock only at Foundry

48 Point — 3A 6a

6 BROMIDE
Royal Buglers

36 Point — 4A 6a

HOME BRIDE 8
Elegant position for
maid desiring travel

30 Point — 5A 8a

2 MODERN ROSES
Beautiful exhibit placed
among leading features

24 Point — 5A 10a

SECURE DESIGN
Attractive typography
from distinctive design
should help production

18 Point — 9A 15a

CHARMING SEASONS
Delightful party of European
excursionists and tourists are
traveling amid southern cities

14 Point — 12A 24a

MOTION PICTURE HOUSES
Draw plans for places to be opened in
heart of this city. Several foreign stars
will have the leading roles next season

8 Point — 22A 42a

BOUNDLESS PROSPECTS
Excellent opportunities present
themselves to investors who have
sufficient capital. Many citizens
migrating to unexplored regions

12 Point — 16A 32a

STOP RUSHING
Careless drivers given
plenty of warning and
must take consequence

6 Point — 23A 45a

CONNECTICUT IS BEAUTIFUL
Mountains and small lakes where
sport and scenery appeal to all are
only a part of nature's gift to this
wonderful section of New England

10 Point — 21A 42a

FIRM HAS PROSPECTS
Manufacturers of new article
are making giant strides with
assurance of many big orders

Nicolas Cochin

72 Point
3A 5a

Mythical Sights

60 Point
4A 6a

Quickly Displayed

48 Point
5A 8a

Explains Ideal Subject

36 Point
6A 11a

Delightful Chat

24 Point
8A 17a

Stylish Cloak Design

18 Point No. 2
11A 23a

PUBLIC OPINION
Great Questions Debated

18 Point No. 1
15A 28a

SPLENDID SUNRISE
Boy Describes Beautiful Sight

14 Point
18A 37a

REQUIRES EXPERIENCE
Demanded Exceptional Knowledge

12 Point
21A 42a

ADDS MUCH DISTINCTION
Compositors Produce Handsome Effects

10 Point
23A 47a

STYLE OF EIGHTEENTH CENTURY
Recent Exhibition Attracts Famous Printers

8 Point
26A 51a

NICOLAS COCHIN TYPES ARE FAMOUS
Beautifully Printed Specimens Receive Much Praise

6 Point
28A 55a

FRENCH TYPE DESIGNS QUITE DISTINCTIVE
Excellent Results Obtained Interested Desirable Customer

Characters in Complete Font

A B C D E F G
H I J K L M N
O P Q R S T U
V W X Y Z & $
1 2 3 4 5 6 7 8 9 0
a b c d e f g h i j k
l m n o p q r s t u v
w x y z ff fi fl ffi ffl
. , - ' " " : ; ! ?
( ) — « » *

Lining Figures have been added to the series to meet the requirements of the American printer

Original French Figures
Put up in separate fonts and furnished only when specially ordered

$ 1 2 3 4 5 6 7 8 9 0

MODERNISTIC DECORATORS NO. 3

Nicolas Cochin Italic

NICE *Graceful Style*
48 Point
5A 9a

Elegant Display Line NOTICE
36 Point
6A 11a

MODERN HOUSES ERECTED
Splendid Apartments Magnificently Decorated
24 Point
8A 15a

Characters in Complete Font

A B C D E F G
H I J K L M N
O P Q R S T U
V W X Y Z &
$ 1 2 3 4 5 6 7 8 9 0
a b c d e f g h i
j k l m n o p q r
r s t u v w x y z
ff fi fl ffi ffl & « »)
. , - ' : ; ! ?

Lining Figures have been added to the series to meet the requirements of the American printer

Original French Figures
Put up in separate fonts and furnished only when specially ordered
$ 1 2 3 4 5 6 7 8 9 0

YOUNG SOLDIER
Service medal awarded man when first enlistment expired
18 Point Nº 2
12A 24a

GRAND RECEPTION
Distinguished Guests Delighted
18 Point Nº 1
13A 26a

DESERVING CHARITIES
Supplies for earthquake victims sent from emergency storehouses instantly
14 Point
19A 37a

MUNICIPAL GOVERNMENT
Highway commissioner appoints deputies to patrol indian reservation fearing outbreaks
12 Point
22A 43a

DISTINCTIVE QUALITIES NOTED
Up-to-date typographers will quickly observe the versatility of this harmonious type series for catalogues, booklets, or other advertising matter
10 Point
23A 47a

SUNSETS OF SOUTHERN CALIFORNIA
Here as the sun sets the natural colors change and the hills seem to be bathed in transparent films of beautiful ever-changing shades, creating a scene of rare beauty
8 Point
25A 50a

ITALIC DESIGN OF EXCEPTIONAL BEAUTY
The italic associate of Nicolas Cochin is indeed a very suitable one. It follows closely some of the graceful cursive lettering of the most famous masterly engravers of the seventeenth century
6 Point
26A 52a

MODERNISTIC DECORATORS NO. 3

Cochin & Cochin Italic

14 Point 16A 32a

DISCOVERS HISTORIC BOOKS
Metropolitan collector secures fifteenth
century religious books in fine condition

14 Point 18A 37a

HAND DECORATED LATIN BIBLE
Collector discovers splendidly preserved volumes
in a monastery situated far away in mountains

12 Point 21A 42a

COLLECTOR OF RELIGIOUS EDITIONS
University professor possesses remarkable library
which will probably be presented to his alma mater

12 Point 23A 46a

NOVEL METHOD OF COLLECTING BOOKS
Naude had peculiar ideas regarding the buying of rare
books. His favorite plan was to buy whole libraries in the
gross, speculative lots as the other dealers called them

10 Point 24A 48a

CRAFTSMEN HAVE BEEN REWARDED
Eminent watch manufacturer rewards employees
for many years of faithful service while building up
a business that has become internationally famous

10 Point 26A 51a

DISTINCTIVE DESIGN ENHANCED BOOK
Among kings and princes it is well to meet one man of
letters, and he, the greatest of the age, a bibliophile
to wit. The enemies and rivals of Moliere were always
reproaching him for his great love of rare old editions

8 Point No. 2 27A 53a

ECCENTRIC RULER EMBELLISHED HIS RARE BOOKS
Perhaps the name of booklover could scarcely be applied to Henry III
for he probably never read the works that were bound for him in the
most elaborate way; however, he showed interest in the art of printing

8 Point No. 2 27A 55a

BEAUTIFUL BOOKS NUMEROUS IN BYGONE CENTURIES
Colbert, the celebrated French statesman, was a bibliophile who did not read
but who amassed beautiful books and looked forward, as business men do,
to the day when he would have time to study them. After Grolier, De Thou
and Mazarin, Colbert possessed probably the most elaborate private library
in Europe. The ambassadors of France were charged to procure rare volumes

8 Point No. 1 31A 62a

NUMEROUS WOMEN OF NOBILITY HAD LIBRARIES
So general and ardent has the love of good books been in France,
that it would be a very simple thing to write a sort of bibliomaniac
history of that country which would prove of the greatest interest

8 Point No. 1 33A 65a

LITERATURE AND HISTORIES OF EARLIEST PERIODS
People who wanted to gain Colbert's favor approached him with presents
of books, and the city of Metz presented him with two real curiosities: the
famous Metz Bible and the Missal of Charles the Bald. The Elzevirs
sent to him their finest examples, though Colbert probably saw more of
the fine bindings and the gilt covers of his books than of their contents

6 Point 39A 75a

LURE OF EXQUISITE BINDINGS HAS LONG BEEN POTENT AT THE FRENCH COURT
As a patron of all the arts, Francis I was naturally an admirer of good bindings. The fates of books
were very curiously illustrated by the story of the copy of Homer, which Aldus, the famous Venetian
printer, presented to Francis I. This volume was owned for awhile by a leading English statesman

The Cochin Series is made only in the sizes shown above

The Cochin Italic Series is made only in the sizes shown above

---

Characters in Complete Font

A B C D E F G H I J K L
M N O P Q R S T U V W
X Y Z & $ 1 2 3 4 5 6 7 8 9 0
a b c d e f g h i j k l m n o p
q r s t u v w x y z ff fi fl ffi ffl
. , - ' : ; ! ? " " ( ) — « » *

Characters in Complete Font

A B C D E F G H I J K L
M N O P Q R S T U V W
X Y Z & $ 1 2 3 4 5 6 7 8 9 0
a b c d e f g h i j k l m n n
o p p q r r s s t t u v w x y z ff
fi fl ffi ffl . , - ' : ; ! ? " " ( ) « »

MODERNISTIC DECORATORS NO. 3

Gravure Series

72 Point 4A 5a

HONEST Sailors 3

60 Point 5A 7a

8 Interesting APPEAL

48 Point 5A 9a

EXHIBITS Rarest Antique

42 Point 6A 10a

10 Mail Order ADVERTISING

36 Point 6A 10a

DESIGNING Artistic Booklet Covers

30 Point 7A 12a

High-class PRINTING

24 Point 9A 16a

MAGNIFICENT Apartment

18 Point 12A 23a

Finest Selection of DRESS GOODS

14 Point 17A 33a

COUNTRIES Visited by American Citizens

12 Point 19A 37a

PREFERENCE FOR HIGH-CLASS ENGRAVING
Essentially Desirable in Fine Advertising Display

Figures

$ 1 2 3 4 5 6 7 8 9 0

Characters

A B C D E F G H I
J K L M N O P Q R
S T U V W X Y Z &
a b c d e f g h i j
k l m n o p q r s t u
v w x y z ff fi fl ffi ffl
. , - ' ' : ; ! ?

Cast on Art Line

:[101]:

Raleigh Cursive

NEW
Jackmurd
ALL MODELS
NOW AVAILABLE FOR
Quick Delivery
•
Convertibles
Sedans
Victorias
Roadsters
•
JACKMURD MOTORS

RALEIGH CURSIVE WITH BERNHARD BOOKLET

Bristol
A NEW DEAL IN
HOTELS

RALEIGH INITIAL   RALEIGH CURSIVE AND STYMIE LIGHT

Characters

A B C D E F G H
I J K L M N O
P Q R S T U
V W X Y Z & $
a b c d e f g h i j k l m
n o p q r s t u v w x y z
ar er ir as es is us . , - ' ' : ; ! ?
1 2 3 4 5 6 7 8 9 0

72 Point 3A 4a
Highest Realm

60 Point 4A 7a
Magnificent Gowns

48 Point 5A 10a
Enterprising Diplomatist

42 Point 6A 11a
Bulgaria Imported Biplanes

36 Point 6A 11a
Delightful Saxophone Orchestra

30 Point 7A 13a
Noted Educator Attending Convention

24 Point 9A 18a
Beautiful Women Handsomely Gowned

18 Point 15A 28a
Typographic Specimen Deserved Honorable Mention

14 Point 21A 41a
Recent Developments in Horticulture Exciting Considerable Interest

12 Point 22A 45a
Wonderful Reception Tendered International Heroes During Celebration

10 Point 27A 55a
Exhibition of Rare Curios and Fine Antiques Continues to Attract Notable Connoisseurs

Sizes 24 to 72 Point cast on Angle Body

Raleigh Initials

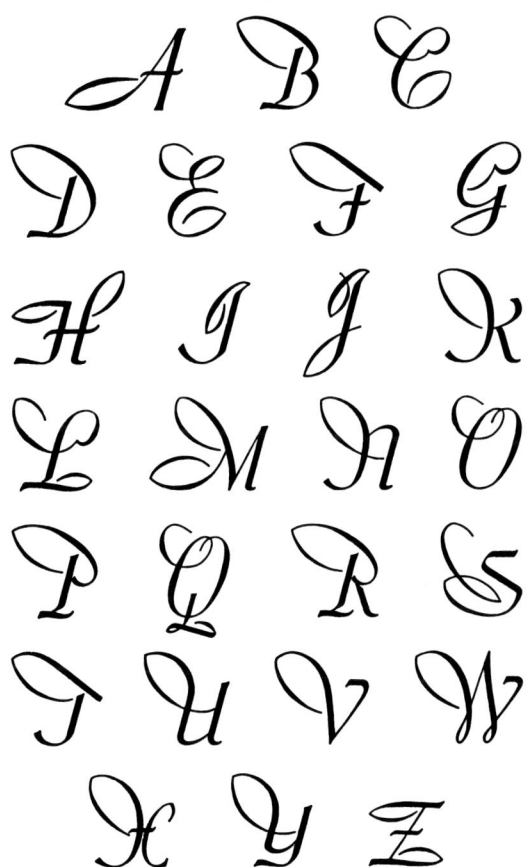

Initials J and Q cast on size larger body
26 characters made in all sizes

96 Point

84 Point

72 Point

60 Point

54 Point

48 Point

36 Point

An Exhibition

OF SCULPTURE BY REUBEN HALS,

CALLED THE RACE OF MAN, WILL

BE OPENED TO THE PUBLIC FROM

FEBRUARY SECOND TO TWELFTH

AT THE MOLIERE ART GALLERIES

RALEIGH INITIAL   RALEIGH CURSIVE AND 18 POINT MODERNISTIC BORDER NO. 78

Cheltenham Oldstyle

72 Point — 3A 4a
8 Authority

60 Point — 3A 4a
Right Styles 5

48 Point — 4A 8a
2 Money Lender

42 Point — 5A 8a
Regiment Inspected

36 Point — 5A 8a
DEPORTS MINER
Questioned Legislation

Characters in Complete Font

A B C D E F G
H I J K L M N O
P Q R S T U V
W X Y Z & $ 1 2
3 4 5 6 7 8 9 0
a b c d e f g h i j
k l m n o p q r r s
t u v w x y z ff fi fl
ffi ffl Qu ct st ¶])
' " . , - ' : ; ! ?

Characters] ' " not made for 30, 36, 42, 48, 60 and 72 Point sizes

11 Point carried in stock only at Foundry

Cheltenham Oldstyle

MODERN NIC-NACS

30 Point — 6A 10a
MONEY PROMISED
Organizations contributing
extensively toward project

24 Point — 6A 12a
IMPROVING GARDENS
Japanese chrysanthemum more
mystifying and greatly admired

18 Point — 10A 21a
MOISTENED
Quaint buildings
interested author

14 Point — 15A 30a
IMPERFECTION
Golden opportunities
awaiting every youth

12 Point — 18A 38a
BROWN OCTOBER
Nature bedecks autumnal
woodlands so unstintingly
and sublimely each season

10 Point — 21A 42a
REFINED DRAPERIES
Beautifully illustrated booklets present inexpensive decorative schemes and harmonious color combinations for bright homes

8 Point — 24A 48a
INTERNATIONAL RECORD
Expert craftsmen magically produce wonderful instrument which reveals almost incredible improvement over everyday music producing machines

6 Point — 24A 48a
SOUTHERN RIDING ACADEMY
Thorough instruction in horsemanship and other outdoor activities imparted by eleven courteous instructors. Our carefully trained saddle horses insure safety and the immense well-lighted riding arena makes instruction possible notwithstanding climatic conditions

Cheltenham Italic

Characters in Complete Font

A B C D E F G H
I J K L M N O P
Q R S T U V W
X Y Z & $ 1 2
3 4 5 6 7 8 9 0
a b c d e f g h i j
k l m n o p q r s t
u v w x y z & ff fi
fl ffi ffl . , - ' : ; ! ?

The following special characters are supplied with all fonts from 6 to 14 Point inclusive. They are put up in separate fonts from 18 to 72 Point inclusive, and are furnished only when specially ordered

A B D E G M N P
R T V h J r v w y Qu

11 Point carried in stock only at Foundry

CHELTENHAM ITALIC

GRAYBAR COMBINATION BRACKETS, GROUP D USED WITH 18 POINT TEAGUE BORDER NO 1810

72 Point — 3A 4a
Reported 2

60 Point — 3A 5a
3 Stylish Bag

48 Point — 4A 9a
Author Replying

42 Point — 5A 8a
Mortgage Satisfied

36 Point — 5A 11a
BUYING HOMES
Real Estate Bargains

30 Point — 7A 11a
HONOR SCHOLAR
Students contribute much amusement for graduates

24 Point — 7A 12a
SECURE PERFORMER
Eastern instrumentalist giving demonstrations during sojourn

10 Point — 20A 46a
BOUGHT RESIDENCE
Leading magazine and book publisher buys historic edifice situated in picturesque valley and remodels it for exhibition

8 Point — 23A 46a
NUMEROUS MERCHANTS
Several investigators report foreign financiers satisfied with conditions between international business men that bespeak commercial prosperity

6 Point — 22A 46a
EMINENT ARTISTS LECTURED
Prominent printers congregate in spacious auditorium and listen attentively to expert designer speaking about the application of modern art to printing. Definite plans are being made by advertising and publishing company for additional educational talks

18 Point — 11A 21a
RENOUNCE
Many important discoveries made

14 Point — 15A 28a
HIDE FIGURES
Exchanges machine after prolonged trial

12 Point — 17A 36a
SECURES DESIGN
Display of newest styles drew immense crowds of motorists to annual show

:[105]:

Cheltenham Medium

72 Point — 3A 4a

Nightly 6

60 Point — 3A 6a

3 Repeater

48 Point — 4A 7a

Dandy Baby 8

42 Point — 5A 8a

21 ROMANTIC
Historical Study

36 Point — 5A 9a

MAGIC WORDS 2
Important Message

30 Point — 6A 10a

RIVER CLUB TENNIS
5 Matches Great Event

24 Point — 7A 14a

SIGNS OF PROSPERITY 1
Country Grange Attractions

Characters in Complete Font

A B C D E F G H
I J K L M N O P
Q R S T U V W
X Y Z & $ 1 2
3 4 5 6 7 8 9 0
a b c d e f g h i j
k l m n o p q r r s
t u v w x y z ct st
. , - ' : ; ! ?

The following characters are furnished with all fonts from 6 Point to 18 Point inclusive

ff fi fl ffi ffl

The Incomparable Cheltenham Family

DECORATIONS: UNITS FROM MODERN NIC-NACS

18 Point — 11A 21a

IMPORTUNE
Frank criticism
stimulates help

10 Point — 19A 38a

ESCAPE HOT SPELL
Many who like outdoor
recreation defer taking
their vacation until cool
September winds come

14 Point — 15A 28a

FINE AMBITION
Industrious printer
shows artistic taste
for finest sketching

8 Point — 22A 45a

ACQUIRES RARE PRINTS
Those hoping to collect prints
could select one department,
and find an active and trusted
print dealer who is assuredly
in sympathy with such efforts

12 Point — 17A 34a

DISCOVER TRUTH
Merchants convinced
that advertising would
market their products

6 Point — 26A 50a

PUBLIC SCHOOLS PROGRESS
The prevailing and ancient method
of taking and training apprentices
can not and does not create skilled
workmen. Instruction in printing is
being given nowadays in our public
schools with many excellent results

Cheltenham Medium Italic (Non-Kerning)

Characters in Complete Font

A B C D E F G H
I J K L M N O P
Q R S T U V W
X Y Z & $ 1 2
3 4 5 6 7 8 9 0
a b c d e f g h i j
k l m n o p q r s t
u v w x y z ct st
ff fi fl ffi ffl . , - ' : ; ! ?

Cheltenham Medium Italic

DECORATIONS: UNITS FROM MODERN NIC-NACS

72 Point — 3A 4a
Buyers 5

60 Point — 3A 5a
6 Avoiding

48 Point — 4A 6a
Special Offer 1

42 Point — 5A 7a
3 BLIND MICE
Lovely Styling 8

36 Point — 5A 8a
FINE DIAMOND
2 Beautiful Homes

30 Point — 6A 9a
MEN ANNOUNCE 4
Indoor Championships

24 Point — 7A 12a
ELITE COUNTRY CLUB
Offers Gala Entertainment 7

18 Point — 10A 20a
UPHOLDING
Knight plowed
fertile meadow

14 Point — 15A 28a
RETURNS FISH
Careful sportsman
lost dandy pickerel
before leaving boat

12 Point — 18A 35a
GRAND STEAMER
Magnificent transport
brings returning army
from turbulent section

10 Point — 19A 38a
RARE GEMS GIVEN
Generous magnate will
award prize to students
finishing college course
in practical advertising

8 Point — 22A 43a
DRIVER FIXED BRAKES
Every good chauffeur should
regularly inspect entire body
of his automobile. If bolts or
nuts become worn and loose
do not neglect proper repairs

6 Point — 24A 48a
PROFIT SURPRISES PRINTER
New inventions gradually replaced
methods in vogue forty odd years
ago when every artistic compositor
was an expert rule twister. Efficient
production and quality work make
the hard working job printer happy

Cheltenham Bold

120 Point — 3A 4a

Sight 2

96 Point — 3A 4a

5 Maple

84 Point — 3A 4a

Camp 6

72 Point — 3A 4a

3 Printer

60 Point — 3A 5a

Mythical 4

48 Point — 4A 6a

8 EXPLORE
Original Girls

Characters in Complete Font

A B C D E F G H
I J K L M N O P
Q R S T U V W
X Y Z & $ 1 2
3 4 5 6 7 8 9 0
a b c d e f g h i
j k l m n o p q r
r s t u v w x y z
. , - ' : ; ! ?

Cheltenham
⚜ BOLD ⚜
CHARACTER FROM MODERNISTIC BORDER NO. 73

42 Point — 4A 8a

Might

36 Point — 5A 8a

HORN
Grated

30 Point — 6A 10a

ENTIRE
Delivery

24 Point — 6A 13a

NEITHER
Simplified

18 Point — 10A 20a

NICKNAME
Honest Sport

14 Point — 14A 26a

REPRODUCES
Quaint Drawing

12 Point — 17A 33a

DESCRIBE SCENE
Entering Battlefield

10 Point — 18A 37a

SOLDIERS REJOICE
Timely reconnoitering
narrowly averted war

8 Point — 22A 45a

INDUSTRIOUS WORKER
Diligent mechanic becomes
department superintendent

6 Point — 24A 48a

BOLD MOUNTAIN CLIMBERS
Encounter many hardships while
making perilous journey upward

Cheltenham Bold Italic

Characters in Complete Font

A B C D E F G H
I J K L M N O P
Q R S T U V W
X Y Z & $ 1 2
3 4 5 6 7 8 9 0
a b c d e f g h i
j k l m n o p q r
s t u v w x y z
. , - ' : ; ! ?

Sizes 24 to 72 Point furnished also on Angle Body

---

72 Point — 3A 5a

Regular 9

60 Point — 4A 6a

2 Complains

48 Point — 4A 6a

Gigantic Sale 5

Cheltenham Bold Italic

42 Point — 5A 7a

3 MINERALS
Specimen Gem

36 Point — 5A 8a

MORTGAGES 1
Payable Monthly
Legal Compound

30 Point — 6A 9a

4 FINE EFFICIENT
Advertisers Prospect
Showy Organization

12 Point — 15A 32a
GUIDES DESIGN
Sought suggestions wandering through picturesque valleys

10 Point — 16A 34a
NOTED GROUNDS
Children frolic midst wonderful botanical garden and enjoy the exhilarating climate

8 Point — 20A 42a
COMPLIMENTS ARTIST
Many entertaining exhibits of painting are displayed in the main room. The library habitue will be interested in these fascinating art works

6 Point — 20A 42a
SOLDIERS IN MANEUVERS
Numerous troops forming with beautiful accuracy along road passed inspections and started active work. Quickly establish permanent headquarters while zephyrs sharpen their appetite

24 Point — 7A 11a
REOPEN
City folks interested

18 Point — 9A 20a
SPECIMEN
Brochure by old artificer delights boy

14 Point — 14A 28a
DISTRIBUTER
Urchins pleased with many gifts donated weekly by the merchant

Cheltenham Bold Condensed

72 Point — 3 A 4 a

1Hunts Quality

60 Point — 3 A 4 a

Designs Boudoir 2

48 Point — 4 A 8 a

9 BROUGHT RADIOS
Graphic Art Displayed

Characters in Complete Font

A B C D E F
G H I J K L
M N O P Q R
S T U V W X
Y Z & $ 1 2 3
4 5 6 7 8 9 0
a b c d e f g
h i j k l m n
o p q r r s t
u v w x y z
. , - ' : ; ! ?

42 Point — 5 A 8 a

MODERN GOWNS
Elicited Admiration

$ 1 2 3 4 5 6 7 8 9 0

36 Point — 5 A 8 a

STRANGE REMEDIES
Beautiful Girls Embark

24 Point — 8 A 16 a

ENHANCING
Beautiful star
shining bright

12 Point — 21 A 44 a

DEFENDS DOCTRINE
Honor system becomes
main discussion among
professors at meetings

10 Point — 22 A 46 a

POSTPONE PROGRAM
Curtail winter concerts of
symphony orchestra until
arrival of eminent soloists

30 Point — 7 A 13 a

CONDENSED LINES HELP
Enabled job printers to save
valuable space when needed

18 Point — 12 A 26 a

IMPROVEMENT
Enlarged interior
has pleasing look

14 Point — 17 A 36 a

HEROIC REGIMENT
Springfield holds fine
banquet for the many
men who gained fame

8 Point — 27 A 54 a

ERECTED BEAUTIFUL HOME
Retired manufacturer purchases
tract adjoining present property
for building magnificent mansion

6 Point — 30 A 60 a

OFFICIAL REFUSES NOMINATION
Government officer declared principal
reason for not accepting situation was
remuneration. This created quite some
comment among several acquaintances

Cheltenham Bold Extra Condensed

Characters in Complete Font

A B C D E F G H I J
K L M N O P Q R S
T U V W X Y Z & $
1 2 3 4 5 6 7 8 9 0
a b c d e f g h i j k l m n
o p q r r s t u v w x y z
ff fi fl ffi ffl . , - ' : ; ! ?

---

120 Point — 3 A 4 a
Engine 4

96 Point — 3 A 4 a
1 Company

84 Point — 3 A 4 a
Machinery 8

72 Point — 3 A 5 a
6 Graphic Arts

60 Point — 3 A 5 a
Liquidate Debts 3

48 Point — 6 A 9 a
5 SPRING FASHIONS
Automobile Showings

$1234567890

---

14 Point — 20 A 40 a
ENERGETIC PLANS
Serious development undertaking finished

12 Point — 24 A 48 a
LEADING GYMNASIUM
Many contestants report intense activity at camps

10 Point — 27 A 54 a
NOTEWORTHY DECISION
Important questions settled during informal conference between opposing societies

8 Point — 33 A 68 a
INDEMNIFIED MANUFACTURER
Erecting monstrous warehouse of standardized materials as required by the fire insurance underwriters

6 Point — 36 A 73 a
NUMEROUS CHANGES IN SCHEDULE
Excursion steamers crowded to capacity with smiling throngs of July vacationists returning home after enchanting pleasure jaunts to mountain and seashore resorts

---

42 Point — 6 A 10 a
Red Eagle

36 Point — 6 A 10 a
Night Hawk

30 Point — 8 A 14 a
FOREBODING
Hemispherical

24 Point — 10 A 19 a
DISCOMPOSURE
Brief Exploration

18 Point — 15 A 31 a
PERFECT SPECIMEN
Kinder Characteristic

:[111]:

Cheltenham Bold Extended

72 Point — 3A 4a
Nails 5

60 Point — 3A 4a
Hunters

48 Point — 3A 4a
Excursion

42 Point — 3A 5a
REDUCING
Best Mark 3

36 Point — 3A 5a
INSPECTORS
Unique Mode

30 Point — 4A 7a
PERFORMANCE
Entertain Society

24 Point — 5A 9a
PLEASANT SINGER
Swedish Nightingale

Characters in Complete Font

A B C D E F G
H I J K L M N
O P Q R S T U V
W X Y Z & $ 1 2
3 4 5 6 7 8 9 0
a b c d e f g h i
j k l m n o p q r
r s t u v w x y z
. , - ' : ; ! ?

CHELTENHAM BOLD EXTENDED
PENLINE FLOURISHES 7203L AND 7203R GROUP 4

18 Point — 7A 13a
BROKEN
Solicitors
mystified

14 Point — 10A 21a
REMINDER
Companion
encouraged
further trial

12 Point — 12A 25a
NOURISHING
Food scientist
makes rations
very tempting

10 Point — 13A 28a
INSTRUCTION
Extra buildings
provide golden
opportunity for
additional class

8 Point — 15A 30a
MINIATURE ROSE
Swiss horticulturist
exhibits interesting
hardy varieties that
brought loud praise
from noted growers

6 Point — 17A 35a
RAINBOW CREATION
Beautiful satin ribbons
help in conveying that
distinctive atmosphere
of rare refinement and
good taste so desirable
and universally sought

Cheltenham Wide

72 Point — 3A 4a
Signifies 8

60 Point — 3A 4a
MOTIONS
Rejuvenate

48 Point — 4A 8a
DEMAND 93
Select Quality

42 Point — 4A 8a
BAKED CAKE
Invites Neighbor

36 Point — 5A 8a
REAL PRINTING
25 Elegant Layouts

30 Point — 5A 10a
PUBLICITY STUNTS
Distinguish Advertising

Characters in Complete Font

A B C C D E F G H I
J K L M N O P Q R
S T U V W X Y Z & $
1 2 3 4 5 6 7 8 9 0
a b c d e f g h i j k l
m n o p q r r s t u v
w x y z ff fi fl ffi ffl
Qu ct st ¶)] ' "
. , - ' : ; ! ?

Characters] ' " not made for 30, 36, 42, 48, 60 and 72 Point sizes

11 Point carried in stock only at Foundry

Cheltenham Wide

24 Point — 6A 12a
GHERKIN
Stimulating
the appetite

18 Point — 10A 21a
NEIGHBORS
Hold rehearsal
of playlet early

14 Point — 15A 30a
BURN CHURCH
Historical building
and art collections
completely ruined

12 Point — 18A 38a
FORTUNE SMILED
Diamond miner found
indescribable beauties
after wearisome quest

10 Point — 21A 42a
DEFECTS REVEALED
Notable professors bring
remarkable photographs
for use in scientific study

8 Point — 24A 48a
CONCERNING DREAMERS
Natural ability without energy
is always deplorable and often
terminates in complete despair

6 Point — 24A 48a
ENERGETIC FOLKS ADVANCE
Lazy men are most certain of failure
while active men invariably succeed
in most fields. This statement should
be carefully considered by everyone

Cooper Series

72 Point   3A 3a

GUIDE delayed 6

60 Point   3A 4a

1 delightful MAIDEN

48 Point   3A 6a

FINE GOLD
3 parking rules

36 Point   4A 7a

QUAINT SHOP
harmony prevailed

30 Point   5A 9a

SPRING CHORUS
paint sylvan landscape

24 Point   6A 10a

IMPORTS FURNITURE
firm received large shipment

18 Point   9A 18a

MODERN PICTURES SHOWN
SPECIAL attraction pleases hundreds

16 Point   11A 20a

PROGRESSIVE REPORTS MADE
BANKERS anticipated greater prosperity

---

14 Point   13A 26a

APPROVES MODEST STYLES
SEVERAL attractive samples shown

12 Point   16A 32a

IMPROVED DECORATION SOUGHT
LARGE building employed mysterious design

10 Point   20A 40a

UNIVERSALLY IMPROVED CONDITIONS
REGULAR monthly statements show improvement

8 Point   22A 44a

REMARKABLE SYMPHONIC PROGRAM RENDERED
GRAND opening highly impressed critical cosmopolitan audience

6 Point   24A 48a

PROPERTY OWNERS HOLDING FOURTH CONVENTION
SUBURBAN residents make application for needed traffic improvements

---

Characters in Complete Font

A B C D E F G H I J
K L M N O P Q R S
T U V W X Y Z & $
1 2 3 4 5 6 7 8 9 0
a b c d e f g h i j k
l m n o p q r s t u
v w x y z . , - ' : ; ! ?
¶ [— · ❧ ✿ ⁓ ⁓

Characters ❧ ⁓ made only in sizes from 6 to 36 Point

Characters ff fi fl ffi ffl made only in sizes from 6 to 18 Point

Small Caps in sizes from 6 to 18 Point are put up separately and furnished only when specially ordered

:[114]:

Cooper Italic (Non-Kerning)

HOME supreme 8

5 introducing NIECE

MENTIONING PRODUCTION
famous corporation increasing force

OPERATION IMPROVED SURGEON
restricted habits and recreation prolong life

PRONOUNCE METHOD INDISPENSABLE
maintaining improved typographic service becoming purpose of largest printing and advertising concerns

WONDERFUL IMPROVEMENTS CONTEMPLATED
impressive assortment of new models exhibited at automobile show presages continuation of development for motor industry

GREAT RESULTS ACCOMPLISHED BY DOING WORK WELL
preference for high-class printing is justified from the standpoint of sound business and also from an admiration for clever, discernible craftsmanship

NICE TIME

2 beautiful rug

SEND REPORT

financial problems

BRIGHT SOLDIER

displays nice uniform

GOVERNMENT BONDS

broker considering investment

MODERN TYPES DESIGNED

insure distinctive typographic effect

PUBLICITY PRINTING EXHIBIT

display in newspapers pleased advertisers

Characters in Complete Font

A B C D E F G H I J
K L M N O P Q R S
T U V W X Y Z & $
1 2 3 4 5 6 7 8 9 0
a b c d e f g h i j k
l m n o p q r s t u
v w x y z ff fi fl ffi ffl
. , - ' : ; ! ? ( )

Characters ff fi fl ffi ffl made only in sizes from 6 to 18 Point

Cooper Black

120 Point 3A 3a

OIL sold

96 Point 3A 3a

half 8

72 Point 3A 3a

BE paid

60 Point 3A 4a

3 days IN

48 Point 3A 4a

BOLD style

42 Point 3A 4a

4 stage HITS

36 Point 3A 4a

REAL position

30 Point 4A 7a

inspected HOMES

24 Point 5A 9a

PINK drapery

18 Point 6A 13a

delighted FRIEND

14 Point 10A 20a

MAYOR greatly pleased

12 Point 13A 26a

BEAUTIFUL SPRING COATS
finely tailored sport costume

10 Point 14A 28a

ENTRANCING MUSICAL DRAMA
collegiate glee club has rehearsal

8 Point 16A 32a

METROPOLITAN BUSINESS INCREASED
builder receives many encouraging reports

6 Point 18A 36a

NOTED JURIST GIVES IMPORTANT DECISION
this long disputed question satisfactorily settled

Characters in Complete Font

A B C D E F G H I J
K L M N O P Q R S
T U V W X Y Z & $
1 2 3 4 5 6 7 8 9 0
a b c d e f g h i
j k l m n o p q r
s t u v w x y z
. , - ' : ; ! ? ﬆ • —]

:[116]:

Cooper Black Italic

120 Point 3A 3a

SIX tails

24 Point 5A 10a

HOME delights

18 Point 6A 15a

indisputable STORY

14 Point 10A 23a

CHARMING lace displays

12 Point 13A 26a

investigated annual REPORTS

10 Point 14A 28a

CROWDS welcome arctic explorer

8 Point 16A 32a

**DISCOVERS UNTOLD MINERAL WEALTH
young traveler described unexploited region**

6 Point 19A 38a

**ROMANTIC ADVENTURE LIES BEYOND HORIZON
wanderlust victims always enjoy the wide open spaces**

Characters in Complete Font

A B C D E F G H I J
K L M N O P Q R S
T U V W X Y Z & $
1 2 3 4 5 6 7 8 9 0
a b c d e f g h i
j k l m n o p q r
s t u v w x y z . ,
- ' : ; ! ? [ ] · — ( )

The following characters are fonted separately and furnished
only when separately ordered

A B D E F G M N
P R T Y

96 Point 3A 3a

shift 4

72 Point 3A 4a

NO mail

60 Point 3A 4a

5 built UP

48 Point 3A 4a

MEN signed

42 Point 3A 4a

sold 28 LOTS

36 Point 3A 5a

REAL publicity

30 Point 4A 8a

duplicates ORDER

Cooper Hilite

120 Point 3A 3a

BIG girl

96 Point 3A 3a

thin ICE 2

24 Point 5A 9a

RECOGNITION
elegant lecture

18 Point 6A 13a

ORIENTAL CARPET
beautiful tapestries

72 Point 3A 3a

HIS job

60 Point 3A 4a

high BIT

48 Point 3A 4a

SIX forty 5

36 Point 3A 4a

largest HARE

30 Point 4A 7a

MODERN RINKS
delight juveniles

Characters in Complete Font

A B C D E F G H
I J K L M N O P
Q R S T U V W
X Y Z & $ 1 2
3 4 5 6 7 8 9 0
a b c d e f g h i
j k l m n o p q
r s t u v w x
y z . , - ' : ; ! ?
q · —]

:[118]:

Parsons Series

72 Point — 3A 4a
5 Holiday

60 Point — 3A 4a
Developed

48 Point — 3A 7a
NUMEROUS
2 Employment

36 Point — 3A 8a
6 GRAND BIRDS
Some Magnificent

30 Point — 4A 10a
ROMAN SCHOLAR
Education propelling
force in craftsmanship

24 Point — 5A 12a
AMERICAN development
Intrepid explorers continue
trail completely unmolested

18 Point — 7A 21a
EXHIBITION
New products
put on display

14 Point — 9A 27a
MOST Delightful
Originality marks
the Parsons types

12 Point — 10A 30a
FINE Complimentary
Things have been said
of this series by all the
printing trade papers

10 Point — 12A 36a
MANY NEW FEATURES
Embodied in the Parsons
design have made it liked
by clever advertising men

8 Point — 14A 42a
THOSE LONG ASCENDERS
And descenders help to give
effects that are certainly very
novel and also very attractive
if used with pleasing restraint

6 Point — 16A 46a
FOR CERTAIN FORMS OF JOB
Work, in which there are not too
many lines, this type provides all
the most important advantages of
hand lettering; that is, informality
and distinction, qualities that are
of value in securing the attention

◄ Parsons ►

Characters in Complete Font

A A B C D E F G H I J
K L M M N N O P Q R
S T T U V W X Y Z q
& $ 1 2 3 4 5 6 7 8 9 0
a b c d e f g h i j k l m
o p q r s t u v w x y z ff
fi fl ffi ffl . , - ' : ; ! ? — [ ]

All fonts contain a few of the long Ascenders and
Descenders. These are cast on double the regular
body, excepting those for the 14, 60 and 72 point,
which are cast on 30, 108 and 120 point bodies

b d g h k l p y

All sizes are very easily justified with spaces and
quads, thus assuring quick and perfect alignment

Characters ff fi fl ffi ffl made only in 6 to 18 point sizes

Nubian Series

dorian
NOVELTY SHOP

ROCK & RYE

.79 Frosted Rock and Rye Bottles, sterling silver trimmed.

•

Airplane Travelers

24.60 Zipper Bag of Moire used as a back rest. Quilted throw of lamb's wool.

•

KID MULES

10.98 High heeled, silver lined. Ultra modern.

NOVELTY SHOP
dorian

NUBIAN AND BERNHARD GOTHIC LIGHT

72 Point 3A 4a
Sharp

60 Point 3A 4a
Garden

48 Point 3A 4a
Query 89

42 Point 3A 5a
Syndicates

36 Point 4A 6a
Oriental 492

30 Point 5A 7a
Oil Gun

24 Point 5A 9a
Quits Job

18 Point 6A 11a
**DESIGNED
Many Boats**

14 Point 9A 17a
**MODEL SHOP
Pays Dividend**

12 Point 11A 21a
**GARDEN
Help Man**

10 Point 12A 24a
**BOUNDED
Rapid Shot**

8 Point 14A 28a
**DRY BRUSH
Queries artist
about designs**

6 Point 15A 30a
**EASTER SALES
Many bargains in
beautiful baskets**

Characters

A B C D E F G
H I J K L M N
O P Q R S S T
U V W X Y Z &

a b c d e f g h i
j k l m n o p q
r s t u v w x y z
. , - ' ' ; ! ?

The following characters are cast recessed in sizes from 24 to 72 Point

A F L P T V W Y

1 2 3 4 5 6 7 8 9 0 $

GALLIA SERIES

72 Point 3 A
KINGS

60 Point 3 A
BINDER

48 Point 4 A
RUG SALE

36 Point 6 A
NICE DESIGN

30 Point 8 A
SAMPLE GOWNS

24 Point 9 A
CHARMING SINGER

18 Point 12 A
BRIGHT COLORS PLEASED

14 Point 15 A   **12 Point 16 A**
SCORE BOARDS   MODEL PICTURE

Characters

A A B C D E E F G H I J
K L M N O P Q R R S S
S SS T T U V W X Y Z &
$ 1 2 3 4 5 6 7 8 9 0 . , ~ ' : ; ! ?

:[121]:

FLATTERY
OF FOX

◆

TOWN COATS
BY MAY

◆

AMAZING
SOFTNESS

◆

WORTHY
COLLECTION

GALLIA WITH BODONI ITALIC

FOOD
FOR THOSE
WHO KNOW

CHOICER, fresher foods, and better balanced portions, French cuisine, at less than you would expect to pay. Luncheon 60c. Dinner 75c. Cocktails 25c. No cover charge.

JAY'S
123 HADON STREET

GALLIA WITH BODONI FAMILY
CALENDAR AUXILIARY GROUP F CHARACTER 39

Parisian Series

VISIT THE FLORIST SHOP

at JOY'S

A separate little shop has been set apart for your delectation .. Fresh cut flowers always on hand. See the Geranium display

— JOY'S

TYPOGRAPHIC DOT AND MODERN NIC-NACS
3 POINT MODERNISTIC BORDER NO. 4

---

72 Point   3 A   4 a
RUN Quickest

60 Point   4 A   6 a
Delightful IDEAS

48 Point   6 A   9 a
BUYS Rare Hyacinth

42 Point   7 A   10 a
Merchant Imported LACE

36 Point   7 A   11 a
JOINT Convention Approved

30 Point   8 A   14 a
International Photographer FOUND

24 Point   10 A   17 a
RURAL HOME
Picturesque Cottage

18 Point   14 A   30 a
SPLENDID SONG
Played Latest Rhapsody

14 Point   19 A   38 a
ENDEARING CHARM
Symphony Rendition Exquisite

12 Point   23 A   46 a
BRIGHT SELECTION
Lauded European Thespians

10 Point   26 A   53 a
SUPERFINE QUALITY
Extraordinary Display Pleases

8 Point   27 A   Made in Caps only
DEALERS ENTHUSIASTIC
MADE ELABORATE PLAN
FOR MONTHLY MEETING

6 Point   28 A   Made in Caps only
THE METROPOLITAN COLLEGE
COMMENCEMENT EXERCISES
STUDENT RECEIVED DIPLOMA

Characters

A B C D E F G H I
J K L M N O P Q R
S ſ T U V W X Y Z &
a b c d e f g h i j k l m n
o p q r ſ s t u v w x y z
. , - ' ' : ; ! ?

The following characters are cast recessed in 60 and 72 Point sizes

A F L ſ T V W Y

1 2 3 4 5 6 7 8 9 0 $

:[122]:

Camelot Oldstyle

36 Point   6A 9a
BRIGADIER
Managerial

30 Point   6A 13a
DESCENDING
Recapitulation

24 Point   8A 15a
SPECTROSCOPE
Electric Separator

18 Point   12A 23a
NUMEROUS POEMS
Pleasant Country Ride

12 Point   16A 40a
HAND LETTER DESIGN
Beautiful letters imparted
a feeling of class to every
ordinary piece of printing

10 Point   18A 40a
DISTINGUISHED CUSTOMER
Magnificent stage costumes
displaying appropriate taste
brought unstinted approval

8 Point   20A 52a
DREAMER BUILDS MODERN EDIFICE
Enthusiastic architect praises work
and originality of young unknown
who had just finished new building

6 Point   25A 50a
MAGNIFICENT SHOWINGS HELP SALES
Carefully planned and printed publicity
cannot fail to inspire confidence in your
product by its unconscious appeal to the
esthetic sense of the average individual

Characters in Complete Font
A B C D E F G H I J K L M M N O
P Q R R S ʃ T U V W X Y Z &
$ 1 2 3 4 5 6 7 8 9 0 a a b c d e f
g h h i j k l m m n o p q r s t u v
w x y z ff fi fl ffi ffl ct . , - ' : ; ! ?

Hyancinthe
Creations

The Hyancinthe Shop
North Bloomfield Center

Adonis Series

24 Point   8A 16a
Exceptional Clothing Bargain
5 Modernistic Textile Designs

18 Point   13A 26a
Beautiful Lettering Attractively Handled
Imparted Charm to Every Advertisement

14 Point   18A 36a
Newest Models in Streamlined Effects Thrill Critics
Eagerly Await Opening of International Exposition

12 Point   21A 42a
Uncover New Evidence of Ancient South American Culture
Civilization More Idealistic in Some Degree Than Our Own

10 Point   25A 50a
More advertisers are calling for uncommon type designs and layouts
that will give their products a certain elusive air of cultured refinement

8 Point   26A 52a
Brilliant and almost unbelievably hazardous undertaking finally succeeds after
countless days of unmitigated toil and patient struggling against recalcitrant foe

Characters
A A A B B C D E
F G G H I J K L M
N O P Q R S T U
V V W W X Y Z &
a b c d e f g h i
j k l m n o p r
s s t u v w x y z
. , - ` ' : ; ! ?

Figures for Adonis
1 2 3 4 5 6 7 8 9 0 $

Della Robbia

72 Point — 3A 4a

SERIES 1

QuickSet

60 Point — 3A 4a

24 ARCH

Rare Prints

48 Point — 4A 8a

MEETING 5

Special Agent

42 Point — 5A 9a

8 EMPLOYES

Oppose Striking

General Offices

36 Point — 4A 9a

DRIVE

Myriad

30 Point — 5A 11a

PERISH

Liquidity

24 Point — 7A 12a

NIMROD

Rhapsodist

Deplorable

18 Point — 9A 18a

KNAPSACK

Underhanded

Hieroglyphics

14 Point — 13A 26a

DISJUNCTION
Prominent exhibit
secures first prize
at agricultural fair

12 Point — 16A 33a

UNEXPERIENCED
Big municipal pageant
thrilled large gathering
of enthusiastic citizens

10 Point — 18A 36a

MAIN CONCOURSE
Discerning photographer
secures wonderful views
for suburban newspaper

8 Point — 23A 46a

EXCELLENT PROGRAMME
Impressive demonstration marked
arrival of distinguished foreigners
who have come for trade meeting

6 Point — 26A 52a

PROFESSIONAL INFORMATION
Manufacturing companies amalgamated
their research departments in order that
greater efficiency might be secured. This
necessitated many changes in personnel

36 Point Della Robbia Figures

$1234567890

Characters in Complete Font

A B C D E F G H I J J
K L M N O P Q R R S T
U V W X Y Z Qu ¶ &
$ 1 2 3 4 5 6 7 8 9 0
a b c d e f g h i j k l m n o
p q r s t u v w x y z Qu ct
ff fi fl ffi ffl . , - ' ‥ : ; ! ?

54 Point carried in stock only at Foundry

:[124]:

★ *Liberty Series*

72 Point   3A 9a

Automobile Oiled

60 Point   4A 12a

Membership Gaining

48 Point   4A 16a

Elegant Hosiery Displayed

42 Point   4A 16a

Radio Broadcasting Program

36 Point   5A 17a

Attractively Decorated Auditorium

30 Point   6A 22a

Beautiful Engravings Sold Quickly

24 Point   7A 26a

Extraordinary Typographic Effects Obtained

18 Point   10A 40a

Unusual Demonstration Marks Thirtieth Anniversary

14 Point   14A 55a

Beautiful Landscapes Exhibited at Metropolitan Museum of Art

12 Point   16A 63a

Graduates Received Handsome Diplomas at the Annual Commencement Exercises

---

The New Low Priced RADIO

La Petite

A Handful of RADIO

... You've always wanted to own one of these compact little **RADIOS** *... Now is your* **C H A N C E** *...*

PETITE RADIO COMPANY

LIBERTY SERIES WITH BODONI AND ITALIC
GRAYBAR COMBINATION BRACKETS GROUP G

Characters

A B C D E F G
H I J K L M N
O P Q R S T U
U V W X Y Z & $
a b c d e f g h i j k l
m n o p q r s t u v w
x y z . , - ' : ; ! ?
1 2 3 4 5 6 7 8 9 0

★ Cast on straight body and can be justified with regular quads

Announcement Roman

36 Point — 6A 11a
ENDURANGE REGORD
Equestrians Complimented

30 Point — 7A 14a
DELIGHTFUL ADVENTURE
Ancient Clipper Ship Welcomed

24 Point — 9A 13a
REAL SCIENTIFIC INSTRUCTION
Prominent speaker announces a series
of lectures regarding muscular exercise

18 Point — 14A 28a
PERT DAMOSEL BEGUILES NEW STUDENT
Charming oriental perfumes gently wafted through
the atmosphere bring back long-forgotten memories

Characters in Complete Font

A B B G D D E F G
H I J K L M M N N
O P P Q R R S T U
V V W W X Y Z &
$ 1 2 3 4 5 6 7 8 9 0
a b c d e f f g h i j k
l m n o p q r s t u v
w x y z ff fi fl ffi ffl
fa fe fo fr fu ng ry ty
. , - ' ' : ; ! ?

Characters ng ry ty not made for
6 Point and 8 Point sizes

---

14 Point — 21A 40a
ELEGANT MERCHANDISE
Business promoters developing
experimental suburban hamlet

12 Point — 22A 44a
HELD SECRET CONFERENCE
Negotiations quickly discontinued
notwithstanding pacifying actions

10 Point — 25A 50a
PROPOSE DEVELOPMENT FUND
Magnanimous building superintendent
distributes numerous gratuities among
diligent employees for efficient services

8 Point — 26A 50a
BIG COLLEGES RESUME ACTIVITIES
Students hastening back to classrooms from
long vacation are enthusiastic over prospect
of being promoted before commencing terms

6 Point — 27A 53a
MODIFY PLANS FOR APARTMENT HOUSE
Draughtsmen hurriedly prepare numerous designs
for manufacturer who contemplates increasing the
production of large factory despite repeated warning
from friends and associates opposing the agreement

Stylish Hats
from Paris

THESE hats are imported by
this company direct from the
leading French designer and
have been conceded the most
exclusive of all foreign goods

FIFTEEN DOLLARS TO
SIXTY DOLLARS

MAKLEN & CO.
Rutherford Boulevard

Modern
Suit
Pump

New for wear
with the

Spring
Suit

$8.50

NUREMBAR'S

ANNOUNCEMENT SERIES WITH BODONI

Announcement Italic

```
Characters in Complete Font
A B B C D D E F G
H I J K L M M N N
O P P Q R R S T U
V V W W X Y Z &
$ 1 2 3 4 5 6 7 8 9 0
a b c d e f f g h i j k
l m n o p q r s t u v
w x y z ff fi fl ffi ffl
fa fe fo fr fu ng ry ty
. , - ' ' : ; ! ?
Characters ng ry ty not made for
6 Point and 8 Point sizes
```

36 Point   6 A 11 a

HARMONIOUS CHORD
Large Entranced Audience

30 Point   7 A 13 a

STRENUOUS SPORTSMEN
Brilliant Maneuvering Cheered

24 Point   8 A 16 a

SILENCE IS A GOLDEN VIRTUE
An honest and courageous person will
seldom question the integrity of others

18 Point   13 A 24 a

PERFECT WORKMANSHIP BRINGS PRAISE
Real satisfaction comes from doing one's work in
a manner that precludes the possibility of criticism

14 Point   20 A 40 a

RAILROAD EXCURSIONS
Throngs appreciated splendid
train service and amusements

12 Point   22 A 44 a

PRINTERS DESIRE INCOME
Handsome type faces are business
creators which help multiply trade

10 Point   23 A 47 a

IMPRESSING NOTED TEACHER
Remember to choose your friends very
thoughtfully and wisely. The man who
believes in nobody is not to be trusted

8 Point   25 A 50 a

DECREASED PRINTING EXPENSES
Inefficiency sometimes intrudes itself under
the most successful management. The great
fault often lies in poor printing equipments

6 Point   26 A 52 a

FINE COMPOSITION AND PERSONALITY
Many good talkers lose their argument because of
a disagreeable personality, just as good copy often
fails because of unattractive display. Personality
like composition always pays the largest dividends

A
GREAT SALE
OF
BOUGLÉ
SUITS

(THREE)
(PIECE)

$17.50

Hand-Loomed
☆
Non-Stretch
☆
Ten Colors
☆
LUCILE

The House of

Mallingfriend

2468 Raymond Street
Chicago

*Desires to call the attention of the public
to the annual exhibit of*

Spring and Summer
Gowns

*Our sunlit rooms permit
selections to be made undisturbed in an
atmosphere of pleasing privacy*

Monday, Tuesday, Wednesday
February 24, 25, 26

ANNOUNCEMENT ITALIC WITH BODONI BOOK

Civilité Series

48 Point — 4A 12a
Designer Exhibited Quaint French Specimen

36 Point — 5A 15a
Beautiful Composition Awarded Graphic Arts Medal

30 Point — 6A 18a
Advertising Proficiency Explained
Enterprising Merchant Adopted System

14 Point — 3A 39a
Patriotic Societies Donate Emblems
Historic Mansion Restored to Former Beauty
Valuable Colonial Manuscript

24 Point — 8A 24a
Beautiful Decorations Reproduced
Handwriting Expert Signed Legal Document

12 Point — 15A 45a
President Issued Eighth Annual Statement
Big Munition Corporation Secured Large Contracts
Board of Directors Hold Conference

18 Point — 10A 30a
Tourists Charter Palatial Steamship Majestic
Delightful Inland Scenery Inspired Brazilian Ornithologists

10 Point — 17A 51a
Quaint New England Colonial Residence
University Arranges Important Shakespearean Pageant
Wonderful Landscape Photography

Characters in Complete Font

A B C D E E F G H H I J K
L M N O P Q R S T U V W
X Y Z & $ 1 2 3 4 5 6 7 8 9 0
a a b c d d e e f g g h h i j k l m m n y o p
q r s s t t u v w x y z nd ye . , - ' ' : ; ! ?

ENGRAVERS BOLD

36 Point   3 A
SUM

30 Point   4 A
KING

24 Point   5 A
MIRTH

18 Point No. 2   7 A
ESTATES

18 Point No. 1   8 A
DISHONOR

12 Point No. 3   10 A
BOLD MINER

12 Point No. 2   12 A
IDEAL FRIENDS
MODERN PRICE

12 Point No. 1   17 A
PROMINENT DRIVER
MODERN PURCHASE

6 Point No. 5   16 A
DISTINGUISHED PAINTER
KNIGHT PROCURES HOME

6 Point No. 4   20 A
REPRODUCED FAMOUS MASTER
ARCHITECTURAL SUPERVISORS

6 Point No. 3   27 A
REMARKABLE SPECIMEN COLLECTIONS
AMERICAN CONTRACTORS INSTRUCTED

6 Point No. 2   30 A
MANY BRIGHT PRINTERS MOVING NORTHWARD
INSTRUCTORS PRESENT VEXATIOUS PROBLEMS

6 Point No. 1   34 A
SEVERAL MAGNIFICENT SCENES INSPIRED DESIGNER
ENTERTAINERS DEMANDED INSURANCE PROTECTION
SOME ROMANTIC ESCAPADES RECENTLY DISCLOSED

CHARACTERS

A B C D E
F G H I J
K L M N O
P Q R S T
U V W X Y
Z & $ 1 2 3
4 5 6 7 8 9 0
. , - ' : ; ! ?

The following overhanging characters are
supplied with each font except
6 Point Nos. 1 and 2

A F P T V W Y

READINGS
FROM
DICKENS
BY ALICE N. REID
ELOCUTIONIST

MISS REID HAS BEEN
DELIGHTING LARGE
AUDIENCES FOR THE
PAST FOUR SEASONS

WEDNESDAY EVENING
JUNE TENTH

AT THE
BIRGEN AUDITORIUM
SOUTH BURLING STREET
MERIDEN

ENGRAVERS ROMAN

24 Point   5 A
BRING
HOPES

18 Point   8 A
MARKER
EXPIRES

12 Point No. 43   11 A
FILE REPORT
PRINT CARDS

12 Point No. 42   13 A
NICER SPECIMEN
ELEGANT MENUS

12 Point No. 41   17 A
SOUND INVESTMENTS
UNUSUAL SIMPLICITY

CHARACTERS
A B C D E F G
H I J K L M N
O P Q R S T U
V W X Y Z & $
1 2 3 4 5 6 7 8 9 0
. , - ' : ; ! ?
A V W Y overhanging characters in each font

6 Point No. 43   18 A
ATTENDS ANNUAL MEETING
STOCK EARNING DIVIDENDS
OFFICIALS HIGHLY PLEASED

6 Point No. 42   23 A
AUTOMOBILE INSURANCE POLICIES
DIGNIFIED BUSINESS STATIONERY
INTERESTING DOCUMENTS SIGNED

6 Point No. 41   34 A
SET BUSINESS FORMS IN THIS ATTRACTIVE FACE
PRODUCES WONDERFUL STEEL ENGRAVED EFFECT
CHOSEN BY DISCRIMINATING BUYER OF PRINTING

ENGRAVERS BODONI

24 Point No. 12 7A

REJOICING COMPOSES

24 Point No. 11 8A

GYMNASIUM HISTORIANS

18 Point No. 10 9A

NICE MANSION SINKING FUND

18 Point No. 9 11A

BUSINESS HOUSE STRONG METHOD

12 Point No. 8 14A

FINE MOTORS HIDES CHECK

12 Point No. 7 16A

RESIGNS OFFICE BEING INSPIRED

12 Point No. 6 20A

NEW STYLE SHOWN PRINTER HONORED

12 Point No. 5 24A

CHOICE RELIC BOUGHT COMPETENT ENGINEER

Characters in Complete Font

A B C D E F
G H I J K L M
N O P Q R S T
U V W X Y Z
& $ 1 2 3 4
5 6 7 8 9 0
. , - ' ' : ; ! ?

The following overhanging characters supplied only with fonts No. 7 to No. 12 inclusive

A F L P T V W Y

6 Point No. 4 20A

EFFORT BROUGHT SUCCESS
INSTRUCTOR ENCOURAGED
FINEST SPECIMENS SHOWN

6 Point No. 3 25A

EXCEPTIONAL ANNOUNCEMENTS
MADE WONDERFUL IMPRESSION
CAUSING FAVORABLE COMMENT

6 Point No. 2 30A

REPORTS SATISFACTORY ADJUSTMENT
MERCHANT HAS PROSPEROUS SEASON
SCHOOL TEACHERS ATTEND BANQUET

6 Point No. 1 36A

MONTHLY STATEMENTS PLEASED DIRECTORS
SUBMITTED INTERESTING FINANCIAL REPORT
PRINTER DESCRIBES ARTISTIC COMPOSITION

RAILROAD SECURITIES

H. E. ROBERTS & COMPANY

STOCK BROKERS

PHONE: KING 513

MERIDAN BUILDING
CHICAGO

EDGAR H. MORRISON

18 EAST 24TH STREET
PITTSBURGH

RICHMOND & THOMKINS OF EASTON TAKE GREAT PLEASURE ANNOUNCING THAT

MR. H. S. BRACKEN

HAS BEEN ADMITTED TO PARTNERSHIP IN THE COMPANY. HE WILL TAKE CHARGE OF THE CLOTHING DEPARTMENT, SUCCEEDING MR. T. H. JANIS, WHO RETIRES AFTER MANY YEARS OF FAITHFUL SERVICE.

RICHMOND & THOMKINS
T. H. RICHMOND, PRESIDENT

NOVEMBER 6, 1935

BRANDON SERIES

CHARACTERS IN COMPLETE FONT

A B C D E F G
H I J K L M N
O P Q R S T U
V W X Y Z &
$ 1 2 3 4 5 6 7
8 9 0 . , - ' : ; ! ?

No figures made for 6 Point No. 0

24 Point   6 A
STRONG BANKS
RIGHT NUMBER

18 Point No. 2   8 A
LEADING BROKERS
HARMONIOUS PLAN

AN EVER POPULAR
TYPE FACE

18 Point No. 1   9 A
INQUISITION
PROSPECTUS

12 Point No. 4   12 A
REMINISCENCE
ENTERPRISING

12 Point No. 3   14 A
HUGE MONUMENT
RETURNED PRIZE

12 Point No. 2   18 A
NOTED MUSIC SOCIETY
BRITISH OCEAN LINER

12 Point No. 1   21 A
MOTION PICTURE STUDIOS
TYPE DESIGNS IMPROVED

6 Point No. 3   18 A
HONORED MARINE REGIMENTS
PRAISE INGENIOUS MECHANIC

6 Point No. 2   22 A
EASTERN COLLEGE HEADS CONVENE
INTERESTING SUBJECTS DISCUSSED

6 Point No. 1   26 A
LARGE FRENCH CRUISER ENTERED HARBOR
DEVISED CREDIT SYSTEM FOR MERCHANTS

6 Point No. 0   36 A
MANY SENATORS ATTEND MEMORIAL DAY EXERCISES
HUMOROUS COMEDIANS DELIGHT MIRTHFUL CHILDREN

CARD LIGHT LITHO

12 Point No. 4   12 A
FOREIGN PERFORMER
SUBSTITUTE REPORTS

12 Point No. 3   15 A
DETERMINED GUARDSMEN
SOLDIERS REORGANIZING

12 Point No. 2   17 A
HEROIC GRENADIERS RETURN
PLUMED KNIGHTS MARCHING

12 Point No. 1   22 A
RENUMBERING
BRIGHT MINDS

6 Point No. 4   21 A
BOLD FISHERMEN
HANDSOME HOME

6 Point No. 3   24 A
INGENIOUS MARINER
EXPERIENCED FIRMS

6 Point No. 2   28 A
DETERMINED SALESMEN
SECURED NEW MEMBERS

6 Point No. 1   30 A
DECREASING PRODUCTIONS
MODERN GOWNS EXHIBITED

CHARACTERS IN COMPLETE FONT

A B C D E
F G H I J K
L M N O P
Q R S T U
V W X Y Z
& $ 1 2 3 4
5 6 7 8 9 0
. , - ' : ; ! ?

Litho Roman

72 Point — 3 A 4 a

Regalia

60 Point — 3 A 4 a

Sculptor

48 Point — 3 A 4 a

BIG Daily

36 Point — 3 A 6 a

Majestic FIRE

30 Point — 4 A 8 a

TIME 32 Seconds

24 Point — 5 A 9 a

Bought New MOTOR

18 Point — 8 A 14 a

NOTICE Foreign Diplomat

14 Point — 11 A 21 a

Merchant Invests 49 THOUSAND

12 Point — 13 A 26 a

EXCELLENT Display Composition Wins

10 Point — 15 A 28 a

TYPOGRAPHERS EARNED REPUTATION
Preference for High-Grade Printing is Justified

8 Point — 18 A 34 a

PREDICT IMPROVEMENT IN INDUSTRIAL SITUATION
Leading Automobile Manufacturers Express Optimistic Views

6 Point — 20 A 38 a

AMERICAN TYPE DESIGNS SET THE FASHION EVERYWHERE
Discriminating Advertisers Recognize Importance of Modern Typography

---

Characters in Complete Font

A B C D E F G H I
J K L M N O P Q R
S T U V W X Y Z & $
1 2 3 4 5 6 7 8 9 0
a b c d e f g h i j k
l m n o p q r s t u v
w x y z . , - ' : ; ! ?

Litho Roman

BRASS RULE NO. 13212   PINNATE BORDER UNIT

FIRST NATIONAL BANK OF DUBOIS
DUBOIS, MASSACHUSETTS

Being a brief review of the advantages of placing your money with the largest and best bank in this fast growing community

GOUDY ORNAMENT

OFFICERS
James D. Holt . . President
Adam Hoyt . Vice-President
Charles N. Bahr . . Cashier

6 POINT TEAGUE BORDER NO. 614

Invitation Series

24 Point — 8 A 16 a
MASQUERADING
Exquisite Harmony

18 Point — 12 A 22 a
IMPROVE BROCHURE
Finish Original Specimen

14 Point — 16 A 32 a
MERITORIOUS CHARACTER
Recognizing Distinctive Qualities

12 Point — 18 A 36 a
UNIQUE PRODUCTION VIEWED
Magnificent specimen of typography
thrilled enthusiastic college students

10 Point — 20 A 40 a
LIBRARY TRUSTEES HEAR REPORT
Helpful suggestions welcomed by officers
at annual meeting held in library building

Characters in Complete Font

A B C D E F
G H I J K L
M N O P Q R
S T U V W X
Y Z & $ 1 2 3
4 5 6 7 8 9 0
a b c d e f g h
i j k l m n o p
q r s t u v w x
y z ff fi fl ffi ffl
. , - ' ' : ; ! ?

8 Point — 23 A 44 a
BIDS RECEIVED FOR BOOK
Contract awarded to competitor
submitting finest example of art

6 Point — 24 A 47 a
STUDYING FOREIGN EXAMPLES
Bright craftsmen study all periodicals
in their constant search for good ideas

ELITE
FINISHING SCHOOL

An organization of
unusual excellence
which meets every
demand of patrons
who desire nothing
but the best. Every
teacher is a leader
in his especial field

◆◆◆

Chauncey M. Barns
Principal
29 East Boulevard
Columbus

HAFTEL ORNAMENT NO. 3602

Invitation Shaded

Earl Sandringham Hotel

Invitation Matinee Dansant

Given for the benefit of the

Mount Pleasant Dispensary

Saturday, October Eighteenth

Two Dollars   Three to six o'clock

Characters in Complete Font
A B C D E F G H I J K L M N O P Q R S T U V W
X Y Z & $ 1 2 3 4 5 6 7 8 9 0 a b c d e f g h i j k l
m n o p q r s t u v w x y z ff fi fl ffi ffl o'c . , - ' ' : ; ! ?
Character o'c made only in sizes from 10 to 18 Point

---

24 Point — 6 A 10 a
BURNISHING
Inspired Singer

18 Point — 9 A 18 a
SPRING MODELS
Enchanting Damsel

14 Point — 13 A 25 a
HANDSOME LIBRARY
Quickly Impressed Ladies
Distributed Old Specimen

12 Point — 15 A 30 a
DANCING INSTRUCTORS
Lessons Given Each Monday
Helping Ambitious Students

10 Point — 16 A 32 a
SOCIETY MAIDENS ELOPED
Purely Unsophisticated Gambol
Brought Joyous Reconciliations

Typo Roman

24 Point No. 1 8A 16a

Metropolitan Securities Company
Independent Organization

24 Point No. 2 9A 18a

Engravings Satisfactorily Reproduced
Unabridged Encyclopedia

18 Point No. 1 12A 24a

Distinguished Scholars Receiving Diplomas
Nineteen Graduates Honored

18 Point No. 2 15A 30a

Newspapers Launched Big Advertising Campaign
Remarkable Journalistic Enterprise

14 Point 17A 34a

Magnificent Specimens of Swiss Architecture Exhibited
Modernistic Designs Receive Most Notice
American Graphic Arts Society

12 Point 19A 38a

Impressive Ceremonies Mark Opening of Suburban Highway
Numerous State Officials Attend Celebration
Laud Splendid Improvement

10 Point 20A 41a

Delightful Entertainment and Dance Concludes Quarterly Conference
Symphony Orchestra Renders Delightful Music
Excellent Banquet Arranged

Characters in Complete Font

A B C D E F G H I J K L M
N O P Q R S T U V W X Y Z
& $ 1 2 3 4 5 6 7 8 9 0
a b c d e f g g h i j k l m n o p
q r s t u v w x y z ff fi fl ffi ffl
o' r. ay ay, ty . , - ' ' : ; ! ?

Typo Roman Shaded

24 Point No. 1 8A 16a

Metropolitan Securities Company
Independent Organization

24 Point No. 2 9A 18a

Engravings Satisfactorily Reproduced
Unabridged Encyclopedia

18 Point No. 1 12A 24a

Distinguished Scholars Receiving Diplomas
Nineteen Graduates Honored
Relatives Delighted

18 Point No. 2 15A 30a

Newspapers Launched Big Advertising Campaign
Remarkable Journalistic Enterprise
Editors Enjoy Speakers

14 Point 17A 34a

Magnificent Specimens of Swiss Architecture Exhibited
Modernistic Designs Receive Most Notice
American Graphic Arts Society
Lexington Parkway

12 Point 19A 38a

Impressive Ceremonies Mark Opening of Suburban Highway
Numerous State Officials Attend Celebration
Laud Splendid Improvement

Characters in Complete Font

A B C D E F G H I J K L M
N O P Q R S T U V W X Y Z
& $ 1 2 3 4 5 6 7 8 9 0
a b c d e f g g h i j k l m n o p
q r s t u v w x y z ff fi fl ffi ffl
o' r. ay ay, ty . , - ' ' : ; ! ?

THERMO TYPES

24 Point No. 109 11 A
COMPOSING

24 Point No. 108 13 A
INSTRUCTIONS

18 Point No. 107 15 A
ACKNOWLEDGED

18 Point No. 106 18 A
SHREWD INVESTOR

12 Point No. 105 23 A
PRINTING KNOWLEDGE

12 Point No. 104 27 A
DISTINGUISHED REPUBLICAN

12 Point No. 103 32 A
MAGNIFICENT PAINTING EXHIBITED

6 Point No. 102 31 A
FORMER AMBASSADOR HOMEWARD BOUND
PRESIDENT MENTIONS NOTABLE SENATOR

6 Point No. 101 43 A
SWEDISH ACTRESS GIVES WONDERFUL PERFORMANCE
THEATRICAL PROFESSION REJOICES WITH RISING STAR

6 Point No. 100 50 A
MOUNTAIN CLIMBING CONTESTS PROVED INVIGORATING EXERCISE
SUMMER VACATIONISTS ENTHUSIASTICALLY APPLAUD CONTESTANTS

24 Point No. 209 9 A
IMPROVES

24 Point No. 208 11 A
REMARKING

18 Point No. 207 13 A
DISCOURAGED

18 Point No. 206 15 A
EXPERT PRINTER

12 Point No. 205 19 A
GRAIN HARVESTING

12 Point No. 204 24 A
MYSTERIOUS DETECTIVE

12 Point No. 203 28 A
SPONSOR UNIQUE RECEPTION

6 Point No. 202 29 A
LUMBERMEN AWAITING CONVENTIONS
PROMINENT DELEGATES INTERVIEWED

6 Point No. 201 36 A
TREMENDOUS BUSINESS FOLLOWS DEPRESSION
SATISFIED CUSTOMERS RETURNING ABUNDANTLY

6 Point No. 200 45 A
FIRST VICE-PRESIDENT INTRODUCES IMPORTANT CHARTER
EUROPEAN BANKERS DISCUSS AMERICAN CREDIT SYSTEMS

24 Point No. 309 8 A
REQUIRE

24 Point No. 308 9 A
QUALITIES

18 Point No. 307 11 A
DISCRETION

18 Point No. 306 13 A
HIRES SINGER

12 Point No. 305 16 A
PUBLISH NAMES

12 Point No. 304 19 A
WONDERFUL HOUSE

12 Point No. 303 24 A
CHILDREN ENACT DRAMA

6 Point No. 302 23 A
PARISIAN MILLINERY ENCHANTS
HUNDREDS VISITED SHOWROOM

6 Point No. 301 31 A
HOLD MARVELOUS PAINTING EXHIBITION
CONGRESSMAN BUYS EXHIBITED PICTURE

6 Point No. 300 36 A
INDIAN POLOISTS DISPLAYED FINE SPORTSMANSHIP
NORWEGIAN HORSEMEN MAKE BRILLIANT SHOWING

CHARACTERS IN COMPLETE FONT

A B C D E F G
H I J K L M N
O P Q R S ſ T
U V W X Y Z & $
1 2 3 4 5 6 7 8
9 0 . , - ' ' : ; ! ?

The following characters are cast recessed in the 24 Point sizes only

A F L P T
V W Y

THERMO TYPES ARE LABOR-SAVING

The example below shows why Thermo Types are labor-saving. The measure is 21 ems pica. You wish to use the largest 24 Point (No. 309) for the name FRAMINGDALE, and it comes

Measure is 21 ems pica

FRAMINGDALE
FRAMINGDALE

out one pica too long. Simply change the R and N to 24 Point No. 209 and you have the correct measure within a point or two. Each series is the same in weight, size for size. The type is fitted point set and is practically self-spacing.

Heavy Copperplate Gothic

24 Point No. 30 — 6 A
ENDANGER

24 Point No. 29 — 7 A
INSTRUCTION

18 Point No. 30 — 9 A
ERASED MARKS

18 Point No. 29 — 11 A
DEPTH MEASURED

12 Point No. 28 — 13 A
KNOWLEDGE SOUGHT

12 Point No. 27 — 16 A
FOUND HANDSOME BOOK

12 Point No. 26 — 19 A
SEVEN SCHOLARS FURNISHED

12 Point No. 25 — 24 A
INTERNATIONAL BOATING CONTEST

6 Point No. 24 — 21 A
DEMONSTRATION SATISFACTORY
MODERN LABOR-SAVING DEVICES

6 Point No. 23 — 26 A
COLLEGE PROFESSOR RETURNS REPORT
DEPARTMENT OFFICIAL CORRECTS NOTE

6 Point No. 22 — 32 A
JUDGE HONORED FAMOUS EUROPEAN LIBRARIAN
NEWSPAPER PUBLISHED BIOGRAPHY OF VISITOR

6 Point No. 21 — 37 A
RAPID CALCULATING MACHINE PROVES VERY EFFICIENT
SEVERAL LEADING BUSINESS MEN ENDORSED INVENTION

Characters in Complete Font

A B C D E F G H I
J K L M N O P Q
R S T U V W X Y
Z & $ 1 2 3 4 5 6
7 8 9 0 . , - ' : ; ! ?

Our Birthday

While serving the public for the past twenty-five years we have made a reputation for ourselves of which we are proud. To-day we celebrate our

Twenty-Fifth Anniversary

In honor of this important event patrons of our store will be given the benefit of a thirty per cent reduction on all merchandise in the building. This liberal offer is for to-day only. Do not fail to take advantage of it

Broad Department Store
Chester, Indiana

Light Copperplate Gothic

Characters in Complete Font

A B C D E F G H I
J K L M N O P Q
R S T U V W X Y
Z & $ 1 2 3 4 5 6
7 8 9 0 . , - ' : ; ! ?

6 Point No. 4 — 21 A
PREPARED ELEMENTARY COURSE
SCHOOL TEACHERS DIRECT BOYS

6 Point No. 3 — 26 A
INTERNATIONAL IMPROVEMENT SOCIETY
FOREIGN BRANCH OFFICES CONSIDERED

6 Point No. 2 — 32 A
AMERICAN RAILROADS CHANGE TIME SCHEDULE
COMMUTERS REJOICED WHEN THEY HEARD NEWS

6 Point No. 1 — 37 A
FURNISHED APARTMENT HOUSE NOW BEING REMODELED
WORK TO BE DONE BEFORE THE COLD WEATHER ARRIVES

24 Point No. 10 — 6 A
RENUMBER

24 Point No. 9 — 7 A
HARMONIOUS

18 Point No. 10 — 9 A
MONTH ENDING

18 Point No. 9 — 11 A
EXCEPTING RULES

12 Point No. 8 — 13 A
SPECIMEN EXHIBITION

12 Point No. 7 — 16 A
REPRODUCTION INSURED

12 Point No. 6 — 19 A
SPECIALIZING MACHINE WORK

12 Point No. 5 — 24 A
FURNISHED MODERN DEPARTMENT

LOUIS PINE, PRESIDENT   JOHN LIONS, TREASURER

MONROE BANK
CAPITAL and SURPLUS
$975,000

•

ANNUAL REPORT

NORTH REVINGTON BOULEVARD   CHICAGO

Light Copperplate Gothic Condensed

Characters in Complete Font
A B C D E F G H I J K L M N
O P Q R S T U V W X Y Z & $
1 2 3 4 5 6 7 8 9 0 . , - ' : ; ! ?

The Montauk Dramatic Society

A Society Composed of
Members of the Metropolitan Church
Will Present

The Prodigal Son

A Sketch in Four Acts

At the Church Auditorium

Manhattanville, New York

Wednesday Evening, February Twenty-Fourth

---

12 Point No. 36 — 26 A
Engraving Exhibited
Delightful Musicale

12 Point No. 35 — 29 A
Fine Oration Delivered
Professor Lauds Judge

6 Point No. 34 — 27 A
Fine Wedding Announcement
Praise Artistic Workmanship
Displays Excellent Specimen

6 Point No. 33 — 31 A
Apartment Exclusively Decorated
Remarkable Landscape Paintings
Many Beautiful Scenes Exhibited

6 Point No. 32 — 37 A
Good Typography Sought by Advertiser
Programs Arranged for Church Social
Plan Tremendous Advertising Campaign

6 Point No. 31 — 42 A
Organized New Merchandizing Headquarters
Hat Manufacturers Hold Annual Convention
Several Interesting Resolutions Submitted

24 Point No. 40 — 8 A
BRIDGES

24 Point No. 39 — 10 A
PROSPECT

18 Point No. 40 — 11 A
EXPOSITION

18 Point No. 39 — 14 A
HUMORESQUE

12 Point No. 38 — 18 A
PLEASING SHOW
FRENCH ACTORS

12 Point No. 37 — 22 A
MODERNIZED HOME
RAREST DRAPERIES

Heavy Copperplate Gothic Condensed

24 Point No. 20 — 8 A
HONORS

24 Point No. 19 — 10 A
EXCLUDED

18 Point No. 20 — 11 A
IMPRESSIVE

18 Point No. 19 — 14 A
EMBANKMENT

12 Point No. 18 — 18 A
MODERN HOMES
FINE MERCHANT

12 Point No. 17 — 21 A
SPLENDID EXAMPLE
BEAUTIFUL GARDEN

12 Point No. 16 — 25 A
REMARKABLE STORIES
EXQUISITE APARTMENT

12 Point No. 15 — 29 A
SIMPLICITY OF DESIGNING
NOVEL SPECIMEN SHOWN

6 Point No. 14 — 27 A
EXTRAORDINARY IMPROVEMENT
ACQUIRED MODERN BUILDINGS
INDUSTRIAL TREND IMPROVING

6 Point No. 13 — 31 A
SUBMITS VERY INTERESTING REPORT
NATIONAL BOARD OF UNDERWRITERS
ENCOURAGING INDUSTRIAL OUTLOOK

6 Point No. 12 — 37 A
IMPROVED FINANCIAL CONDITIONS SHOWN
ADVERTISING CAMPAIGNS BEING PLANNED
GOOD TYPE DESIGNS COMMAND ATTENTION

6 Point No. 11 — 42 A
PROGRESSIVE MANUFACTURER ORDERS PRINTING
MOST ADVERTISERS PREFER HAND COMPOSITION
HANDSOME TYPE FACES CREATE MORE BUSINESS

Characters in Complete Font
A B C D E F G H I J K L M N
O P Q R S T U V W X Y Z & $
1 2 3 4 5 6 7 8 9 0 . , - ' : ; ! ?

Business Stimulated

An Artistic Piece of Printing Usually Attracts
The Eyes of Business Men in Not Only Your Own
But in Every Other Line. With Our Facilities for
Producing Artistic Printing Your Business Can
Be Stimulated No Matter What You Make or Sell

Artistic Printing Company
Advertising Designers and Typographers
Poughkeepsie, New York

Light Copperplate Gothic Extended

24 Point No. 70 — 5 A
ENSURED

24 Point No. 69 — 6 A
RIGHTEOUS

18 Point No. 70 — 8 A
INSTRUCTIVE

18 Point No. 69 — 9 A
FOREIGN BIRTH

12 Point No. 68 — 11 A
SMART EXECUTOR

12 Point No. 67 — 13 A
PRODUCING FIGURES

12 Point No. 66 — 15 A
MECHANICS PROSPERING

12 Point No. 65 — 18 A
HISTORIC BANKING CONCERN

6 Point No. 64 — 17 A
ENTHUSIASTIC ADVERTISER
SHOWING ARTISTIC DESIGN

6 Point No. 63 — 22 A
IMPORTANT BANQUET ARRANGED
MANY NOTED SPEAKERS PRESENT

6 Point No. 62 — 26 A
INTERNATIONAL ROWING CHAMPIONSHIP
MAGNIFICENT BRONZE TROPHY AWARDED

6 Point No. 61 — 30 A
CONTEMPLATE REMARKABLE DEMONSTRATION
PRESIDENT ATTENDS IMPRESSIVE CEREMONIES

CHARACTERS IN COMPLETE FONT

A B C D E F G
H I J K L M N O
P Q R S T U V
W X Y Z & $ 1 2
3 4 5 6 7 8 9 0
. , - ' : ; ! ?

BAKER-RICHMOND COMPANY
MADISON SQUARE, ST. LOUIS, MISSOURI

OUR MR. JACKSON WILL CALL ON YOU SEPTEMBER 24TH
WITH AN UNUSUAL SHOWING OF USEFUL AND ARTISTIC

SILVERWARE

MR. JACKSON RANKS AMONG THE LEADING AUTHORITIES
ON SILVERWARE, AND WE SINCERELY BELIEVE YOU WILL
FIND HIS VISIT VERY INTERESTING AND OF REAL VALUE

BAKER-RICHMOND COMPANY

AUGUST NINTH

Heavy Copperplate Gothic Extended

CHARACTERS IN COMPLETE FONT

A B C D E F G
H I J K L M N O
P Q R S T U V
W X Y Z & $ 1 2
3 4 5 6 7 8 9 0
. , - ' : ; ! ?

6 Point No. 74 — 17 A
CONCERT SINGERS RETURN
BEAUTIFUL WINTER HOMES

6 Point No. 73 — 22 A
ILLUSTRATED WESTERN SCENERY
VARIOUS KINDS OF LARGE SHOWS

6 Point No. 72 — 27 A
NEW MACHINE BREAKS RACING RECORD
HIGH-GRADE SHOES SOLD REASONABLY

6 Point No. 71 — 30 A
NEW YORK CENTRAL TRAVELS ALONG HUDSON
COUNTRY WINDOW DISPLAYS VERY ATTRACTIVE

24 Point No. 80 — 5 A
MENDING

24 Point No. 79 — 6 A
DISREPUTE

18 Point No. 80 — 7 A
COLD WINDS

18 Point No. 79 — 8 A
NUMBER FOUR

12 Point No. 78 — 11 A
FROZEN CHICKEN

12 Point No. 77 — 13 A
NOTED AUTOMOBILE

12 Point No. 76 — 15 A
MERCHANTS CROWDING

12 Point No. 75 — 18 A
NUMEROUS HOMES DESIRED

MRS. EDNA BROWNSON

TAKES GREAT PLEASURE IN INVITING YOU
TO BE PRESENT AT HER

SECOND VIOLIN RECITAL

SUNDAY AFTERNOON, SEPTEMBER FIRST
THREE FORTY-FIVE O'CLOCK

MENDLESHON DRAWING ROOMS
NORTHSHORE MANOR

FOR THE BENEFIT OF AGED MUSICIANS

Copperplate Gothic Italic

Characters in Complete Font

A B C D E F G
H I J K L M N
O P Q R S T U
V W X Y Z & $
1 2 3 4 5 6 7
8 9 0 . , - ' : ; ! ?

6 Point No. 54 — 21 A
STRAIGHTFORWARD APPRENTICE
NOTABLE LEGISLATORS ELECTED

6 Point No. 53 — 25 A
PROFESSIONAL ACTIVITIES CONDEMNED
STORES ENJOYED PROSPEROUS SEASON

6 Point No. 52 — 32 A
BRILLIANT ENTERTAINMENT CLOSES PAGEANTRY
MISUNDERSTANDING CAUSES SERIOUS BLUNDER

6 Point No. 51 — 37 A
WONDERFUL RESULTS SECURED BY SIMPLIFIED PROCESS
ELECTRICIANS DISCUSS NUMEROUS TOPICS OF INTEREST

24 Point No. 60 — 6 A
HUNDREDS

24 Point No. 59 — 8 A
EXPOUNDING

18 Point No. 60 — 9 A
MAGNIFICENCE

18 Point No. 59 — 11 A
RECONSTRUCTION

12 Point No. 58 — 12 A
PERMANENT SERVICE

12 Point No. 57 — 16 A
LEGENDARY HAPPENINGS

12 Point No. 56 — 18 A
DASHING OFFICER PROMOTED

12 Point No. 55 — 22 A
ENTHUSIASTIC VOYAGERS RETURN

FOURTH SEASON

DRAMATIC GUILD

DECEMBER
ROMEO AND JULIET
ACADEMY OF MUSIC

SEASON TICKETS ARE NOW ON SALE

Copperplate Gothic Bold

24 Point No. 50 — 6 A
EMBRACED

24 Point No. 49 — 7 A
RETRIBUTION

18 Point No. 50 — 9 A
NECROMANCER

18 Point No. 49 — 11 A
UNCOMPROMISING

12 Point No. 48 — 13 A
MYSTERIOUS SEARCH

12 Point No. 47 — 16 A
FINANCIAL ADJUSTMENTS

12 Point No. 46 — 19 A
DISTINGUISHED PHILOSOPHER

12 Point No. 45 — 24 A
BRILLIANT INSTRUCTOR RESIGNED

6 Point No. 44 — 22 A
SUPERINTENDENT ENCOURAGED
MECHANIC PATENTED INVENTION

6 Point No. 43 — 25 A
PERIODICAL ILLUSTRATORS BANQUETED
BUILDS EXTENSIVE STEEL WAREHOUSES

6 Point No. 42 — 34 A
ESTABLISHED SEVENTEEN NORTHERN BRANCHES
HASTEN ARRANGEMENTS FOR INVITATION DANCE

6 Point No. 41 — 37 A
MANUFACTURING BUILDER SECURES FACTORY CONTRACT
FREIGHT CONFERENCE ADJOURNS AFTER PRELIMINARIES

Characters in Complete Font

A B C D E F G
H I J K L M N
O P Q R S T U
V W X Y Z & $
1 2 3 4 5 6 7
8 9 0 . , - ' : ; ! ?

SLOAN & BUCHANAN

MANAGING AGENTS AND DIRECTORS FOR THE PRINCIPAL
FOREIGN AND DOMESTIC COMPANIES

INSURANCE

PITTSBURGH — INDIANAPOLIS — CINCINNATI

BANK GOTHICS

Bank Gothic Light

18 Point No. 10 10 A
MECHANICS

18 Point No. 9 12 A
REPRODUCED

12 Point No. 8 15 A
SECURED HOME

12 Point No. 7 17 A
CLEVER SALESMAN

12 Point No. 6 21 A
SUPERIOR INSURANCE

12 Point No. 5 24 A
ENTERPRISING EXHIBITOR

6 Point No. 4 21 A
BEAUTIFUL SUMMER GARDENS
TENNIS CHAMPION SURPRISED

6 Point No. 3 25 A
AMERICAN PRESIDENT ENTERTAINED
REMARKABLE MECHANICAL EXHIBITS

6 Point No. 2 29 A
ARTIST ILLUSTRATING WESTERN SCENERY
FIRM ESTABLISHING NORTHERN BRANCH

6 Point No. 1 35 A
ARCHITECTURAL INSTITUTE GIVING EXHIBITION
BRILLIANT PAGEANT CLOSING ENTERTAINMENT

Bank Gothic Medium

18 Point No. 20 10 A
EXTENDING

18 Point No. 19 12 A
BENEVOLENT

12 Point No. 18 15 A
GRAND SCENES

12 Point No. 17 17 A
HISTORIC VOLUME

12 Point No. 16 21 A
STEADY EMPLOYMENT

12 Point No. 15 24 A
ENCOURAGING SYMPTOM

6 Point No. 14 21 A
INTERESTING COVER DESIGNS
PROMOTES REAL INVESTMENT

6 Point No. 13 25 A
MODERNISTIC OFFICE STATIONERY
PRINTING INSTRUCTORS ENGAGED

6 Point No. 12 29 A
DISTINCTIVE PRINTING RECEIVED AWARD
CUSTOMER DESIRES ARISTOCRATIC TYPE

6 Point No. 11 35 A
ADMIRES DIGNIFIED COMMERCIAL STATIONERY
REPRODUCE FINE ENGRAVED ANNOUNCEMENT

Bank Gothic Bold

18 Point No. 30 9 A
PRODUCED

18 Point No. 29 11 A
DISTINGUISH

12 Point No. 28 13 A
MODERN RADIO

12 Point No. 27 16 A
BANK TREASURER

12 Point No. 26 20 A
ECONOMIC METHODS

12 Point No. 25 24 A
DESIRABLE PRODUCTION

6 Point No. 24 21 A
**SUBMIT INTERESTING REPORT
NATIONAL BANK STATEMENTS**

6 Point No. 23 25 A
**UNUSUAL OPPORTUNITY OFFERED
HANDSOMELY BOUND DICTIONARY**

6 Point No. 22 29 A
**COMPETENT MECHANIC MADE FOREMAN
MANUFACTURING CONCERN PROSPERED**

6 Point No. 21 34 A
**INTERNATIONALLY PROMINENT TYPOGRAPHER
EXHIBITED WONDERFUL PRINTING SPECIMENS**

Characters in Complete Font

A B C D E F G H I J K L M N O P Q R S T U V W X Y Z &
$ 1 2 3 4 5 6 7 8 9 0 . , - ' ' : ; ! ?

Characters are the same in Light, Medium and Bold

FRANK PANKEY, JR.
TREASURER

MANUFACTURERS
FOR
BOTTLERS
EXCLUSIVELY

•

MEMBER OF
WESTERN MANUFACTURERS
OF SODA WATER
FLAVORS

GEORGE M. CHAPMAN
PRESIDENT

GIBSON-KINNEY COMPANY
MANUFACTURING CHEMISTS

ESTABLISHED 1896
TELEPHONE MAIN 1301

1027 RIVER STREET

DANTOWN, IOWA

CHARLES E. MEISTER
CHEMIST

FLAVORS
CERTIFIED COLORS
ACIDS
COMPOUNDS
GINGER ALE
EXTRACTS
ETC.

VOCATIONAL CAMEO 3616

Bank Gothics Condensed

Bank Gothic Condensed Light

18 Point No. 40   13 A
MODERN HOUSE

18 Point No. 39   15 A
INCREASED ORDER

12 Point No. 38   17 A
PURCHASED BUILDING

12 Point No. 37   20 A
IMPROVING PRODUCTIONS

12 Point No. 36   25 A
REPORT SPLENDID CONDITION

12 Point No. 35   29 A
MANUFACTURERS CALLED MEETING

6 Point No. 34   25 A
DISTINGUISHED LAWYER RECEIVED AWARD
EUROPEAN THESPIANS HELD CONVENTION

6 Point No. 33   30 A
EXHIBITING DIGNIFIED COMMERCIAL STATIONERY
REPRODUCED FINE ENGRAVED ANNOUNCEMENTS

6 Point No. 32   35 A
MODERNISTIC EMBELLISHMENT PLEASED TYPOGRAPHER
CRAFTSMAN CREATED MANY ORIGINAL COVER DESIGNS

6 Point No. 31   40 A
MANY CUSTOMERS ARE DEMANDING ARISTOCRATIC TYPE FACES
PROSPEROUS MANUFACTURING CONCERN PROMOTED FOREMAN

Bank Gothic Condensed Medium

18 Point No. 50   12 A
REGAL EMPIRES

18 Point No. 49   15 A
STYLISH LINGERIE

12 Point No. 48   17 A
MODERNIZED SKETCH

12 Point No. 47   19 A
EXCLUSIVE ATMOSPHERE

12 Point No. 46   23 A
BEAUTIFUL SUMMER GARDEN

12 Point No. 45   27 A
INTERESTING COVER DESIGN SOLD

6 Point No. 44   25 A
ARTIST ILLUSTRATING WESTERN SCENERY
FIRM ESTABLISHING NORTHERN BRANCH

6 Point No. 43   28 A
ARCHITECTURAL INSTITUTE GIVING EXHIBITION
BRILLIANT PAGEANT CLOSES ENTERTAINMENT

6 Point No. 42   33 A
CONCERN ORDERED MODERNISTIC OFFICE STATIONERY
MANY PROMINENT PRINTING INSTRUCTORS ENGAGED

6 Point No. 41   38 A
AMERICAN PRESIDENT ENTERTAINED DISTINGUISHED ENVOYS
SHOWN NUMEROUS REMARKABLE MECHANICAL INNOVATIONS

Bank Gothic Condensed Bold

18 Point No. 60   11 A
RIGHT DESIGN

18 Point No. 59   13 A
DESCRIBES SHIP

12 Point No. 58   15 A
RURAL MERCHANTS

12 Point No. 57   17 A
SPLENDID ATTRACTION

12 Point No. 56   21 A
ORDERS COLORFUL GOWNS

12 Point No. 55   25 A
FRENCH AIRPLANE TRIUMPHANT

6 Point No. 54   22 A
**BROKER SUBMITS EXCELLENT REPORT
MARKET NATIONAL BANK STATEMENTS**

6 Point No. 53   26 A
**UNUSUAL OPPORTUNITY OFFERED DIRECTOR
HANDSOMELY EMBELLISHED DICTIONARIES**

6 Point No. 52   31 A
**COMPETENT YOUNG CRAFTSMAN GETS PROMOTION
MACHINE MANUFACTURING CONCERN PROSPERED**

6 Point No. 51   35 A
**INTERNATIONALLY PROMINENT TYPOGRAPHERS CONVENED
EXHIBITS SEVERAL WONDERFUL TYPOGRAPHIC SPECIMENS**

Characters in Complete Font

A B C D E F G H I J K L M N O P Q R S T U V W X Y Z &
$ 1 2 3 4 5 6 7 8 9 0 . , - ' ' : ; ! ?

Characters are the same in Light, Medium and Bold

FOR LARGER SIZES OF BANK GOTHIC CONDENSED MEDIUM SEE POSTER GOTHIC, PAGE 185

PEERLESS AUTOMATIC UNIT

•

THE PEERLESS AUTOMATIC UNIT WILL HANDLE THE FULL RANGE OF STOCK, STARTING WITH 13-POUND FOLIO, UP TO 10 OR 12-PLY CARDBOARD. IT WILL ALSO FEED BLOTTERS, ENVELOPES, TAGS, CARDS, AND EVEN CERTAIN FOLDED JOBS THAT ARE TO BE IMPRINTED. THERE IS AN ENDLESS VARIETY OF WORK WHICH THE PEERLESS WILL DO QUICKER AND BETTER THAN CAN BE DONE ON A PRESS FED BY HAND

AMERICAN TYPE FOUNDERS SALES CORPORATION

AMERICAN
INSTRUMENTS OF UNUSUAL
EXCELLENCE

KINGSMAN PIANOS

ON DISPLAY
AT THE MUSIC SHOW
HARMONY HALL

KINGSMAN PIANO COMPANY
PHILADELPHIA

Blair Series

24 Point No. 2 — 5 A
NICHE

24 Point No. 1 — 6 A
URBAN

18 Point No. 2 — 8 A
SQUIRM

18 Point No. 1 — 9 A
REPENTS

12 Point No. 4 — 11 A
MORTGAGE
BIG SIPHON

12 Point No. 3 — 14 A
INSPIRED HIM
HIDES CHECK

12 Point No. 2 — 16 A
PRINTING TRUE
MOSAIC DESIGN

12 Point No. 1 — 18 A
RAMBLING NOMAD
HELPED CAPTIVES

6 Point No. 4 — 16 A
MODERN ORCHESTRA
SHIP FOLDERS QUICK

6 Point No. 3 — 19 A
EXPERIENCED WORKERS
BUILD SUBURBAN SHOP

6 Point No. 2 — 23 A
PRUDENT ADVERTISERS SAVE
RARE DRAWING GIVEN WRITER
QUAINT FURNITURE EXHIBITS

6 Point No. 1 — 29 A
NEAT TYPOGRAPHIC SPECIMEN BOOK
CANADIAN CRAFTSMEN BANQUETING
IDAHO SENATOR DELIVERED ORATION

CHARACTERS IN COMPLETE FONT

A B C D E F G
H I J K L M N O
P Q R S T U V
W X Y Z & $ 1 2
3 4 5 6 7 8 9 0
. , - ' : ; ! ?

6 Point No. 0 carried in stock only at Foundry

SECOND ANNUAL

WHIMSICAL DANCE

OF THE

ROXBURY CLUB

FRIDAY EVENING — MARCH TENTH

Steelplate Gothic Shaded

CHARACTERS IN COMPLETE FONT

A B C D E F G H I J K L M
N O P Q R S T U V W X Y Z
& $ 1 2 3 4 5 6 7 8 9 0
. , - ' : ; ! ?

THE NORTHERN

OF NEW YORK

THE LEADING PERIODICAL IN ITS FIELD

ANNOUNCES

THE APPOINTMENT OF

MR. ALEXANDER JACKSON

AS THE EDITOR-IN-CHIEF

---

12 Point No. 73 — 17 A
MERCHANDISE
SHOWING FINE
NEW METHODS

12 Point No. 72 — 19 A
FOURTH ANNUAL
DECEMBER CLUB
FLAG EXHIBITION

12 Point No. 71 — 23 A
MANY INTERESTING
PAPERS EXHIBITED
BENEFITING LOCAL
FLOWER MERCHANT

6 Point No. 74 — 28 A
DISTINGUISHED BANKER
BESTOWS COMPLIMENTS
UPON DARING OFFICERS
AND MEMBERS OF FORCE

6 Point No. 73 — 32 A
PROMINENT EASTERN WRITER
RECOVERS FRENCH PICTURES
DURING THE RECENT DISPLAY
BY PROMINENT CONNOISSEUR

24 Point No. 72 — 6 A
BANKS
HEDGE

24 Point No. 71 — 8 A
EMBARK
SECOND

18 Point No. 72 — 9 A
NOMADIC
KINGDOM

18 Point No. 71 — 11 A
RESIDENCE
DIRECTORS

12 Point No. 74 — 14 A
DEMOLISHING
AMENDMENTS

Comstook

36 Point   3 A 4 a
HERB
Spent

30 Point   4 A 5 a
MUSIC
Elderly

24 Point   5 A 7 a
NIMROD
Regicide

18 Point   7 A 10 a
ENSURING
Habilitated

14 Point   9 A 15 a
BRIGHT BLUE
Seoure Result

12 Point No. 1   12 A 20 a
INSURED MINER
Request Granted

12 Point No. 2   15 A
HISTORIC DESIGNS
KNIGHTS CONVENE
EXQUISITE DINNER

12 Point No. 3   18 A
EUROPEAN COSTUMERS
ORCHESTRAS ENGAGED
HUMOROUS COMEDIANS

Characters in Complete Font

A B C D E F G H I J
K L M N O P Q R S
T U V W X Y Z & $
1 2 3 4 5 6 7 8 9 0
a b c d e f g h i j k l
m n o p q r s t u v
w x y z . , - ' : ; ! ?

JOHNSON & BOSTWICK
DRUGGISTS

62 STUYVESANT TERRACE

TELEPHONE 123   ELMFORD, MD.

COMSTOCK WITH CASLON NO. 471 AND ITALIC   TELEPHONE CAST CUT NO. 1802

Engravers Shaded

Characters in Complete Font

A B C D E F G
H I J K L M N
O P Q R S T U
V W X Y Z & $
1 2 3 4 5 6 7 8 9 0
. , - ' : ; ! ?

The following overhanging characters are supplied with each font

A F L P T V W Y

MISS ELINORE HICKSON

42 HUNEKER PLACE

18 Point No. 1   6 A
PAYING
DEVICE

18 Point No. 2   7 A
MONDAY
PARTIES

12 Point No. 1   10 A
MAY DAYS
REGILDER
AUDITORS

12 Point No. 2   12 A
DESIGN GIFT
ART EDITOR
RIGHT BOND

12 Point No. 3   16 A
AMERICA FIRST
GIRL NEIGHBOR
RESERVE BANK

6 Point No. 1   18 A
HANDSOME DESIGNS
BRIGHT SPRING DAY
MORNING EXERCISE
FINE ARTS DIVISION

6 Point No. 2   21 A
THE MUNICIPAL COUNCIL
INVESTIGATED REPORTS
TAXPAYER COMPLAINED
EXHIBITION OF POTTERY

6 Point No. 3   25 A
COMPLIMENT GREAT ORATOR
SCHOOLS OBSERVED EASTER
MANY PROMINENT IN CHURCH
COLORFUL MUSICAL SERVICE

Antique Shaded

72 Point — 3 A 4 a
Curls 2

60 Point — 3 A 4 a
5 Money

48 Point — 3 A 4 a
CRIMES 8
Large haul

42 Point — 3 A 4 a
4 DOCTORS
Advise quiet

36 Point — 3 A 4 a
FIRST SALE 3
Suits and Coats

30 Point — 4 A 6 a
ANNUAL DANCE
1 Elite Patronized

24 Point — 4 A 7 a
REBUS
Musing
an hour

18 Point — 7 A 11 a
EMBERS
Boy scout
tends fire

14 Point — 9 A 17 a
MUSICALE
Big receipts
benefit poor

12 Point — 10 A 20 a
NUMBERING
Inventor likes
the intricately
fitted machine
to work nicely

10 Point — 12 A 22 a
INSTRUCTORS
Reads literature
containing most
beautiful phrase
written in years

8 Point — 14 A 26 a
MERCHANT SAILS
Around the world in
about seven months
combining pleasure
with business spirit

★ ANTIQUE SHADED ★
6 POINT MODERNISTIC STARS NO. 2

Characters in Complete Font

A B C D E F G
H I J K L M N
O P Q R S T U V
W X Y Z & $ 1 2
3 4 5 6 7 8 9 0
a b c d e f g h i
j k l m n o p q r
s t u v w x y z
. , - ' ' : ; ! ?

[144]

Royal Script

*An interesting display
of the latest*
Mid-Winter Fashions
*awaits your approval
and offers great
variety at*

The Elite Shop
*Broadway and Grand
San Francisco*

Lucille Harmon

Miss Florence Burke

Piano Instruction

Sniffin Ornament
No. 7

48 Point   3A 6a
Defended
36 Point   4A 11a
Magniloquent
30 Point No. 551   4A 12a
Lids Replaced
30 Point No. 552   4A 12a
Beautiful Home
24 Point No. 551   6A 18a
Stylish Decorators
24 Point No. 552   6A 18a
New Samples Given
18 Point No. 551   7A 21a

*Regular Customer
Admire Ideal Proposal*

12 Point No. 551   9A 36a

*Distinguished Gentleman
Merchants Entertaining Diplomat*

Characters in Complete Font

A B C D E F G H I J K L M N O P Q
R S T U V W X Y Z & $ 1 2 3 4 5 6 7 8 9 0
a b c d e f g h i j k l m n o p q r s t u v
w x y z . . . , = ' : ; ! ?

Typo Script and Typo Script Extended

Typo Script

60 Point — 3A 8a
Hesperian

48 Point — 3A 10a
Rhapsodical

36 Point — 4A 14a
Beautiful Girls

30 Point — 4A 17a
Captivated Knight

24 Point — 6A 20a
Delightful Atmosphere
Summer Homes

18 Point — 8A 24a
Mighty Behemoth
President Invited Everybody
Bought Automobile

14 Point — 8A 32a
Remarkable Personality
Famous English Psychologist Returns
Cordial Reception
Entertained Vast Assemblage

Characters in Complete Font
A B C D E F G
H I J K L M
N O P Q R S T
U V W X Y Z &
$ 1 2 3 4 5 6 7 8 9 0
a b c d e f g h i
j k l m n o ó p q r
s s t u v w x y z
. ‹ , ; - ' : ; ! ? , ,

Typo Script Extended

Characters in Complete Font
A B C D E F
G H I J K L
M N O P Q R
S T U V W X
Y Z & $ 1 2 3
4 5 6 7 8 9 0
a b c d e f g h i
j k l m n o ó p q
r s s t u v w x y z
. ‹ , ; - ' : ; ! ? , ,

24 Point — 6A 18a
Government
Large Aeroplanes

18 Point — 8A 24a
Delightful Chat
Pleasant Surroundings

14 Point — 8A 32a
Manufactured Fabric
Building Terminal Extension

12 Point — 10A 40a
Preferred Stockholders
Marine International Companies
Insurance Division

60 Point — 3A 7a
Majestic

48 Point — 3A 9a
Knapsack

36 Point — 4A 12a
Synchronize

30 Point — 4A 14a
Depositors
Redfield Bank

Typo Upright Bold and *Typo Upright*

Typo Upright Bold

60 Point — 3 A 9 a
Hieroglyphical

48 Point — 3 A 10 a
Mysterious Story

36 Point — 4 A 13 a
Wonderful Decoration

30 Point — 5 A 16 a
Acknowledges Qualification

24 Point No. 1 — 7 A 20 a
Purchased Magnificent Portrait

24 Point No. 2 — 8 A 23 a
Compiled Very Interesting Reports

18 Point — 9 A 29 a
Discovered Extraordinary Metamorphosis

14 Point — 11 A 32 a
Beautiful Rose
Displays Fine Flowers

12 Point — 11 A 45 a
Successful Business
Banking Situation Pleases

Characters in Complete Font

A B C D E F G H I J K L
M N O P Q R S T U V W
X Y Z Th Tu & $ 1 2 3 4 5 6
7 8 9 0 a b c d e f g h i j k l
m n o o' p q r s s' t u v w x y z
. , ' ' . . ' , ; - ' : ; ! ?

Typo Upright

18 Point — 9 A 35 a
Prominent Jurist Given Agreeable Surprise

14 Point — 9 A 44 a
Finest Specimens
Exquisite Type Designing

12 Point — 10 A 48 a
Brilliant Scholars
Professor Awarded Prizes

48 Point — 3 A 10 a
Best Encyclopedia

36 Point — 4 A 14 a
Metropolitan Theatres

30 Point — 5 A 18 a
Smart Handwriting Expert

24 Point No. 1 — 6 A 21 a
Beautiful Engravings Duplicated

24 Point No. 2 — 7 A 26 a
Customers Admire Aristocratic Letter

Characters in Complete Font

A B C D E F G H I J K L
M N O P Q R S T U V W
X Y Z & Tu Th $ 1 2 3 4 5 6 7
8 9 0 a b c d e f g h h i j k l m
n o o' p q r s s' t u v w x y z
rs of . , ' ' . . ' , ; - ' : ; ! ?

Typo Shaded

48 Point — 3A 12a

Reproduce
Magnificent

36 Point — 4A 15a

Lithographed
Design Pleasing

30 Point — 5A 18a

Highest Quality
Kentucky Tobaccos

24 Point No. 1 — 6A 22a

Suspend Judgment
Night Editions Helped

24 Point No. 2 — 8A 25a

Invention Safeguarded
Royalty Cheered Acrobats

18 Point — 10A 32a

Extraordinary Manuscript
Delightful Country Residences
Important Structures

14 Point — 12A 40a

Wonderful Encyclopedias Bought
Unprejudiced Photographer Exonerated
Remarkable Demonstrations

Elizabeth Rembrandt

Philadelphia

Announcing a special
showing of

Dainty Silk Lingerie

in the latest and most
distinctive designs

Exhibited on the third floor in the
Fashion Department

Wednesday May fifth

Half after three

Pinnate Border No. 9

Characters in Complete Font

A B C D E F G H I J
K L M N O P Q R S
T U V W X Y Z Th Tu
& $ 1 2 3 4 5 6 7 8 9 0
a b c d e f g h i j k l m n
o p q r s 's t u v w x y z
. , ' . . , , - ' : ; ! ?

Typo Text and Waldorf Text

Typo Text

24 Point 4A 11a
Beautiful Parks

18 Point 6A 18a
Recently Established

14 Point 9A 28a
Given Delightful Surprise
Honorable Mention

12 Point 11A 31a
Entertains Celebrated Violinist
Requests Introduction

10 Point 11A 34a
Diplomatic Methods Solve Problem
Noteworthy Achievement

8 Point 14A 40a
Popular Artist Displays Masterpiece
Valuable Information Concerning Exhibition
Artistic Paintings Recognized

1 2 3 4 5 6 7 8 9 0

24 Point Figures set solid

12 Point Chic Border No. 4

Characters in Complete Font

A B C D E F G H I
J K L M N O P Q R
S T U V W X Y Z &
$ 1 2 3 4 5 6 7 8 9 0
a b c d e f g h i j k
l m n o p q r s t u
v w x y z ff fi fl ffi ffl o'c
. , - ' : ; ! ?

Character o'c made only in sizes from 8 to 18 Point

Betrothed
Marjorie Eleanor Baskerville
and
Raymond Henderson

Waldorf Text

CHARACTERS

A B C D E F G H I
J K L M N O P Q R
S T U V W X Y Z &
1 2 3 4 5 6 7 8 9 0
a b c d e f g h i j k l m
n o p q r s t u v w x y z
. , - ' : ; ! ?

1 2 3 4 5 6 7 8 9 0

36 Point 4A 12a
Splendid
Scenic Route
Production

24 Point No. 2 5A 15a
Manhattan
Sculpture Studio
Beauty Parlor

24 Point No. 1 6A 18a
Exceptional
Window Displays
Costumers

18 Point 9A 27a
Twenty-second
Annual Entertainment
Successful

14 Point 12A 33a
Recently Purchased
New Theological Seminary
Most Modern

Engravers Text

24 Point No. 1   8A 22a
Southern Progressive Association
Noted Speakers Introduced

24 Point No. 2   9A 27a
Handsome Building Lately Constructed
Modernized Effect Procured

18 Point No. 1   13A 38a
East Greenpoint Military Academy
Third Regimental Band Entertains Troopers
Delightful Programme Enjoyed

18 Point No. 2   14A 42a
President Appoints New Chairman
Cosmopolitan Securities Corporation Lauded
Elegant Brochure Printed

14 Point   18A 53a
Advertising Designers Praise Artist
Picturesque Landscapes Accurately Photographed
Best Commercial Stationery

12 Point   20A 60a
Third Anniversary
County Historical Society
Highest Ideal

10 Point   23A 68a
Grand Entertainment
Church Auditorium Dedicated
Visitors Welcome

Characters in Complete Font

A B C D E F G H
I J K L M N O P
Q R S T U V W
X Y Z & $ 1 2
3 4 5 6 7 8 9 0
a b c d e f g h i
j k l m n o p q r
s t u v w x y z
. , - ' ' : ; ! ?

★

American Type
"The Best in Any Case"

Mr. and Mrs. Reginald Harper

request the honor of

your company at the marriage of their daughter

Jacqueline Marie

to

Mr. Alfred Bruce Saylor

on the evening of Wednesday, the first of October

at half after seven o'clock

at Six hundred and ten Richelieu Place

Kingsland, Wyoming

Wedding Text

1 2 3 4 5 6 7 8 9 0

48 Point Figures set solid

Nobby Decorator No. 3602

48 Point 4A 10a
Important

42 Point 4A 11a
Quiet Parks

36 Point 4A 13a
Very Brightly

30 Point 5A 15a
Sculptor Helped

24 Point No. 1 6A 18a
Appreciation
Distinctive Portrait

24 Point No. 2 7A 19a
Reliable Methods
Noted Lawyer Elected

18 Point No. 1 9A 30a
Proposed Library
Valuable Records Intact

18 Point No. 2 10A 30a
Fitting Memorial
Erecting Beautiful Statues

14 Point 13A 40a
Receive Unique Design
Talented Decorators Gratified

12 Point 12A 45a
Quaint Paintings
Enthusiastic Art Critic
Magnificent

8 Point 16A 54a
Awarded Scholarships
Holding Impressive Ceremony
Made Valedictorian

10 Point 15A 50a
Cordial Reception
Most Graceful Dancer
Entertainment

6 Point 18A 60a
Distinguished Personality
Congenial Representative Secured
Inspiring Confidence

Characters in Complete Font

A B C D E F G H
I J K L M N O P Q
R S T U V W X Y Z
& $ 1 2 3 4 5 6 7 8 9 0
a b c d e f g h i j k l m
n o p q r s t u v w x y z
vv rd o'c st th . , - ' : ; ! ?

Character o'c made only in sizes from 6 to 18 Point

Janet Savoy

extends a most cordial invitation to
you to inspect a complete
assortment of

Excellent Gowns

designed by popular
modistes

Tuesday, October Eighth

Kenilworth Parkway
Sayerville

Shaw Text

48 Point — 4 A 8 a

Repudiated

36 Point — 4 A 11 a

Decides Position

30 Point — 5 A 14 a

Enlivening Crowds

24 Point — 5 A 16 a

Geographic Study
Practical Development

Characters in Complete Font

A B C D E F G
H I J K L M N
O P Q R S T U V
W X Y Z & $ 1 2
3 4 5 6 7 8 9 0
a b c d e f g h i
j k l m n o p q r
s t u v w x y z o'c
. , - ' : ; ! ?

Character o'c made only in sizes from 8 to 18 Point

---

18 Point — 8 A 25 a

Ardent Support
Begins New Method

12 Point — 15 A 45 a

Possessed Originality
Reliable Business Policies
Artistic Designing

10 Point — 16 A 50 a

Excitement Subsiding
Delivered Forceful Lecture
Generous Rewards

14 Point — 13 A 38 a

Produce Fine Printing
Obtaining Desirable Results

8 Point No. 1 — 18 A 54 a

Used Appropriate Type Faces
Satisfied Customer Repeats Order
Extraordinary Performance

8 Point No. 2 — 22 A 65 a

Great Demonstrations Everywhere
Many Celebrated People Arriving Daily
Entertain Distinguished Guest

Permit us to extend the personal services and courtesy of

Miss Elsie May Bosworth

Special Designer of

The Ladies' Apparel Department

who will assist you and afford you every consideration

in the selection of your hats and gowns

Rodman Company

Please present this card

---

1 2 3 4 5 6 7 8 9 0

48 Point Figures set solid

AMERICAN
TYPE FOUNDERS
SALES
CORPORATION

Freehand Series

48 Point 6A 10a

Dignified Printer

36 Point 6A 10a

Fine Musical Program

30 Point 8A 14a

Semi-annual Golf Tourney

24 Point 10A 18a

Now in Progress
Notable Embroidery Exhibitions

18 Point 14A 28a

Fancy Skating Display
Summer Vacations Will Soon Be in Order
Healthful Games

14 Point 21A 40a

Masterpieces Bought
Nine Day Cruise to the West Indies & South America
Coerce Metropolitan Author

12 Point 22A 42a

Brochure Won Trophy
Steamship Companies Report European Tours Very Popular
National Association of Scribes

10 Point 25A 49a

Seventh Regimental Dance
Meeting of the Board of Education Voted to Erect New High School
Legislative Manual for Government

8 Point 27A 53a

Choicest Educational Literature
Philadelphia Girls Friendly Society
Horticultural Exposition

6 Point 29A 58a

International Yacht Racing Contests
Weekly Meeting of Southern Negro Guild
Eighth Financial Statement

Characters in Complete Font

A B C D E F G H I J
K L M N O P Q R S
T U V W X Y Z & $
1 2 3 4 5 6 7 8 9 0
a b c d e f g h i j k
l m n o p q r s t u
v w x y z ff fi fl ffi ffl
. , - ' ' : ; ! ?

Greeting Monotone

24 Point 9A 20a

Many Happy Returns

18 Point 14A 28a

Greetings for CHRISTMAS

14 Point 22A 43a

HOLIDAY MAIL HEAVY
Exports to Foreign Countries Increase

12 Point 23A 45a

ANNUAL CHARITY BALL
Benefit Performance for Out of Work Fund

10 Point 24A 48a

INDEPENDENCE DAY PARADE
Celebrated with Athletic Events and Fireworks

Characters in Complete Font

A B C D E F G H I J K L M N O
P Q R S T U V W X Y Z & $ 1 2 3 4
5 6 7 8 9 0 a b c d e f g h i j k
l m n o p q r s t u v w x y z ff fi fl ffi ffl
Ct Th . , - ' ' : ; ! ?

:[153]:

Engravers Old English

72 Point — 3 A 5 a
Bible

60 Point — 3 A 5 a
Picked

48 Point — 3 A 7 a
Explain
Teach

42 Point — 4 A 7 a
Loadstar
Speak

36 Point — 4 A 8 a
Handicraft
Refusal

30 Point — 5 A 11 a
Pyrotechnics
Chorister

24 Point — 5 A 12 a
Advocate
Entertained
Banker

18 Point — 8 A 22 a
Incantation
Holiday Social
Venetians

14 Point — 10 A 33 a
Finished Manse
Pleasant Reception
Mademoiselle

12 Point — 13 A 37 a
Guardianship
Twelve Modistes
Wonderful

10 Point — 14 A 44 a
Racer Rewarded
Fine Entertainment
Yuletide Tale

8 Point — 16 A 48 a
Elaborate Reception
One Hundred Thousand
Tenth Pedagogue

6 Point — 16 A 50 a
Impressive Presentation
Builders Recommend Actor
Dedication Ceremonial
Reports Harmony

Characters in Complete Font

A B C D E F G
H I J K L M
N O P Q R S T
U V W X Y Z & $
1 2 3 4 5 6 7 8 9 0
a b c d e f g h i j k l
m n o p q r s t u v w x
y z ff fi fl ffi ffl Æ o'r
. , - ' " : ; ! ?

Character o'r made only in sizes from 6 to 18 Point

1 2 3 4 5 6 7 8 9 0

60 Point Figures set solid

Cloister Black

1 2 3 4 5 6 7 8 9 0
60 Point Figures set solid

12 Point — 12 A 36 a
Exceptionally
Serving Luncheon
Tournament

10 Point — 14 A 42 a
Elected Secretary
Officiating Conductor
Congressional

8 Point — 16 A 52 a
Delightful Confections
Acknowledgment Registered
United Congregation

6 Point — 17 A 55 a
Theological Organization
Insurance Company Courageous
September Testimonial
First Exposition

24 Point — 5 A 14 a
Yachting
Educational
Anchor

18 Point — 8 A 22 a
Graduation
Testamentary
Statutes

14 Point — 10 A 32 a
Horticulturist
Wasted Program
Bridesmaid

Characters in Complete Font

A B C D E F
G H I J K L
M N O P Q R
S T U V V W
W X Y Z & $
1 2 3 4 5 6 7 8 9 0
a b c d e f g h i j
k l m n o p q r s
t u v w x y z ct ll
. , = ' : ; ! ?

72 Point — 3 A 5 a
Brief

60 Point — 3 A 6 a
Debut

48 Point — 4 A 7 a
Knights
Nectar

42 Point — 4 A 8 a
Musicale
Width

36 Point — 4 A 9 a
Respirator
Counsel

30 Point — 5 A 11 a
Index Leased
Handicap

American Text

72 Point 3A 5a

Scripture Quoted

60 Point 3A 8a

German Philosopher

48 Point 4A 10a

Distinguished Theologian

42 Point 4A 11a

Eulogize University Graduate

36 Point 4A 13a

Mystic Shrine Dedicates Building

30 Point 5A 15a

Exceptionally Artistic Programmes

24 Point 7A 19a

Provident Building and Loan Association
New Series Recently Opened

18 Point 9A 30a

Distinguished German Visitor Unveiled Monument
Many Diplomats Attend Ceremonies

Figures

1 2 3 4 5 6 7 8 9 0 $

Melodious
"Linda di Chamounix"
at the **REX**

The Opera in Review at The
⋅REX⋅

CHARACTERS

A B C D E F G
H I J K L M N
O P Q R S T U
V W X Y Z &

a b c d e f g h i
j k l m n o p q r
s t u v w x y z
. , - ' ' : ; ! ?

Hobo Series

48 Point — 3A 5a

SPORTING
37 Athletes

36 Point — 4A 6a

SWEET MUSIC
Dance Acrobat

24 Point — 6A 11a

48 NOTABLE CRITICS
Enjoy Radio Programs

18 Point — 9A 18a

FRAGRANT LILAC PERFUME
Gayly Decorated Auditoriums

14 Point — 12A 23a

PRINT SOCIAL ANNOUNCEMENTS
Excellent Letter for Society Printing

12 Point — 15A 29a

NEW PAPER INCREASES CIRCULATION
Progressive Merchant Regular Advertiser

10 Point — 17A 35a

NOTED ARCHITECT DESIGNS MODERN HOMES
Suburban Realty Company Erects Quaint Building

8 Point — 20A 39a

FINE MUSICAL PROGRAM
Applaud Fine Violin Soloist

6 Point — 24A 48a

RUNNERS TRAIN FOR MARATHON
Noted Athletes Enter Great Struggle

Characters In Complete Font

A B C D E F G H I
J K L M N O P Q R
S T U V W X Y Z &
$ 1 2 3 4 5 6 7 8 9 0
a b c d e f g h i j k
l m n o p q r s t u v
w x y z . , - ' : ; ! ?

Cast without descenders on Title Line

WANDELING
AUTO TIRES

● Manufactured to satisfy the natural demand for service and for mileage, two important elements that determine the very life of a tire. Wandeling tires give you service of a kind that is peculiarly satisfying, with unusual freedom from troubles.

Manufactured by the
WANDELING TIRE COMPANY
CHICAGO, ILLINOIS

BROADWAY SERIES

½ PRICE
SALE

SUITS
TOP COATS

NO CHARGE FOR
ALTERATIONS

19⁵⁰

BECKS

VALUES TO THIRTY DOLLARS

72 Point 3 A
HERDS

60 Point 3 A
IGNORE

48 Point 3 A
GRANTED

42 Point 4 A
DELUSIONS

CHARACTERS

A B C D E F
G H I J K L
M N O P Q R
S ſ ſſ T U V
W X Y Z & $
1 2 3 4 5
6 7 8 9 0
. , - ' : ; ! ?

36 Point 5 A
BURN

30 Point 6 A
CHAFE

24 Point 8 A
EXPORT

18 Point 10A
ROMANTIC
RED ROSES

14 Point 13A
DRAMATIC
FINISHING

12 Point 14A
HISTORICAL
NEW HOMES

10 Point 17A
FINE ORCHIDS
MODELS HOME

8 Point 19A
MOUNTAIN LAKES
EMPIRE FOUNDER

6 Point 20A
BEAUTIFUL COSTUMES
EXHIBIT INTERESTING

:[158]:

Broadway Condensed

72 Point 3 A 4 a

NICE Style

60 Point 3 A 5 a

Largest SITE

48 Point 4 A 7 a

CLEVER Knight

42 Point 5 A 7 a

Exquisite MODELS

36 Point 5 A 8 a

BUILDS New Cottage

30 Point 6 A 10 a

Finest Zinc ETCHING

24 Point 8 A 13 a

MODERN Designs Please

10 Point 20 A 39 a
SPLENDID SPECIMEN
Electrical Expositions

8 Point 22 A 43 a
BANKER MADE DECISION
Mayor Questions Legality

6 Point 24 A 48 a
MIDSUMMER VACATIONISTS
Holiday Resorts Are Crowded

18 Point 11 A 20 a
HUGE Cylinder

14 Point 15 A 29 a
Splendid DESIGNS

12 Point 17 A 34 a
EXPORTS FINE LINEN
Receives Big Shipment

NEW AND USED

Motor Cars

BARGAINS IN
NEW AND REBUILT
TRUCKS AND
CARS OF
ALL MAKES

Automobile Exchange

MADISON SQUARE

Characters

A B C D E F G H I J
K L M N O P Q R S ʃ
ʃʃ T U V W X Y Z &
$ 1 2 3 4 5 6 7 8 9 0
a b c d e f g h i
j k l m n o p q r
s t u v w x y z
. , - ` ´ : ; ! ?

:[159]:

BOUL MICH

72 Point 3 A
CHARM

60 Point 3 A
BRIDGES

48 Point 4 A
FURNISHED

42 Point 5 A
SYMBOLIZES

36 Point 6 A
FINE BUILDING

30 Point 7 A
BRIGHT GIRLS

24 Point 9 A
SPLENDID SCENE

20 Point 10 A
ENGLISH CRAFTSMEN

18 Point 11 A
NICE DESIGN

14 Point 14 A
GEOGRAPHY

16 Point 13 A
RICH MAIDEN

12 Point 15 A
MODERNISTIC

One more month and it will be SPRING

Everything for the Garden

GARDEN SHOP
PORTLAND STREET

BOUL MICH AND STYMIE LIGHT
CALENDAR SILHOUETTE, SERIES J, NO. 2

CHARACTERS

A B C D E F G
H I J K L M N
O P Q R S T U
V W X Y Z & S
1 2 3 4 5
6 7 8 9 0
. , - ' " : ; ! ?

:[160]:

Hollywood Series

NEW HOTEL ROOMS

Newly furnished and decorated 2-room suites in the modern and period styles, complete with serving pantries and all of the latest improvements. Rents reasonable

SEND FOR DESCRIPTIVE FOLDER

HOTEL PINES

PEQUOIT PARK

HOLLYWOOD AND GOLD RUSH PENLINE FLOURISH

---

72 Point 3A 4a
FINER Catalog

60 Point 3A 6a
Splendid DESIGN

48 Point 5A 8a
DESIRABLE Quietude

42 Point 5A 9a
Prosperous MERCHANT

36 Point 5A 10a
ORDERS Bank Investigated

30 Point 6A 12a
International Parleys CONTINUED

Characters

A B C D E F G H I
J K L M N O P Q R
S T U V W X Y Z &
a b c d e f g h i j k l
m n o p q r s t u v
w x y z . , - ' ' : ; ! ?

Superior $ furnished with all sizes from 24 to 72 Point

Special Characters made in all sizes and fonted separately

E F M OO S T U Y a r s

---

24 Point 8A 15a
ANNUAL DANCES
Delightful Evening

18 Point 12A 24a
BANKERS CONVENED
Extraordinary Session

14 Point 16A 30a
EXCLUSIVE APARTMENTS
Demands Steadily Increase

12 Point 18A 36a
WONDERFUL SPECIMEN
Exclusive Border Design

10 Point 20A 40a
PRESIDENTIAL RECEPTION
Accorded Visiting Diplomat

8 Point 22A 43a
INCREASED TOURIST BOOKING
Steamship officials predict quick
return to more normal conditions

6 Point 23A 46a
BUSINESS FUTURE ENCOURAGING
Wisest industrialists and merchants
throughout the nation are optimistic

1 2 3 4 5 6 7 8 9 0 $ $

Rosetti Series

Come to the Elizabeth Garden Salon

For a slender figure

A healthy body

A superb and graceful carriage

ASK ABOUT THE NEW FACE TREATMENT

ELIZABETH GARDEN

ATLANTIC CITY

ROSETTI SERIES AND BERNHARD GOTHIC LIGHT

Characters

A A B B C D D
E Œ F Ƒ G H I J K
L M (M N N O P P
Q R R S T T U V
W W X Y Y Z & $
1 2 3 4 5 6 7 8 9 0
a a b c d e f g h i j k
l m n o p q r s t u v w
x y z et st . , - ' ' : ; ! ?

The following characters are cast recessed in sizes from 24 to 72 Point

A F L P T V W Y

---

72 Point 3A 4a
MEN Delayed

60 Point 3A 5a
Beautiful SIGNS

48 Point 4A 6a
HEARS Philosopher

42 Point 5A 8a
Display Latest GOWNS

36 Point 6A 10a
FRENCH Diplomat Sailed

30 Point 7A 12a
Splendid POEMS

24 Point 8A 16a
REDUCING PRICES
Dainty Silk Garments

18 Point 13A 26a
COLORFUL INDIAN RUG
Modernistic Design Pleases

14 Point 19A 38a
OPERA SINGER VISITS SWEDEN
European Thespians Honor Judge

12 Point 21A 42a
SUBMIT GOOD REPORT
Stockholders Well Satisfied

10 Point 25A 50a
ENCOURAGE DAILY EXERCISE
Health and strength is the reward to those who practice calisthenics

8 Point 26A 52a
EXCELLENT METHOD APPROVED
Many prominent educators endorsed newest systems of vocational training practiced in schools and institutions

6 Point 27A 54a
WAY TO AVOID FUTURE DEPRESSIONS
Progressive merchants appreciate the many benefits obtained by advertising constantly in prominent newspapers and by direct mail

EAGLE BOLD

96 Point 3 A

SIDE

CHARACTERS IN COMPLETE FONT

ABCDEFGHIJ
KLMNOPQRS
TUVWXYZ&$
1234567890
.,-''"";!?

Letters A, F, L, P, T, V, W, Y, are cast recessed in all sizes
At least one such character included in every font

84 Point 3 A

PAIR

72 Point 3 A

MEND

60 Point 3 A

KING

48 Point 3 A

MINER

42 Point 4 A

RETAIN

36 Point 5 A

SINGERS

30 Point 6 A

REMINDER

24 Point 7 A

MODERNIZED

18 Point 10 A

EAGLE BOLD TYPE

GADGETS
FOR SPRING DAYS

and nights—choose them last, but they're likely to be first in your affection. We make unusual little things.

PARRAN
FOUR WEST PALM STREET

EAGLE BOLD BODONI 12 POINT MODERNISTIC BORDER NO. 37 6 POINT MODERNISTIC STARS NO. 2

Agency Gothic

120 Point 3 A
MODERNIZE

96 Point 3 A
NICE PRINTING

84 Point 3 A
BRIGHT COLORS

72 Point 4 A
CHARMING DESIGN

60 Point 5 A
EXPENSIVE FURNITURE

48 Point 5 A
ADVERTISING

36 Point 8 A
SALES INCREASE

CHARACTERS

A A B C
D E F G
H I J K
L M M
N O P Q
R S T U
V W X Y
Z & $ ¢
1 2 3 4
5 6 7 8
9 0
. ' - `
. ,
: ; ! ?

Agency Gothic Open

DESIRING

120 Point 3 A

SPECIMENS

96 Point 3 A

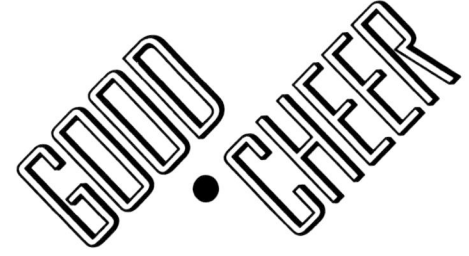

Announcing another meeting of the REGAL SOCIAL CLUB, on Wednesday Evening, in the Dining Room of **REX HOTEL**

JANUARY 10th

•

AGENCY GOTHIC OPEN, FRANKLIN GOTHIC AND P. T. BARNUM

BURNISHED

84 Point 3 A

CHARACTERS

A B C D E F G
H I J K L M N O
P Q R S T U V W
X Y Z & $ 1 2 3
4 5 6 7 8 9 0 ¢
. , - ' ' : ; ! ?

FINE DESIGNS

72 Point 4 A

MODERN HOUSE

60 Point 5 A

ATTRACTIVE SALES

48 Point 5 A

:[165]:

Raleigh Gothic Condensed

Other sizes in preparation

144 Point 3A Font contains two punctuation marks (? !), also period and comma which may be justified into position with quads to form other punctuation marks

ABCDEFGHIJKL
MNOPQRSTUV
WXYZ& $12345

Above Character Cast on 72 Point Body

67890-AKMNS

Raleigh Gothic Condensed Figures, as well as Grotesque Characters A, K, M, N, S, shown above, are not included in the regular font

Newport Series

72 Point — 3A 5a

HOMES Decorated

Descenders cast on 78 Point body

60 Point — 4A 6a

Enthusiastic SPEAKER

Descenders cast on 66 Point body

48 Point — 5A 8a

MODERN System Adopted

Descenders cast on 54 Point body

42 Point — 5A 10a

Promote Gigantic ENTERPRISE

36 Point — 6A 10a

REMARKABLE Australian Biography

30 Point — 7A 14a

36 Oldest Apartment Houses REMODELLED

24 Point — 9A 18a

CITIZENS WELCOMED Great European Philosophers

18 Point — 16A 30a

Excellent Musical Program Distinguished CHURCH ENTERTAINMENT

1 2 3 4 5 6 7 8 9 0 $ *$ *¢

★ Not made in sizes below 24 Point

---

14 Point — 21A 40a

THOUSANDS VISIT EXHIBITION
Fine Paintings Greatly Admired

12 Point — 23A 46a

MELODIOUS THRUSHES RETURNED
Spring Gloaming Inspirited Scholar

10 Point — 27A 54a

PROFITABLE CONIFEROUS WOODLANDS
Northern Operations Increasing Monthly

8 Point — 30A 60a

AUTUMNAL MIGRATION DELIGHTED STUDENTS
Birds travelling into the unknown without any
previous knowledge or experience to ultimately
winter on grounds of which they are ignorant

6 Point — 33A 65a

STUPENDOUS PUZZLE SEEMINGLY INEXTRICABLY MIXED
Everywhere are shorebirds and none have ever travelled
before; this is the first migration. Here is a rabble from
the north, southward bound; no mistakes must be made

CHARACTERS

A B C D E F
G H I J K L
M M N O P
Q R S T U V
W X Y Z &
a b c d e f
g h i j k l m
n o p q r s t
u v w x y z
. , - ' ' : ; ! ?

Alternate Gothic No. 1

72 Point — 3 A 5 a
Symbol

60 Point — 3 A 6 a
BINDERS
Quietude

48 Point — 6 A 10 a
ENCOMIUM
Multiplicity

42 Point — 7 A 10 a
DISCOURAGE
Recapitulate

36 Point — 7 A 13 a
KINDERGARTEN
Bright Scholars

30 Point — 9 A 16 a
DISCOMPOSE
Spendthrifts

24 Point — 11 A 22 a
MODERN GUIDE
Gifted Violinist

18 Point — 16 A 34 a
HONEST MEMBERS
Registers Approval

14 Point — 24 A 48 a
DOMESTIC ENTERPRISE
Establishments opened
long before completion

12 Point — 25 A 50 a
SECURITIES INVESTIGATED
Many stockholders rejoice
on completion of inventory
which proved encouraging

10 Point — 30 A 60 a
REMARKABLE OPPORTUNITIES
New schools install necessary
equipment and capable teacher
gives instruction for operating

8 Point — 32 A 63 a
IMPORTANT SUGGESTION PUBLISHED
Discontinuance of extravagant method
and the practicing of strictest economy
wherever practicable pleased taxpayer

6 Point — 35 A 70 a
PICTURESQUE JOURNEY PLEASING PROFESSORS
There are many beautiful residences along the
well-kept mountain highways. How refreshing
the atmosphere and pleasing the early sunset
after tiresome labors in crowded metropolis

Characters in Complete Font

A B C D E F G H I
J K L M N O P Q R S
T U V W X Y Z & $
1 2 3 4 5 6 7 8 9 0
a b c d e f g h i j k l
m n o p q r s t u v w
x y z . , - ' : ; ! ?

1 2 3 4 5 6 7 8 9 0

60 Point Figures set solid

Alternate Gothic No. 2

1234567890

60 Point Figures set solid

12 Point — 24 A 48 a
ENTERPRISING CITIZEN
Introduces novel system
for finding true valuation
after many futile efforts

10 Point — 26 A 52 a
WONDERFUL GYMNASTICS
Great athletes exhibit skill
and daring to amuse people
who gaze on in amazement

8 Point — 29 A 58 a
PRACTICABILITY DEMONSTRATED
Business men manifesting unusual
interest in novel heating apparatus
which promises great saving of fuel

6 Point — 33 A 65 a
INDEPENDENCE BRINGS US CONFIDENCE
Contradictory as they seem, two things go
together always : manly self-reliance and
manly independence. They are inseparable
attributes to personal courage and dignity

30 Point — 8 A 13 a
HUNDREDS
Graduating

24 Point — 9 A 18 a
MANIFESTED
Remonstrate

18 Point — 15 A 30 a
DEMAND RIGHTS
Judges Expected

14 Point — 20 A 41 a
NEAREST BUILDING
Overhauled recently
for big athletic club

72 Point — 3 A 4 a
Mythic

60 Point — 3 A 5 a
RECORD
Encircle

48 Point — 5 A 9 a
SCHEMER
Influential

42 Point — 6 A 9 a
MUSICIANS
Gesticulate

36 Point — 6 A 12 a
DISTINGUISH
Chamberlains

Characters in Complete Font

A B C D E F G H I
J K L M N O P Q R S
T U V W X Y Z & $
1 2 3 4 5 6 7 8 9 0
a b c d e f g h i j k l
m n o p q r s t u v w
x y z . , - ' : ; ! ?

Alternate Gothic No. 3

72 Point — 3 A 4 a
Maple

60 Point — 3 A 4 a
BOUND
Dignify

48 Point — 5 A 8 a
MODERN
Splendor

42 Point — 5 A 9 a
FINISHING
Gymnasts

36 Point — 6 A 9 a
REMAINDER
Disintegrate

30 Point — 7 A 12 a
SHARPEN
Captivate

24 Point — 8 A 15 a
RIGHTEOUS
Headstrong

18 Point — 12 A 25 a
DISORGANIZED
Restores Order

14 Point — 18 A 35 a
STRANGE CUSTOM
Unusual practices
discontinued here

12 Point — 20 A 40 a
EXCELLENT REPORTS
Promising young man
gets highest average
in recent history test

10 Point — 23 A 46 a
PROPOSE CONFERENCE
Many nationally famous
railroad magnates have
been invited to meeting

8 Point — 27 A 54 a
MEN SHOULD USE DISCRETION
We believe there are many more
good traits in the mind of man,
but few so useful as discretion

6 Point — 30 A 60 a
FUTURE IS REPETITION OF THE PAST
History often repeats itself, making
only such changes of programme as
growths of nations and time require
and should direct man in the future

Characters in Complete Font

A B C D E F G H I
J K L M N O P Q R S
T U V W X Y Z & $
1 2 3 4 5 6 7 8 9 0
a b c d e f g h i
j k l m n o p q r
s t u v w x y z
. , - ' : ; ! ?

1 2 3 4 5 6 7 8 9 0

60 Point Figures set solid

CONDENSED TITLE GOTHIC No. 11

1234567890
60 Point Figures set solid

12 Point — 23 A
DIRECTING CHOIR
CHANGE OBJECTS
REHEARSE OFTEN

10 Point — 27 A
MOST ENTHUSIASTIC
INTRODUCED BRIDES
BEGINS CONVENTION

8 Point No. 112 — 32 A
HONOR INTREPID HUNTER
DELEGATE INVESTIGATING
HONOR CLUB EXECUTIVES

8 Point No. 111 — 37 A
REQUIRED DISTINCTIVE SUITE
GIVE MAGNIFICENT SOUVENIR
HUMOROUS CRITICISM HEARD

6 Point No. 113 — 37 A
FOREIGN SCIENTIST PRAISED WORK
DISTINGUISHED SURGEON REMAINS
YOUNG MECHANIC DECIPHERS CODE

6 Point No. 111 — 45 A
MERCHANT REPLENISHED ENTIRE STOCKS
INGENIOUS MECHANIC EARNS PROMOTION
SOME PHILANTHROPIC GENTLEMAN DINED
EXPENSIVE PRODUCTIONS BROUGHT HERE

30 Point — 9 A
MEANING
BROKERS

24 Point — 13 A
DIMENSION
ENCUMBER

20 Point — 16 A
HIDE BRANCH
CONDUCTORS
MARKED SIZE

16 Point — 20 A
RIGHT GOVERNOR
SPREADING BUSH
COMBS REMOVED

9 and 54 Point carried in stock only at Foundry

CHARACTERS IN COMPLETE FONT

A B C D E F G
H I J K L M N
O P Q R S T U
V W X Y Z & $
1 2 3 4 5 6 7 8 9 0
. , - ' : ; ! ?

72 Point — 3 A
MUCH

60 Point — 3 A
BROKE

48 Point — 5 A
DICTION
SUNDER

42 Point — 5 A
HEROISM
CAMBRIC

36 Point — 6 A
UNRACKED
DESIGNING

EXTRA CONDENSED TITLE GOTHIC No. 12

72 Point — 4 A
FOUNDED REMAINS

60 Point — 4 A
NARCOTIC SHOCKING

48 Point — 8 A
COMPOSITOR MARKS DATE

42 Point — 8 A
DOMESTICATE COUNTY ROAD

CHARACTERS IN COMPLETE FONT

A B C D E F G H I
J K L M N O P Q R S
T U V W X Y Z & $
1 2 3 4 5 6 7 8 9 0
. , - ' : ; ! ?

54 Point carried in stock only at Foundry

36 Point — 9 A
UNDERMINED CONDUCTORS

30 Point — 11 A
ENCUMBERING REPAIRS ROAD

24 Point — 17 A
GRAND WELCOME
BEAUTIFUL GIFTS
SUPERIOR MUSIC

20 Point — 23 A
MYSTERIOUS FIGURES
INGENIOUS WORKMEN
PRODUCTIVE METHOD

16 Point — 26 A
OVERWHELMING DEMANDS
UNUSUAL DEMONSTRATION
NOTEWORTHY APPEARANCE

12 Point — 30 A
MANUFACTURER PROGRESSING
INTELLIGENT SUPERINTENDENT
HIRED INDUSTRIOUS WORKERS

10 Point — 37 A
SCHOLARS ENCOURAGED INSTRUCTOR
TEACHER SUBMITS SPLENDID REPORT
ENTIRE CLASS ATTENDED RECEPTION

12 34 56 78 90

48 Point Figures set solid

Chic Border No. 5

RAILROAD GOTHIC

1234567890
60 Point Figures set solid

14 Point — 19 A
INTERESTING BIOGRAPHERS

12 Point — 20 A
HIGHLANDERS MASTERPIECE

10 Point No. 2 — 24 A
FOREIGN SINGER BLIND MUSICIAN

10 Point No. 1 — 30 A
RECOVERED FRIEND PUBLIC RESOURCES

8 Point No. 2 — 26 A
UNAUTHORIZED FORCE IMPORTANT PAINTING

8 Point No. 1 — 30 A
EXHIBITED CLEAN LEDGER INDIAN MAIDS CAMPING

6 Point No. 5 — 36 A
DISTRICT CHAIRMAN APPOINTED UNCOMPROMISING COMMANDER

6 Point No. 4 — 42 A
REMODELING SUBURBAN FARMHOUSE SOUTHERN CONVENTION ADJOURNED

6 Point No. 3 — 48 A
GOVERNMENT SECURING PLENIPOTENTIARIES CONGRESSIONAL INVESTIGATION SUCCESSFUL ENCOURAGED RESERVATIONS CONFIRMATION

6 Point No. 2 — 54 A
BEAUTIFUL MOUNTAIN RESIDENCES COMPLETED ORGANIZATION IMPROVED DISTRIBUTING CHARGE SEVERAL BOUNTIFUL GENTLEMEN CONTRIBUTING

42 Point — 5 A
BRING IDEAS

36 Point — 6 A
MOUTH REGAIN

30 Point — 8 A
EXPOSED COINAGE

24 Point — 11 A
PROVISION MACHINES

18 Point — 15 A
NECKERCHIEF UNDESIRABLE

54 Point carried in stock only at Foundry

CHARACTERS IN COMPLETE FONT

A B C D E F G H I J K L
M N O P Q R S T U V W
X Y Z & $ 1 2 3 4 5 6
7 8 9 0 . , - ' : ; ! ?

120 Point — 3 A
SIX

96 Point — 3 A
RUN

84 Point — 3 A
KIDS

72 Point — 3 A
HOUR

60 Point — 3 A
BRAIN

48 Point — 4 A
ENGINE

Franklin Gothic

96 Point — 3 A 4 a

Ida

84 Point — 3 A 4 a

Sift

72 Point — 3 A 4 a

Elks

60 Point — 3 A 4 a

Baby

48 Point — 3 A 6 a

Rejoin

42 Point — 4 A 6 a

Nuptial

36 Point — 4 A 7 a

Haughty

30 Point — 5 A 8 a

MAIDS
Repeat

24 Point — 5 A 11 a

QUARTZ
Borough

18 Point — 8 A 17 a

NITROGEN
Hymnology

14 Point — 12 A 24 a

EQUESTRIAN
Popular Story

12 Point — 14 A 29 a

QUICK SERVICE
Important Notes

10 Point — 16 A 32 a

NIGHTINGALES
Bird sanctuaries
become popular
for nature study

8 Point — 19 A 38 a

SUBMERGE BRIDGE
Detour necessitated
selecting altogether
new homeward route

6 Point — 21 A 44 a

BRIGHTEST SUNSHADE
Summer costumes show
most amazing display of
decidedly new colors and
enliven drab city streets

5 Point — 22 A 46 a

SCREEN PLAY FASCINATING
Fancy runs riot under the spell
of motion pictures, for by fairy
enchantment shackles of time
and space fall away and we live
and move amid mystic scenes

4 Point — 20 A 48 a

QUAINT COLONIAL ARCHITECTURE
Interesting old-fashioned villagers
that overflow with shrewd, vinegary
humor inhabit these historic towns
but once their confidence is gained
you discover their sterling qualities

Characters in Complete Font

A B C D E F G
H I J K L M N O
P Q R S T U V
W X Y Z & $ 1 2
3 4 5 6 7 8 9 0
a b c d e f g h i
j k l m n o p q
r s t u v w x y z
. , - ' : ; ! ?

1 2 3 4 5 6 7 8 9 0

60 Point Figures set solid

Franklin Gothic Italic (Non-Kerning)

1234567890

60 Point Figures set solid

10 Point — 15 A 30 a
WINTER HOMES
New departments
showing valuable
household design

8 Point — 18 A 36 a
CONSIDER PROBLEM
Many opportunities for
business boys seeking
more happy prospects

6 Point — 19 A 39 a
SPEAKERS APPLAUDED
Prominent editorial writer
will deliver daily discourse
to former collegians. Some
diagrams shown explained

5 Point — 19 A 38 a
HOME OR OFFICE EFFICIENCY
Frequently this phrase is used in
connection with more production
but the business man will handle
the word with intelligence. There
are different phases of efficiency

18 Point — 8 A 14 a
SPLENDOR
Entertained
their guests

14 Point — 11 A 21 a
HOME GUARD
Enlisted guide
gave watchers
valuable paper

12 Point — 14 A 27 a
PICTURE FOUND
Enchanting scene
recently restored
interested critics

Characters in Complete Font

A B C D E F G
H I J K L M N O
P Q R S T U V
W X Y Z & $
1 2 3 4 5 6 7 8 9 0
a b c d e f g h i j
k l m n o p q r s
t u v w x y z ff fi
fl ffi ffl . , - ' : ; ! ?

72 Point — 3 A 4 a
Gift

60 Point — 3 A 4 a
Sale

48 Point — 4 A 5 a
Night

42 Point — 4 A 6 a
Myths

36 Point — 5 A 7 a
BROKE
Cymbal

30 Point — 5 A 8 a
QUENCH
Replaced

24 Point — 6 A 9 a
DREAMER
Hydropical

Franklin Gothic Condensed

72 Point   3A 4a

Dyke

60 Point   3A 5a

Slight

48 Point   4A 7a

Months

42 Point   5A 8a

BROKEN
Register

36 Point   5A 9a

HUMIDOR
Exploiting

30 Point   6A 10a

NOURISHED
Indigo Gown

24 Point   7A 14a

NOSTRUM
Junior help
impetuous

18 Point   11A 20a

EXTRACTION
Old countries
partly helped
intrepid sons

14 Point   15A 30a

KINDERGARTEN
Healthy children
enjoy embryonic
educational year

12 Point   17A 34a

BRONZE FIGURE
Generous citizen
donates splendid
memorial college

10 Point   19A 38a

MOUNTAIN TRACK
Great geographers
explore unfamiliar
mountainous trails

8 Point   22A 45a

ENCHANTED PARADISE
Startling adventures in
remote islands recently
discovered make movie
picture very interesting

6 Point   24A 46a

PRETTY ORIENTAL VASES
Newest imported novelties
suitable to personal usage
or holiday gifts are found in
greater variety in this store
than ever thought possible

Characters in Complete Font

A B C D E F G
H I J K L M N O
P Q R S T U V
W X Y Z & $ 1 2
3 4 5 6 7 8 9 0
a b c d e f g h i
j k l m n o p q
r s t u v w x y z
. , - ' : ; ! ?

---

1 2 3 4 5 6 7 8 9 0

60 Point Figures set solid

Franklin Gothic Extra Condensed

1
2
3
4
5
6
7
8
9
0

60 Point Figures set solid

14 Point   18 A   36 a
POWERFUL ENGINE
Displays Character

12 Point   21 A   44 a
ENDURANCE CONTEST
Awakened enthusiasm
among local amateurs

10 Point   25 A   48 a
RESTORED CONFIDENCE
Great printing concerns
installed new machinery

8 Point   28 A   55 a
FIRST DEGREE ADMINISTERED
Newly elected members enjoy
banquet after being initiated

6 Point   30 A   60 a
INCREASES SUBURBAN BUSINESS
Merchants insist that advertising
gives business an added stimulus

Characters in Complete Font

A B C D E F G H I
J K L M N O P Q R S
T U V W X Y Z & $
1 2 3 4 5 6 7 8 9 0
a b c d e f g h i
j k l m n o p q r
s t u v w x y z
. , - ' : ; ! ?

42 Point   5 A   9 a
Magnet

36 Point   5 A   11 a
Respited

30 Point   7 A   14 a
High Grade

24 Point   9 A   18 a
DISCOVERED
Stylish Guest

18 Point   14 A   29 a
NOTED FARMER
Invested Capital

120 Point   3 A   4 a
Bait

96 Point   3 A   4 a
Myth

84 Point   3 A   4 a
Rapid

72 Point   3 A   4 a
Ginger

60 Point   3 A   6 a
Defects

48 Point   4 A   8 a
Navigable

GOTHIC CONDENSED TITLE NO. 117

120 Point — 3 A
HINDER

96 Point — 3 A
BANKERS

72 Point — 3 A
MESHING

60 Point — 3 A
BURNISHED

54 Point — 6 A
UNDERMINES

48 Point — 6 A
MERCHANDISE

42 Point — 8 A
HOUSE BUILDING

36 Point — 8 A
UNKNOWN CRIMES

30 Point — 9 A
**SUPERIOR MINE
IS OUR DEMAND**

24 Point — 14 A
**GOOD COMPOSITORS
FOR CLASS PRINTING**

20 Point — 18 A
**DESIGNED FOR SPECIMEN
DISTINCTIVE BOOK COVER**

18 Point — 21 A
**SERVING NEEDS OF CUSTOMER
PLEASING HIS UTMOST DESIRE**

16 Point — 21 A
**SHARP BUSINESS COMPETITION
DEMANDS NEWER EQUIPMENTS
MODERN SHOPS DO FINE WORK**

12 Point — 25 A
**CANNOT BE EXECUTED ON ANY WORN
OUT MACHINERY OR WITH OLD TYPE
NOT IN FIT CONDITION $1234567890**

10 Point No. 1172 — 33 A
SOME HIGH CLASS WORK REQUIRES EXTRA
MACHINES AND IN PRESSROOMS CONTAINING
CORRECT EQUIPMENT THIS PROBLEM CAN BE

10 Point No. 1171 — 39 A
COMPOSITION TODAY IS SIMPLIFIED BY CONFINING
ENERGIES SPENT IN EXECUTING HIGHEST CLASSES
OF PRINTING TO STANDARD OF TYPE FACES NEEDED

8 Point — 44 A
MAXIMUM STRENGTH IN THE FORCEFUL EXPRESSION CONVEYED
BY THE PRINTED WORDS OFTEN CONSTITUTES THE IMPELLING
REASON FOR THE PARTICULAR ADAPTABILITY OF THE GOTHICS

6 Point — 39 A
HEADLETTER PURPOSES ARE WELL SERVED BY THE TITLE CONDENSED
ITS VARIED USES AS A MEMBER OF THE GOTHIC CONSTELLATION BEING
RECOGNIZED WHERE COMPACTNESS IS AN ESSENTIAL REQUISITE FOR

5 Point — 33 A
FIVE POINT SIZE IN THIS GROUP INDISPENSABLE AS ALL PRACTICAL PRINTERS AGREE
ITS INCLUSION STRENGTHENS THE UTILITY OF THE SERIES AND ADDS CHARACTER TO
FINISHED PRINTED PRODUCTIONS THUS CONTRIBUTING PRIME IMPORTANCE TO THIS

1234567890

54 Point Figures set solid

Gothic No. 578

1234567890
60 Point Figures set solid

10 Point — 16 A 30 a
MARINE GUARD
Naval destroyers anchor in harbor to guard interests

8 Point — 20 A 38 a
EMINENT POLITICIAN
Great crowds welcome soldiers on return from battlefields of Flanders

6 Point — 24 A 44 a
LARGE OFFICE BUILDINGS
Happy bank clerks take great delight in the coziness of their new quarters. Beautiful view of river may be had from roof

5 Point — 21 A 38 a
DELIGHTFUL SUMMER OUTINGS
Numerous excursionists line deck of palatial steamboat about to start up the Hudson River. A syncopated jazz band will furnish dance music

24 Point — 5 A 10 a
BONUS
Distinct

18 Point — 8 A 16 a
REIGNED
Magnifies

14 Point — 12 A 23 a
IMPROVING
State House

12 Point — 15 A 27 a
HONORARIUM
English lawyer found evidence

9 and 54 Point carried in stock only at Foundry

Characters in Complete Font

A B C D E F
G H I J K L M
N O P Q R S
T U V W X Y
Z & $ 1 2 3 4
5 6 7 8 9 0
a b c d e f g h i
j k l m n o p q r
s t u v w x y z
. , - ' : ; ! ?

72 Point — 3 A 4 a
Rail

60 Point — 3 A 4 a
Bird

48 Point — 3 A 4 a
MIEN
Ignite

42 Point — 3 A 5 a
EIDER
United

36 Point — 4 A 6 a
BOUGH
Knights

30 Point — 4 A 8 a
NOMADS
Exporting

Gothic No. 544

36 Point   4 A 7 a
NIMBUS
Eclipsing

30 Point   5 A 9 a
MIXTURE
Distinction

24 Point   6 A 12 a
HUMOROUS
Congratulated

18 Point   9 A 19 a
NICE UNIFORM
Excellent Soldier

14 Point   12 A 25 a
GYPSIES CAMPED
Build Splendid Huts

12 Point   14 A 28 a
FRESH ENCOUNTER
Rivals Contested Game

10 Point   17 A 36 a
DANGEROUS MECHANISM
Accidents Fortunately Averted

8 Point   18 A 38 a
ENCHANTING SURROUNDINGS
Grotesquely Painted Establishment

6 Point   18 A 40 a
DELIGHTS INTERESTED AUDIENCE
Noted Actor Scored Wonderful Success

Characters in Complete Font

A B C D E F G
H I J K L M N O
P Q R S T U V
W X Y Z & $ 1 2
3 4 5 6 7 8 9 0
a b c d e f g h i
j k l m n o p q
r s t u v w x y z
. , - ' : ; ! ?

42, 48, 54 and 60 Point carried in stock only at Foundry

PAGEANT
Commemorating the Opening of the Home for Aged Actors

Kenilworth Auditorium
Newark, Kansas
WEEK OF JUNE FIRST

Under auspices of the
ACTORS' WELFARE LEAGUE
of Hudson County

VOCATIONAL CAMEO NO. 7213

---

1 2 3 4 5 6 7 8 9 0

36 Point Figures set solid

AMERICAN TYPE FOUNDERS SALES CORPORATION

Gothic No. 545

1234567890

60 Point Figures set solid

Characters in Complete Font

A B C D E F G
H I J K L M N
O P Q R S T U V
W X Y Z & $ 1 2
3 4 5 6 7 8 9 0
a b c d e f g h i
j k l m n o p q
r s t u v w x y z
. , - ' : ; ! ?

9 and 54 Point carried in stock only at Foundry

72 Point   3 A 4 a

Nod

60 Point   3 A 4 a

Bank

48 Point   3 A 5 a

Expert

42 Point   3 A 6 a

Mikado

10 Point   15 A 30 a

NEW METHOD
Company claims greatly improved facilities caused more production

8 Point   18 A 36 a

RAILROAD BRIDGES
Engineer arranging the many necessary details and superintending the preliminary regulations for immediate building

6 Point   18 A 36 a

BANKING EQUIPMENT
Model conveniences that enhance the satisfaction and accommodations for many depositors are now installed. The gentlemen directing are industrious

18 Point   8 A 17 a

HUNTING
Bought girl nifty tackle

14 Point   11 A 22 a

NEIGHBOR
Companions encountered former mate

12 Point   13 A 26 a

RESOURCES
Maintain some mode of saving for unusual use

36 Point   4 A 6 a

BUNGS
Haughty

30 Point   5 A 8 a

RESUME
Qualifying

24 Point   6 A 10 a

DECISIONS
Metropolitan

Gothic Nos. 520 to 526

48 Point No. 520 — 3 A

USE

42 Point No. 520 — 5 A

NICK

36 Point No. 520 — 5 A

ROAD

30 Point No. 520 — 6 A

BENCH

24 Point No. 520 — 8 A

MISGIVE

18 Point No. 520 — 10 A

INDENTED
REPOSING

12 Point No. 520 — 15 A

**EACH NUMBER
NOTICE FROCK**

10 Point No. 520 — 18 A

**BARGE RETURNING
DISTINCTIVE HOME**

8 Point No. 526 — 20 A

**HIRE CLEVER MECHANIC
UNIQUE MACHINE GIVEN**

8 Point No. 525 — 23 A

**GET PRODUCTION REPORTS
FURNISH CHARMING MUSIC**

6 Point No. 524 — 23 A

**BEAUTIFUL BUILDING
MADE HONOR GUARD
HISTORIC MANSIONS**

6 Point No. 523 — 30 A

ENTERTAINS GOVERNOR
HANDLING HUGE CROWD
SPECTACULAR RESULTS

6 Point No. 522 — 33 A

PURCHASED FINE CALENDAR
EXHIBIT NUMEROUS STYLES
REMARKABLE SCHOLAR WON

6 Point No. 521 — 37 A

RETURN FROM EUROPEAN CLIME
OVERHAUL SEVEN AUTOMOBILES
JUDGE URGES INSPECTION TOUR

Characters in Complete Font

A B C D E
F G H I J K
L M N O P
Q R S T U
V W X Y Z
& $ 1 2 3 4
5 6 7 8 9 0
. , - ' : ; ! ?

54 and 60 Point carried in stock only at Foundry

Gothic Condensed No. 524

24 Point — 10 A 19 a

EXPORTED
Huge Stock

18 Point — 12 A 24 a

DEMANDING
Kept Enough

14 Point — 19 A 33 a

MODERN USAGE
Began Production

12 Point — 22 A 45 a

**MEMBERS RESIGN
Organize Sport Club**

10 Point — 25 A 54 a

**HANDSOME BORDERS
Bought Choice Material**

8 Point — 32 A 65 a

**DESIGNS INTEREST PUBLIC
Spanish Masterpiece Displayed**

6 Point — 31 A 63 a

**GIVE COMICAL PERFORMANCE
Prominent vaudeville actors make
extensive plans for entertainment**

30, 36, 48, 60 and 72 Point carried in stock only at Foundry

Characters in Complete Font

A B C D E F G H I J K L
M N O P Q R S T U V W X
Y Z & $ 1 2 3 4 5 6 7 8 9 0
a b c d e f g h i j k l m
n o p q r s t u v w x y z
. , - ' : ; ! ?

1
2
3
4
5
6
7
8
9
0

36 Point
Gothic No. 520
Figures
set solid

12
34
56
78
90

24 Point
Gothic Condensed
No. 524 Figures
set solid

GOTHIC CONDENSED No. 521

1234567890
60 Point Figures set solid

CHARACTERS IN COMPLETE FONT

A B C D E
F G H I J
K L M N O
P Q R S T
U V W X Y
Z & $ 1 2 3
4 5 6 7 8 9 0
. , - ' : ; ! ?

20 Point — 20 A
SIGNED NOTE
BARS REPORT

16 Point — 24 A
PROCURE ORDER
DESIGN SCENERY

12 Point — 29 A
MANAGERS GATHER
CLEVER INVENTORS

10 Point — 35 A
RESOLUTIONS ADOPTED
SHOE MANUFACTURERS

8 Point — 48 A
EXTRAORDINARY PHOTOGRAPHER
MERCHANT DEMANDED BUILDING

6 Point — 44 A
DISTINGUISHED WRITER RETURNED
INVENTS WONDERFUL INSTRUMENT

9 and 54 Point carried in stock only at Foundry

HARDWARE
MATERIALS FOR CONTRACTORS AND MECHANICS

FARMING AND FACTORY
SUPPLIES

TRACTOR AND AUTOMOBILE
SERVICE STATION

STEPHENER & BUSHSTEIN
OFFICE AND DELIVERY YARD
RUNSDEN CENTER, MAINE

72 Point — 3 A
ROUND

60 Point — 4 A
BORDER

48 Point — 6 A
SECURING

42 Point — 8 A
DIM FIGURE

36 Point — 8 A
HEROES DINE

30 Point — 10 A
GIRLS RECOVER
MARINES HUNT

24 Point — 15 A
NOTED EXPLORER
REFINERS MARCH

Gothic Condensed No. 529

72 Point — 3 A 5 a
Objected

60 Point — 3 A 5 a
DISGUISE

Multiplier

48 Point — 6 A 10 a
EXCURSION

High Country

42 Point — 6 A 11 a
REMODELING

Notable Firms

36 Point — 6 A 12 a
UNDISCOVERED

Spring Mountain

30 Point — 9 A 17 a
COLUMBIAN

Rich Authors

24 Point — 12 A 25 a
REQUIREMENTS

Expects Payment

18 Point — 17 A 36 a
NOMINATE SOLDIER

Country Enthusiastic

14 Point — 22 A 46 a
CHANGING LARGE MAP

Baffling Manufacturers

12 Point — 28 A 55 a
HOLD MOTORCYCLE RACES
Scores of motorcyclists have now signified their intention of riding in endurance races

10 Point — 31 A 65 a
OCEAN LINER CAPACITY TAXED
Large demands for reservation on passenger steamer. Tourists booking ahead for autumn rush

8 Point — 35 A 70 a
EXHIBITS FINER PORTRAIT PAINTING
Magnificent display of these famous paintings; also noted etchings, which are products of the foreign masters

6 Point — 35 A 70 a
CROWD AT SEASHORE LARGEST KNOWN
Extraordinarily warm weather resulted in the greatest gatherings at the seashore hostelries and resorts ever encountered

CHARACTERS IN COMPLETE FONT

A B C D E F G H I
J K L M N O P Q R S
T U V W X Y Z & $
1 2 3 4 5 6 7 8 9 0
a b c d e f g h i
j k l m n o p q r
s t u v w x y z
. , - ' : ; ! ?

1 2 3 4 5 6 7 8 9 0

60 Point Figures set solid

POSTER GOTHIC

1234567890

48 Point Figures set solid

60 Point — 4 A

DINE

48 Point — 4 A

HAND SOME

42 Point — 5 A

CARES SPORT

36 Point — 6 A

MAIDEN REMIND

30 Point — 8 A

PRINTING GIGANTIC

24 Point — 10 A

NEIGHBORS DISTRIBUTE

96 Point — 3 A

MEN

84 Point — 3 A

RIME

72 Point — 3 A

HARK

Characters in Complete Font

A B C D E F G
H I J K L M N
O P Q R S T U
V W X Y Z & $
1 2 3 4 5 6 7
8 9 0 . , - ' ' : ; ! ?

FOR SIZES SMALLER THAN 24 POINT SEE BANK GOTHIC CONDENSED MEDIUM, PAGE 141

News Gothic

72 Point — 3 A 4 a
Right

60 Point — 3 A 5 a
Equity

48 Point — 4 A 8 a
Intrepid

42 Point — 5 A 9 a
Klondike

36 Point — 5 A 9 a
RETURNS
Exposition

30 Point — 6 A 10 a
HISTRIONIC
British Kings

24 Point — 7 A 14 a
REPRODUCED
Neat Pamphlet

18 Point — 11 A 22 a
MENAGERIE
Big elephant
securely tied

14 Point — 15 A 29 a
ENTERPRISING
Cloth merchant
pleasing buyers

12 Point — 17 A 34 a
RECEIVED NICELY
Brilliant statesman
gladly returns after
prolonged absence

10 Point — 21 A 42 a
OBEY INSTRUCTION
Commanding officer
teaches recruits how
hospital tents should
be folded when down

8 Point — 23 A 45 a
MAKING REAL FRIENDS
Good nature is positively
more agreeable than wit.
It gives to the face an air
more benign than beauty

6 Point — 25 A 50 a
ROAD TO EMINENCE HARD
Many say greatness is really
an eminence, the ascent to
which is steep and lofty, and
superior men always display
unusual boldness and vigor

Characters in Complete Font

A B C D E F G H
I J K L M N O P
Q R S T U V W X
Y Z & $ 1 2 3
4 5 6 7 8 9 0
a b c d e f g h i
j k l m n o p q r
s t u v w x y z
. , - ' : ; ! ?

1234567890

60 Point Figures set solid

News Gothic Condensed

1234567890

60 Point Figures set solid

10 Point   26 A   51 a
WORDS BETRAY WISDOM
Consider silently whatever
folks say, because speech
either conceals or reveals
the speaker's inmost soul

8 Point   28 A   55 a
GOOD BOOKS ARE INSPIRING
Remember that chiefly through
books we have intercourse with
master minds, and good books
are now within the reach of all

6 Point   30 A   60 a
DUTIES FAITHFULLY PERFORMED
We require from buildings, as from
men, two kinds of goodness : doing
their practical duties well, and that
they be pleasing while doing them,
which is itself another form of duty

18 Point   15 A   30 a
INSURED SALES
Advertising idea
helped business

14 Point   21 A   40 a
REASON EXPECTED
Our education must
depend upon brains

12 Point   25 A   48 a
RESTORE CONFIDENCE
Wonderful strides made
toward business revival
encouraging merchants

Characters in Complete Font

A B C D E F G H I
J K L M N O P Q R
S T U V W X Y Z & $
1 2 3 4 5 6 7 8 9 0
a b c d e f g h i
j k l m n o p q r
s t u v w x y z
. , - ' : ; ! ?

72 Point   3 A   4 a
Myriad

60 Point   4 A   6 a
Register

48 Point   5 A   8 a
Symbolize

42 Point   5 A   9 a
Eulogistical

36 Point   6 A   9 a
NOURISHING
Gain Strength

30 Point   7 A   14 a
PERSEVERANCE
Capable Scholar

24 Point   10 A   18 a
HANDSOME COVER
Beautiful Designing

News Gothic Extra Condensed

72 Point   4 A 6 a

Relinquish

60 Point   4 A 6 a

Enjoyed Ride

48 Point   6 A 11 a

Hunting Season

42 Point   6 A 13 a

Mysterious Words

36 Point   6 A 13 a

ENCOURAGES ORDER
General Reorganizing

30 Point   9 A 17 a

INVINCIBLE CHARACTERS
Display Indomitable Spirit

24 Point   12 A 23 a

GOLDEN HARVESTING BEGINS
Everybody Enjoying Prosperity

18 Point   19 A 38 a

DIGNIFIED ILLUSTRATION
Catalogue shows various
designs simply arranged

14 Point   25 A 49 a

GREATLY PLEASE INSTRUCTOR
Children studying the histories
of many celebrated statesmen

12 Point   28 A 56 a

QUESTIONS OF GREAT IMPORTANCE
Shrewd advertisers usually require
publications to give facts regarding
circulation and territory they cover

10 Point   31 A 63 a

JOURNALISM OF BENEFIT TO MANKIND
Newspapers are servants of the human
intellect, and their ministry is for good
or for evil, according to the standing or
character of the folks who direct them

8 Point   35 A 70 a

OUR MINDS INCLINE TO DIFFERENT OBJECTS
Many ideas grow better if transplanted into
another mind. That which was a weed in one
mind soon becomes a flower in the other, and
flowers change to weeds in the same manner

6 Point   34 A 68 a

HEALTHFUL RECREATION STIMULATES WORKERS
Recreation is a physical and moral necessity. The
toilworn artisan, stooping and straining over his
task which taxes eye and brain and limb, ought to
have opportunity and means for an hour or more of
healthful relaxation when that task is concluded

12
34
56
78
90

60 Point Figures
set solid

Characters in Complete Font

A B C D E F G H I
J K L M N O P Q R
S T U V W X Y Z & $
1 2 3 4 5 6 7 8 9 0
a b c d e f g h i
j k l m n o p q r
s t u v w x y z
. , - ' : ; ! ?

AMERICAN
TYPE FOUNDERS
SALES
CORPORATION

Lightline Gothic

1 2 3 4 5 6 7 8 9 0

36 Point Lightline Gothic Figures set solid

1 2 3 4 5 6 7 8 9 0

12 Point Lightline Title Figures set solid

Characters in Complete Font

A B C D E F G H I J
K L M N O P Q R S
T U V W X Y Z & $
1 2 3 4 5 6 7 8 9 0
a b c d e f g h i j k l
m n o p q r s t u v w
x y z . , - ' : ; ! ?

LIGHTLINE TITLE GOTHIC

12 Point No. 8   17 A
RECOGNIZES
DISPOSITION

12 Point No. 7   21 A
BURGOMASTER
ENCYCLOPEDIA

12 Point No. 6   24 A
HONEST PERSON
UNION SERVICES

12 Point No. 5   29 A
PICTURESQUE GUIDE
FINANCIAL CREDITOR

6 Point No. 4   26 A
MECHANICAL TRICK
PREVIOUS REPLIES
COMPULSORY PLAN

6 Point No. 3   31 A
BEWILDERING ACTIONS
NATIONAL PARLIAMENT
ILLUSTRATED FEATURE

6 Point No. 2   40 A
FRANK OUTSPOKEN YOUTH
OUTSTANDING SECURITIES
MEMBERS PRAISE OFFICER
NEW TURBINES INSTALLED

6 Point No. 1   46 A
CAPITALIST PURCHASED ESTATE
INTERNATIONAL MAGNATE WEDS
RELATIVES GREATLY SURPRISED
TELEPHONE CONGRATULATIONS

CHARACTERS IN COMPLETE FONT

A B C D E F G H I J K
L M N O P Q R S T U
V W X Y Z & $ 1 2 3
4 5 6 7 8 9 0 . , - ' : ; ! ?

---

36 Point   6 A   9a
Hypothesis

30 Point   6 A   12a
Military Band

24 Point   8 A   14a
EXPENDITURE
Rival Champion

18 Point   11 A   22a
FOREIGN DICTUM
Independent Official

14 Point   17 A   32a
SOCIAL CONFERENCE
Bibliographic Discussion

12 Point   19 A   39a
UNINTERESTING STORIES
Entertain Rich Philanthropist

10 Point   22 A   43a
POPULAR DRAMAS RECALLED
Many famous plays scheduled for
presentation starting next season

8 Point   24 A   47a
NEWSPAPER PUBLISHERS CONVENE
Editors and proprietors have agreed upon
program for their semi-annual conference

6 Point No. 4   26 A   52a
IMPORTANT MATTERS AWAIT SETTLEMENT
Discussion of advertising and circulation among
the numerous topics scheduled for presentation

6 Point No. 3   31 A   61a
PAPER MANUFACTURERS DESCRIBED CONDITIONS
Give lengthy explanation for increasing contract prices of
newsprint despite objections from the weekly newspapers

Bulletin Typewriter

36 Point 4 A 20 a

IMPORTANT ANNOUNCEMENT: Marsh Motor Trucks are now ready for delivery.

24 Point 6 A 30 A

Many Marsh Motor Trucks are picked at random to run their lives out without ever leaving the building.

18 Point 8 A 40 a

In our engineering research laboratories, Marsh Trucks are subject to that investigation which helps to keep Marsh quality.

CHARACTERS IN COMPLETE FONT OF BULLETIN TYPEWRITER

ABCDEFGHIJKLMNOPQRSTUVWXYZ&$1234567890abc
defghijklmnopqrstuvwxyz.,-'":;!?()¯/@¢*%#

Justifiers are sold separately in one and in five pound fonts

---

Jumbo Typewriter

24 Point 6A

NOTICE: MARSH MOTOR COMPANY OFFERS EXTRAORDINARY QUALITY!

CHARACTERS IN COMPLETE FONT OF JUMBO TYPEWRITER

ABCDEFGHIJKLMNOPQRSTUVWXYZ&
$1234567890.,-'":;!?(

Justifiers are sold separately in one and five pound fonts

Typewriter Faces

6 Point AMERICAN TYPEWRITER. Characters 4 Point Set. Imitation typewritten letters have come to occupy an important place in ABCDEFGHIJKLMNOPQRSTUVWXYZ&$1234567890abcdefghijklmnopqrstuvwxyz.,-'"":;!?()¯*@¢/%#
Fractions are fonted $\frac{1}{4}\frac{1}{2}\frac{3}{4}\frac{1}{8}\frac{3}{8}\frac{5}{8}\frac{7}{8}$ and furnished separately

6 Point REPRODUCING TYPEWRITER. Characters 4½ Pt. Set. Imitation typewritten letters have come to occupy an ABCDEFGHIJKLMNOPQRSTUVWXYZ&$1234567890abcdefghijklmnopqrstuvwxyz.,-'"":;!?()¯/%#
Fractions are fonted $1_4 1_2 3_4 1_8 3_8 5_8 7_8 1_3 2_3$ and furnished separately

10 Point AMERICAN TYPEWRITER. Characters 6 Pt. Set. Imitation typewritten letters ABCDEFGHIJKLMNOPQRSTUVWXYZ&$1234567890abcdefghijklmnopqrstuvwxyz.,-'"":;!?()¯*@¢/%#

8 Point REPRODUCING TYPEWRITER. Characters 5 Pt. Set. Imitation typewritten letters have come to ABCDEFGHIJKLMNOPQRSTUVWXYZ&$1234567890abcdefghijklmnopqrstuvwxyz.,-'"":;!?()¯/%#

10 Point ELITE OLIVER TYPEWRITER. Characters 6 Pt. Set. Imitation typewritten ABCDEFGHIJKLMNOPQRSTUVWXYZ&$1234567890abcdefghijklmnopqrstuvwxyz.,-'"":;!?()¯ᴀ=*@¢/%#

10 Point REPRODUCING TYPEWRITER. Characters 6 Point Set. Imitation typewritten ABCDEFGHIJKLMNOPQRSTUVWXYZ&$1234567890abcdefghijklmnopqrstuvwxyz.,-'"":;!?()¯/%#

10 Pt. ELITE UNDERWOOD TYPEWRITER. Characters 6 Point Set. Imitation type- ABCDEFGHIJKLMNOPQRSTUVWXYZ&$1234567890abcdefghijklmnopqrstuvwxyz.,-'"":;!?()¯=°+*§@¢/%#

10 Point NEW MODEL ELITE REMINGTON TYPEWRITER. Characters 5⅝ Point Set. Im- ABCDEFGHIJKLMNOPQRSTUVWXYZ&$1234567890abcdefghijklmnopqrstuvwxyz.,-'"":;!?()¯*@¢/%#
Fractions are fonted $\frac{1}{4}\frac{1}{2}\frac{3}{4}\frac{1}{8}\frac{3}{8}\frac{5}{8}\frac{7}{8}$ and furnished separately

12 Point NEW MODEL UNDERWOOD TYPEWRITER. Characters 1/10 Inch Set. Imitation typewritten letters have come to occupy an important place in the industrial world of today ABCDEFGHIJKLMNOPQRSTUVWXYZ&$1234567890abcdefghijklmnopqrstuvwxyz.,-'"":;!?()¯°*@¢/%# Fractions are fonted $\frac{1}{4}\frac{1}{2}\frac{3}{4}\frac{1}{8}\frac{3}{8}\frac{5}{8}\frac{7}{8}$ and furnished separately

12 Point NEW MODEL REMINGTON TYPEWRITER. Characters 1/10 Inch Set. Imitation typewritten letters have come to occupy an important place in the industrial world of today, ABCDEFGHIJKLMNOPQRSTUVWXYZ&$1234567890abcdefghijklmnopqrstuvwxyz.,-'"":;!?()¯*@¢/%# Fractions are fonted $\frac{1}{4}\frac{1}{2}\frac{3}{4}\frac{1}{8}\frac{3}{8}\frac{5}{8}\frac{7}{8}$ and furnished separately

12 Point UNDERWOOD TYPEWRITER. Characters 7¼ Point Set. Imitation typewritten letters have come to occupy an important place in the industrial world of today, and every printer with business ABCDEFGHIJKLMNOPQRSTUVWXYZ&$1234567890abcdefghijklmnopqrstuvwxyz.,-'"":;!?()¯*@¢/%#$\frac{1}{4}\frac{1}{2}\frac{3}{4}$

12 Point RIBBON-FACE TYPEWRITER. Characters 7 1/4 Point Set. Imitation typewritten letters have come to occupy an important place in the industrial world of today, and every printer with business in- ABCDEFGHIJKLMNOPQRSTUVWXYZ&$1234567890abcdefghijklmnopqrstuvwxyz.,-'"":;!?()¯/%#

12 Point SILK REMINGTON TYPEWRITER. Characters 1/10 Inch Set. Imitation typewritten letters have come to occupy an important place in the industrial world of today, and ABCDEFGHIJKLMNOPQRSTUVWXYZ&$1234567890abcdefghijklmnopqrstuvwxyz.,-'"":;!?()¯*@¢/%# Fractions are fonted $\frac{1}{4}\frac{1}{2}\frac{3}{4}\frac{1}{8}\frac{3}{8}\frac{5}{8}\frac{7}{8}$ and furnished separately

12 Point REMINGTON TYPEWRITER No. 2. Characters 7 Point Set. Imitation typewritten letters have come to occupy an important place in the industrial world of today, and every printer with business instincts ABCDEFGHIJKLMNOPQRSTUVWXYZ&$1234567890abcdefghijklmnopqrstuvwxyz.,,-'"":;!?()¯/%#

12 Point STANDARD TYPEWRITER. Characters 7¼ Point Set. Imitation typewritten letters have come to occupy an important place in the industrial world of today, and every ABCDEFGHIJKLMNOPQRSTUVWXYZ&$1234567890abcdefghijklmnopqrstuvwxyz.,-'"":;!?()¯/%# Fractions are fonted $\frac{1}{4}\frac{1}{2}\frac{3}{4}\frac{1}{8}\frac{3}{8}\frac{5}{8}\frac{7}{8}\frac{1}{3}\frac{2}{3}$ and furnished separately

Justifiers for all typewriter faces are put up in 1-pound and 5-pound fonts and furnished only when specially ordered

BODY TYPE... MODERN AND OLDSTYLE

READABILITY and attractiveness being essential qualities of all printing, the type face for the text matter of booklets and catalogues should be very carefully selected. Foundry type, hand set and perfectly spaced gives the extra touch of artistry that always distinguishes first-class work. An otherwise well planned job can be spoiled by careless handling of important small text matter. Reader interest—the whole purpose of a catalogue—depends upon careful attention to little details not possible except by hand setting. The designs shown in this body type section offer sufficient variety for every purpose and are grouped by sizes for easy comparison. Sizes larger than twelve point, where made, will be found on other pages of this book in the showing of the complete series.

SIX POINT BODONI BOOK AND ITALIC. The body type faces shown on this and accompanying pages are some of the famous types of printing history. They cover a wide range of styles making easy the selection of the correct body type for any piece of printing. The lines have been made long enough to be of service in calculating copy space. All the faces of each size have been grouped together for comparison *of weight and size of face, thereby enabling the printer*

SIX POINT BASKERVILLE ROMAN AND ITALIC. The body type faces shown on this and accompanying pages are some of the famous types of printing history. They cover a wide range of styles making easy the selection of the correct body type for any piece of printing. The lines have been made long enough to be of service in calculating copy space. All the faces of each size have been grouped together for comparison of weight and size of face, *thereby enabling the printer to make the selection of type most*

SIX POINT CLOISTER LIGHTFACE AND ITALIC. The body type faces shown on this and accompanying pages are some of the famous types of printing history. They cover a wide range of styles making easy the selection of the correct body type for any piece of printing. The lines have been made long enough to be of service in calculating copy space. All the faces of each size have been grouped together *for comparison of weight and size of face, thereby enabling*

SIX POINT CASLON NO. 540 AND ITALIC. The body type faces shown on this and accompanying pages are some of the famous types of printing history. They cover a wide range of styles making easy the selection of the correct body type for any piece of printing. The lines have been made long enough to be of service in calculating copy space. All the faces of each size have been grouped together for comparison of *weight and size of face, thereby enabling the printer to make the*

SIX POINT MODERN ROMAN NO. 64 AND ITALIC. The body type faces shown on this and accompanying pages are some of the famous types of printing history. They cover a wide range of styles making easy the selection of the correct body type for any piece of printing. The lines have been made long enough to be of service in *calculating copy space. All the faces of each size*

SIX POINT ROMAN NO. 510 AND ITALIC. The body type faces shown on this and accompanying pages are some of the famous types of printing history. They cover a wide range of styles making easy the selection of the correct body type for any piece of printing. The lines have been made long enough to be of service in calculating copy space. All the *faces of each size have been grouped together for com-*

SIX POINT CASLON OLDSTYLE NO. 471 AND ITALIC. The body type faces shown on this and accompanying pages are some of the famous types of printing history. They cover a wide range of styles making easy the selection of the correct body type for any piece of printing. The lines have been made long enough to be of service in calculating copy space. All the faces of each size have *been grouped together for comparison of weight and size of*

SIX POINT CLOISTER OLDSTYLE AND ITALIC. The body type faces shown on this and accompanying pages are some of the famous types of printing history. They cover a wide range of styles making easy the selection of the correct body type for any piece of printing. The lines have been made long enough to be of service in calculating copy space. All the faces of each size have been grouped *together for comparison of weight and size of face, thereby en-*

SIX POINT GOUDY OLDSTYLE AND ITALIC. The body type faces shown on this and accompanying pages are some of the famous types of printing history. They cover a wide range of styles making easy the selection of the correct body type for any piece of printing. The lines have been made long enough to be of service in calculating copy space. All the faces of *each size have been grouped together for comparison of*

SIX POINT BULMER ROMAN AND ITALIC. The body type faces shown on this and accompanying pages are some of the famous types of printing history. They cover a wide range of styles making easy the selection of the correct body type for any piece of printing. The lines have been made long enough to be of service in calculating copy space. All the faces *of each size have been grouped together for comparison*

SIX POINT GARAMOND AND ITALIC. The body type faces shown on this and accompanying pages are some of the famous types of printing history. They cover a wide range of styles making easy the selection of the correct body type for any piece of printing. The lines have been made long enough to be of service in calculating copy space. All the faces of each *size have been grouped together for comparison of weight*

SIX POINT SCOTCH ROMAN AND ITALIC. The body type faces shown on this and accompanying pages are some of the famous types of printing history. They cover a wide range of styles making easy the selection of the correct body type for any piece of printing. The lines have been made long enough to be of service in calculating copy space. All the *faces of each size have been grouped together for*

SIX POINT CENTURY SCHOOLBOOK AND ITALIC. The body type faces shown on this and accompanying pages are some of the famous types of printing history. They cover a wide range of styles making easy the selection of the correct body type for any piece of printing. The lines have been made long enough to be of service in calculating copy space. *All the faces of each size have been group*

SIX POINT CENTURY CATALOGUE AND ITALIC. The body type faces shown on this and accompanying pages are some of the famous types of printing history. They cover a wide range of styles making easy the selection of the correct body type for any piece of printing. The lines have been made long enough to be of service in calculating copy space. All the faces of each size have *been grouped together for comparison of weight and*

SIX POINT SCHOOLBOOK OLDSTYLE WITH CENTURY SCHOOLBOOK ITALIC. The body type faces shown on this and accompanying pages are some of the famous types of printing history. They cover a wide range of styles making easy the selection of the correct body type for any piece of printing. The lines have been made long enough to be of *service in calculating copy space. All the faces of*

SIX POINT CENTURY OLDSTYLE AND ITALIC. The body type faces shown on this and accompanying pages are some of the famous types of printing history. They cover a wide range of styles making easy the selection of the correct body type for any piece of printing. The lines have been made long enough to be of service in calculating copy space. *All the faces of each size have been grouped together*

SIX POINT BODONI AND ITALIC. The body type faces shown on this and accompanying pages are some of the famous types of printing history. They cover a wide range of styles making easy the selection of the correct body type for any piece of printing. The lines have been made long enough to be of service in calculating copy space. All the faces of each size have been grouped together for comparison of *weight and size of face, thereby enabling the printer to*

Six Point Goudy Catalogue and Italic. The body type faces shown on this and accompanying pages are some of the famous types of printing history. They cover a wide range of styles making easy the selection of the correct body type for any piece of printing. The lines have been made long enough to be of service in calculating copy space. All the faces *of each size have been grouped together for comparison*

SIX POINT CENTURY EXPANDED AND ITALIC. The body type faces shown on this and accompanying pages are some of the famous types of printing history. They cover a wide range of styles making easy the selection of the correct body type for any piece of printing. The lines have been made long enough to be of service in calculating copy space. *All the faces of each size have been grouped together*

Six Point Bookman Oldstyle and Italic. The body type faces shown on this and accompanying pages are some of the famous types of printing history. They cover a wide range of styles making easy the selection of the correct body type for any piece of printing. The lines have been made long enough to be of service in calculating copy space. *All the faces of each size have been*

FIVE POINT ROMAN NO. 527 AND ITALIC. The body type faces shown on this and accompanying pages are some of the famous types of printing history. They cover a wide range of styles making easy the selection of the correct body type for any piece of printing. The lines have been made long enough to be of service in calculating copy space. All the faces of each size have been grouped together for comparison of weight and size of *face, thereby enabling the printer to make the selection*

Six Point Bernhard Gothic Light and Italic. The body type faces shown on this and accompanying pages are some of the famous types of printing history. They cover a wide range of styles making easy the selection of the correct body type for any piece of printing. The lines have been made long enough to be of service in calculating copy space. All the faces have been grouped *together for comparison of weight and size of face, thereby*

Six Point Stymie Light and Italic. The body type faces shown on this and accompanying pages are some of the famous types of printing history. They cover a wide range of styles making easy the selection of the correct body type for any piece of printing. The lines have been made long enough to be of service in calculating copy space. All the faces of each size have been grouped together for com-

FIVE POINT ROMAN NO. 524 AND ITALIC. The body type faces shown on this and accompanying pages are some of the famous types of printing history. They cover a wide range of styles making easy the selection of the correct body type for any piece of printing. The lines have been made long enough to be of service in calculating copy space. All the faces of each size have been grouped together for comparison of weight and size of face, thereby enabling the printer to make the selection of type most appropriate *for the contemplated job—be it booklet, catalog or publication*

BODY TYPE

EIGHT POINT BODONI BOOK AND ITALIC. The body type faces shown on this and accompanying pages are some of the famous types of printing history. They cover a wide range of styles making easy the selection of the correct body type for any piece of printing. The lines *have been made long enough to be of service*

EIGHT POINT BASKERVILLE ROMAN AND ITALIC. The body type faces shown on this and accompanying pages are some of the famous types of printing history. They cover a wide range of styles making easy the selection of the correct body type for any piece of printing. The lines have been made long *enough to be of service in calculating copy space. All*

EIGHT POINT CLOISTER LIGHTFACE AND ITALIC. The body type faces shown on this and accompanying pages are some of the famous types of printing history. They cover a wide range of styles making easy the selection of the correct body type for any piece of printing. The lines *have been made long enough to be of service in calcu-*

EIGHT POINT CASLON NO. 540 AND ITALIC. The body type faces shown on this and accompanying pages are some of the famous types of printing history. They cover a wide range of styles making easy the selection of the correct body type for any piece of printing. *The lines have been made long enough to be of*

EIGHT POINT MODERN ROMAN NO. 64 AND ITALIC. The body type faces shown on this and accompanying pages are some of the famous types of printing history. They cover a wide range of styles making easy the selection of the *correct body type for any piece of printing.*

EIGHT POINT ROMAN NO. 510 AND ITALIC. The body type faces shown on this and accompanying pages are some of the famous types of printing history. They cover a wide range of styles making easy the selection of the correct body type for any piece of printing. *The lines have been made long enough to*

EIGHT POINT CASLON OLDSTYLE NO. 471 AND ITALIC. The body type faces shown on this and accompanying pages are some of the famous types of printing history. They cover a wide range of styles making easy the selection of the correct body type for any piece of printing. The lines have been made *long enough to be of service in calculating copy space.*

EIGHT POINT CLOISTER OLDSTYLE AND ITALIC. The body type faces shown on this and accompanying pages are some of the famous types of printing history. They cover a wide range of styles making easy the selection of the correct body type for any piece of printing. The lines *have been made long enough to be of service in*

EIGHT POINT GOUDY OLDSTYLE AND ITALIC. The body type faces shown on this and accompanying pages are some of the famous types of printing history. They cover a wide range of styles making easy the selection of the correct body type for any piece of *printing. The lines have been made long enough*

EIGHT POINT BULMER ROMAN AND ITALIC. The body type faces shown on this and accompanying pages are some of the famous types of printing history. They cover a wide range of styles making easy the selection of the correct body type for any piece of printing. *The lines have been made long enough to*

EIGHT POINT GARAMOND AND ITALIC. The body type faces shown on this and accompanying pages are some of the famous types of printing history. They cover a wide range of styles making easy the selection of the correct body type for any piece of printing. *The lines have been made long enough to be of*

EIGHT POINT SCOTCH ROMAN AND ITALIC. The body type faces shown on this and accompanying pages are some of the famous types of printing history. They cover a wide range of styles making easy the selection of the correct body type for any piece of printing. *The lines have been made long enough to*

EIGHT POINT CENTURY SCHOOLBOOK AND ITALIC. The body type faces shown on this and accompanying pages are some of the famous types of printing history. They cover a wide range of styles making easy the selection of the correct *body type for any piece of printing. The*

EIGHT POINT CENTURY CATALOGUE AND ITALIC. The body type faces shown on this and accompanying pages are some of the famous types of printing history. They cover a wide range of styles making easy the selection of the correct body type for any piece *of printing. The lines have been made long*

EIGHT POINT SCHOOLBOOK OLDSTYLE WITH CENTURY SCHOOLBOOK ITALIC. The body type faces shown on this and accompanying pages are some of the famous types of printing history. They cover a wide range of styles making easy *the selection of the correct body type for*

EIGHT POINT CENTURY OLDSTYLE AND ITALIC. The body type faces shown on this and accompanying pages are some of the famous types of printing history. They cover a wide range of styles making easy the selection of the correct body type for any piece *of printing. The lines have been made long*

EIGHT POINT BODONI AND ITALIC. The body type faces shown on this and accompanying pages are some of the famous types of printing history. They cover a wide range of styles making easy the selection of the correct body type for any piece of printing. *The lines have been made long enough to*

Eight Point Goudy Catalogue and Italic. The body type faces shown on this and accompanying pages are some of the famous types of printing history. They cover a wide range of styles making easy the selection of the correct body type for any piece of printing. *The lines have been made*

EIGHT POINT CENTURY EXPANDED AND ITALIC. The body type faces shown on this and accompanying pages are some of the famous types of printing history. They cover a wide range of styles making easy the selection of the correct body *type for any piece of printing. The lines*

Eight Point Bookman Oldstyle and Italic. The body type faces shown on this and accompanying pages are some of the famous types of printing history. They cover a wide range of styles making easy the selection of the correct body type for any piece of **printing. The lines have been made long**

Eight Point Piranesi and Italic. The body type faces shown on this and accompanying pages are some of the famous types of printing history. They cover a wide range of styles making easy the selection of the correct body type for any piece of printing. The lines have been made long enough to be of service *in calculating copy space. All the faces of each size have*

Eight Point Bernhard Gothic Light and Italic. The body type faces shown on this and accompanying pages are some of the famous types of printing history. They cover a wide range of styles making easy the selection of the correct body type for any piece of printing. The lines have *been made long enough to be of service in calcu-*

Eight Point Stymie Light and Italic. The body type faces shown on this and accompanying pages are some of the famous types of printing history. They cover a wide range of styles making easy the selection of the correct body type for any piece of printing. *The lines have been made long enough*

Eight Point Bernhard Booklet and Italic. The body type faces shown on this and accompanying pages are some of the famous types of printing history. They cover a wide range of styles making easy the selection of the correct body type for any piece of printing. The lines have *been made long enough to be of service in calcu-*

BODY TYPE

TEN POINT BASKERVILLE ROMAN AND ITALIC. The body type faces shown on this and accompanying pages are some of the famous types of printing history. They cover a wide range of styles making easy the selection of the correct body type for any piece of printing. The lines have been made long enough to be of service in calculating copy space. All the faces of each size have been grouped together for comparison of weight and size of face, thereby enabling the printer *to make the selection of type most appropriate for the contemplated job in*

Ten Point Piranesi and Italic. The body type faces shown on this and accompanying pages are some of the famous types of printing history. They cover a wide range of styles making easy the selection of the correct body type for any piece of printing. The lines have been made long enough to be of service in calculating copy space. All the faces of each size have been grouped together for comparison of weight and size of face, *thereby enabling the printer to make the selection of type most appropriate for*

TEN POINT CASLON NO. 540 AND ITALIC. The body type faces shown on this and accompanying pages are some of the famous types of printing history. They cover a wide range of styles making easy the selection of the correct body type for any piece of printing. The lines have been made long enough to be of service in calculating copy space. All the faces of each size have been grouped together for comparison of weight and *size of face, thereby enabling the printer to make the selection of type*

TEN POINT CASLON OLDSTYLE NO. 471 AND ITALIC. The body type faces shown on this and accompanying pages are some of the famous types of printing history. They cover a wide range of styles making easy the selection of the correct body type for any piece of printing. The lines have been made long enough to be of service in calculating copy space. All the faces of each size have been grouped together for comparison of weight and size of face, thereby enabling the printer *to make the selection of type most appropriate for the contemplated job*

TEN POINT BODONI BOOK AND ITALIC. The body type faces shown on this and accompanying pages are some of the famous types of printing history. They cover a wide range of styles making easy the selection of the correct body type for any piece of printing. The lines have been made long enough to be of service in calculating copy space. All the faces of each size have been grouped together for comparison of weight *and size of face, thereby enabling the printer to make the selec-*

Ten Point Bernhard Booklet and Italic. The body type faces shown on this and accompanying pages are some of the famous types of printing history. They cover a wide range of styles making easy the selection of the correct body type for any piece of printing. The lines have been made long enough to be of service in calculating copy space. All the faces of each size have been grouped together for comparison of weight and size of face, *thereby enabling the printer to make the selection of type most*

TEN POINT BULMER ROMAN AND ITALIC. The body type faces shown on this and accompanying pages are some of the famous types of printing history. They cover a wide range of styles making easy the selection of the correct body type for any piece of printing. The lines have been made long enough to be of service in calculating copy space. All the faces of each size have been grouped together for comparison of *weight and size of face, thereby enabling the printer to make the*

TEN POINT MODERN ROMAN NO. 64 AND ITALIC. The body type faces shown on this and accompanying pages are some of the famous types of printing history. They cover a wide range of styles making easy the selection of the correct body type for any piece of printing. The lines have been made long enough to be of service in calculating copy space. All the faces of each size have *been grouped together for comparison of weight and size*

TEN POINT GARAMOND AND ITALIC. The body type faces shown on this and accompanying pages are some of the famous types of printing history. They cover a wide range of styles making easy the selection of the correct body type for any piece of printing. The lines have been made long enough to be of service in calculating copy space. All the faces of each size have been grouped together for comparison *son of weight and size of face, thereby enabling the printer to make*

TEN POINT ROMAN NO. 510 AND ITALIC. The body type faces shown on this and accompanying pages are some of the famous types of printing history. They cover a wide range of styles making easy the selection of the correct body type for any piece of printing. The lines have been made long enough to be of service in calculating copy space. All the faces of each size have been grouped together for compari- *son of weight and size of face, thereby enabling the printer to*

TEN POINT CENTURY CATALOGUE AND ITALIC. The body type faces shown on this and accompanying pages are some of the famous types of printing history. They cover a wide range of styles making easy the selection of the correct body type for any piece of printing. The lines have been made long enough to be of service in calculating copy space. All the faces of each size have been *grouped together for comparison of weight and size of*

TEN POINT CLOISTER LIGHTFACE AND ITALIC. The body type faces shown on this and accompanying pages are some of the famous types of printing history. They cover a wide range of styles making easy the selection of the correct body type for any piece of printing. The lines have been made long enough to be of service in calculating copy space. All the faces of each size have been grouped together for comparison of weight and *size of face, thereby enabling the printer to make the selection of type*

BODY TYPE

TEN POINT CLOISTER OLDSTYLE AND ITALIC. The body type faces shown on this and accompanying pages are some of the famous types of printing history. They cover a wide range of styles making easy the selection of the correct body type for any piece of printing. The lines have been made long enough to be of service in calculating copy space. All the faces of each size have been grouped together for comparison of weight and size of *face, thereby enabling the printer to make the selection of type most ap-*

TEN POINT SCOTCH ROMAN AND ITALIC. The body type faces shown on this and accompanying pages are some of the famous types of printing history. They cover a wide range of styles making easy the selection of the correct body type for any piece of printing. The lines have been made long enough to be of service in calculating copy space. All the faces of each size have been grouped together for comparison of weight *and size of face, thereby enabling the printer to make the selection*

TEN POINT GOUDY OLDSTYLE AND ITALIC. The body type faces shown on this and accompanying pages are some of the famous types of printing history. They cover a wide range of styles making easy the selection of the correct body type for any piece of printing. The lines have been made long enough to be of service in calculating copy space. All the faces of each size have been grouped to-*gether for comparison of weight and size of face, thereby ena-*

TEN POINT CENTURY OLDSTYLE AND ITALIC. The body type faces shown on this and accompanying pages are some of the famous types of printing history. They cover a wide range of styles making easy the selection of the correct body type for any piece of printing. The lines have been made long enough to be of service in calculating copy space. *All the faces of each size have been grouped together*

Ten Point Goudy Catalogue and Italic. The body type faces shown on this and accompanying pages are some of the famous types of printing history. They cover a wide range of styles making easy the selection of the correct body type for any piece of printing. The lines have been made long enough to be of service in calcu-lating copy space. All the faces of each size have been *grouped together for comparison of weight and size of face*

TEN POINT CENTURY EXPANDED AND ITALIC. The body type faces shown on this and accompanying pages are some of the famous types of printing history. They cover a wide range of styles making easy the selection of the correct body type for any piece of printing. The lines have been made long enough to be of service in calculating copy space. All the faces of each size have *been grouped together for comparison of weight and*

TEN POINT SCHOOLBOOK OLDSTYLE WITH CENTURY SCHOOLBOOK ITALIC. The body type faces shown on this and accompanying pages are some of the fa-mous types of printing history. They cover a wide range of styles making easy the selection of the cor-rect body type for any piece of printing. The lines have been made long enough to be of service in cal-*culating copy space. All the faces of each size have*

TEN POINT CENTURY SCHOOLBOOK AND ITALIC. The body type faces shown on this and accompanying pages are some of the famous types of printing history. They cover a wide range of styles making easy the selection of the correct body type for any piece of printing. The lines have been made long enough to be of service in calculating copy space. *All the faces of each size have been grouped together*

TEN POINT BODONI AND ITALIC. The body type faces shown on this and accompanying pages are some of the famous types of printing history. They cover a wide range of styles making easy the selection of the correct body type for any piece of printing. The lines have been made long enough to be of service in calculating copy space. All the faces of each size have been grouped together *for comparison of weight and size of face, thereby ena-*

Ten Point Bookman Oldstyle and Italic. The body type faces shown on this and accompanying pages are some of the famous types of printing history. They cover a wide range of styles making easy the selection of the correct body type for any piece of printing. The lines have been made long enough to be of service in calcu-lating copy space. All the faces of each size have been *grouped together for comparison of weight and size*

Ten Point Stymie Light and Italic. The body type faces shown on this and accompanying pages are some of the famous types of printing history. They cover a wide range of styles making easy the selec-tion of the correct body type for any piece of print-ing. The lines have been made long enough to be of service in calculating copy space. All the faces of *each size have been grouped together for compari-*

Ten Point Bernhard Gothic Light and Italic. The body type faces shown on this and accompanying pages are some of the famous types of printing history. They cover a wide range of styles making easy the selection of the correct body type for any piece of printing. The lines have been made long enough to be of service in calculating copy space. All the faces of each size have been grouped together for comparison of weight and size *of face, thereby enabling the printer to make the selection of*

BODY TYPE

12 POINT BASKERVILLE ROMAN AND ITALIC. The body type faces shown on this and accompanying pages are some of the famous types of printing history. They cover a wide range of styles making easy the selection of the correct body type for any piece of printing. The lines have been made long enough to be of service in calcu-*lating copy space. All the faces of each size have been grouped*

12 POINT CASLON NO. 540 AND ITALIC. The body type faces shown on this and accompanying pages are some of the famous types of printing history. They cover a wide range of styles making easy the selection of the correct body type for any piece of printing. The lines have been made *long enough to be of service in calculating copy space.*

12 POINT BODONI BOOK AND ITALIC. The body type faces shown on this and accompanying pages are some of the famous types of printing history. They cover a wide range of styles making easy the selection of the correct body type for any piece of printing. The lines have been made long enough to be of service in cal-*culating copy space. All the faces of each size have*

12 POINT BULMER ROMAN AND ITALIC. The body type faces shown on this and accompanying pages are some of the famous types of printing history. They cover a wide range of styles making easy the selection of the correct body type for any piece of printing. The lines have been made long enough to be of service in calcu-*lating copy space. All the faces of each size have been*

12 POINT GARAMOND AND ITALIC. The body type faces shown on this and accompanying pages are some of the famous types of printing history. They cover a wide range of styles making easy the selection of the correct body type for any piece of printing. The lines have been made long enough to be of service in cal-*culating copy space. All the faces of each size have been grouped*

12 POINT CENTURY CATALOGUE AND ITALIC. The body type faces shown on this and accompanying pages are some of the famous types of printing history. They cover a wide range of styles making easy the selection of the correct body type for any piece of printing. The lines have been made long *enough to be of service in calculating copy space.*

12 Point Piranesi and Italic. The body type faces shown on this and accompanying pages are some of the famous types of printing history. They cover a wide range of styles making easy the selection of the correct body type for any piece of printing. The lines have been made long enough to be of service in calculating copy space. All the faces of each size *have been grouped together for comparison of weight and size of face,*

12 POINT CASLON OLDSTYLE NO. 471 AND ITALIC. The body type faces shown on this and accompanying pages are some of the famous types of printing history. They cover a wide range of styles making easy the selection of the correct body type for any piece of printing. The lines have been made *long enough to be of service in calculating copy space. All*

12 Point Bernhard Booklet and Italic. The body type faces shown on this and accompanying pages are some of the famous types of printing history. They cover a wide range of styles making easy the selection of the correct body type for any piece of printing. The lines have been made long enough to be of service in cal-*culating copy space. All the faces of each size have been*

12 POINT MODERN ROMAN NO. 64 AND ITALIC. The body type faces shown on this and accompany-ing pages are some of the famous types of printing history. They cover a wide range of styles making easy the selection of the correct body type for any piece of printing. The lines have *been made long enough to be of service in calculat-*

12 POINT ROMAN NO. 510 AND ITALIC. The body type faces shown on this and accompanying pages are some of the famous types of printing history. They cover a wide range of styles making easy the selection of the correct body type for any piece of printing. The lines have been made long enough *to be of service in calculating copy space. All the faces*

12 POINT CLOISTER LIGHTFACE AND ITALIC. The body type faces shown on this and accompanying pages are some of the famous types of printing history. They cover a wide range of styles making easy the selection of the correct body type for any piece of printing. The lines have been made long enough to be of service in calculating copy space. *All the faces of each size have been grouped together for*

BODY TYPE

12 POINT CLOISTER OLDSTYLE AND ITALIC. The body type faces shown on this and accompanying pages are some of the famous types of printing history. They cover a wide range of styles making easy the selection of the correct body type for any piece of printing. The lines have been made long enough to be of service in calculating copy space. *All the faces of each size have been grouped together for*

12 POINT GOUDY OLDSTYLE AND ITALIC. The body type faces shown on this and accompanying pages are some of the famous types of printing history. They cover a wide range of styles making easy the selection of the correct body type for any piece of printing. The lines have been made long enough *to be of service in calculating copy space. All the faces*

12 Point Goudy Catalogue and Italic. The body type faces shown on this and accompanying pages are some of the famous types of printing history. They cover a wide range of styles making easy the selection of the correct body type for any piece of printing. The lines have been *made long enough to be of service in calculating*

12 POINT SCHOOLBOOK OLDSTYLE WITH CENTURY SCHOOLBOOK ITALIC. The body type faces shown on this and accompanying pages are some of the famous types of printing history. They cover a wide range of styles making easy the selection of the correct body *type for any piece of printing. The lines have*

12 POINT BODONI AND ITALIC. The body type faces shown on this and accompanying pages are some of the famous types of printing history. They cover a wide range of styles making easy the selection of the correct body type for any piece of printing. The lines have been made long enough to be of *service in calculating copy space. All the faces of*

12 Point Stymie Light and Italic. The body type faces shown on this and accompanying pages are some of the famous types of printing history. They cover a wide range of styles making easy the selection of the correct body type for any piece of printing. The lines have been made *long enough to be of service in calculating*

12 POINT SCOTCH ROMAN AND ITALIC. The body type faces shown on this and accompanying pages are some of the famous types of printing history. They cover a wide range of styles making easy the selection of the correct body type for any piece of printing. The lines have been made long *enough to be of service in calculating copy space.*

12 POINT CENTURY OLDSTYLE AND ITALIC. The body type faces shown on this and accompanying pages are some of the famous types of printing history. They cover a wide range of styles making easy the selection of the correct body type for any piece of printing. The lines *have been made long enough to be of service in*

12 POINT CENTURY EXPANDED AND ITALIC. The body type faces shown on this and accompanying pages are some of the famous types of printing history. They cover a wide range of styles making easy the selection of the correct body type for any piece of printing. The *lines have been made long enough to be of ser-*

12 POINT CENTURY SCHOOLBOOK AND ITALIC. The body type faces shown on this and accompanying pages are some of the famous types of printing history. They cover a wide range of styles making easy the selection of the correct body type for any piece of print- *ing. The lines have been made long enough to*

12 Point Bookman Oldstyle and Italic. The body type faces shown on this and accompanying pages are some of the famous types of printing history. They cover a wide range of styles making easy the selection of the correct body type for any piece of printing. The lines have been *made long enough to be of service in cal-*

12 Point Bernhard Gothic Light and Italic. The body type faces shown on this and accompanying pages are some of the famous types of printing history. They cover a wide range of styles making easy the selection of the correct body type for any piece of printing. The lines have been made long enough to be of service in *calculating copy space. All the faces of each size have*

DIAMOND COMBINATION MONOGRAMS

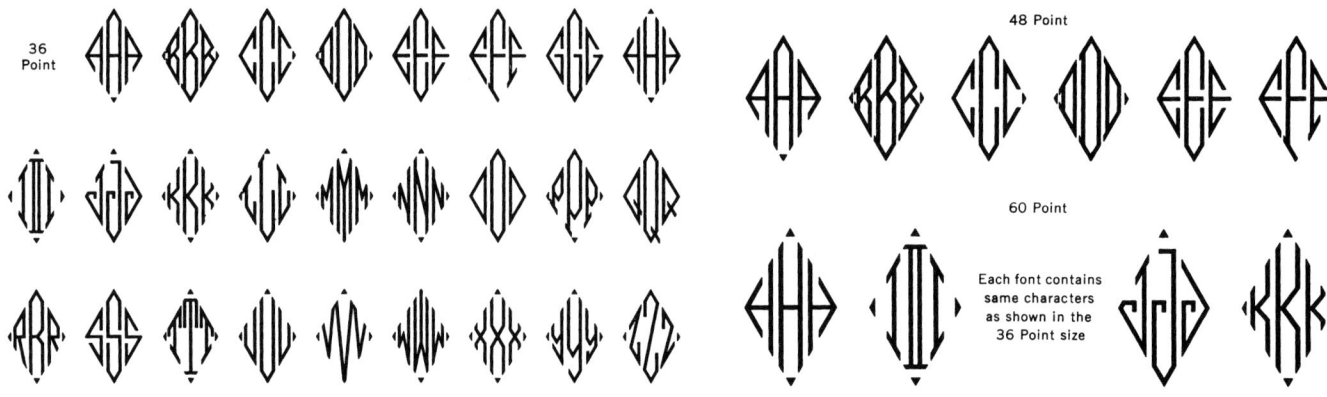

VIRKOTYPE COMBINATION MONOGRAMS
Sold in fonts, or separately in two, three, four and five letter combinations
Series E, 36 Point. Put up in fonts of one type each, 81 characters

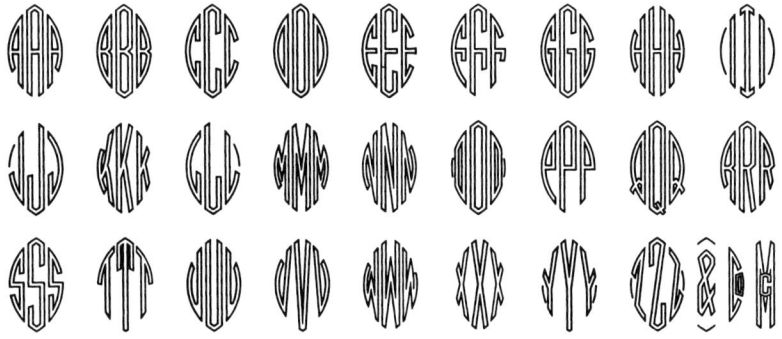

Series F, 36 Point—Color for Series E. Put up in fonts of one type each, 81 characters

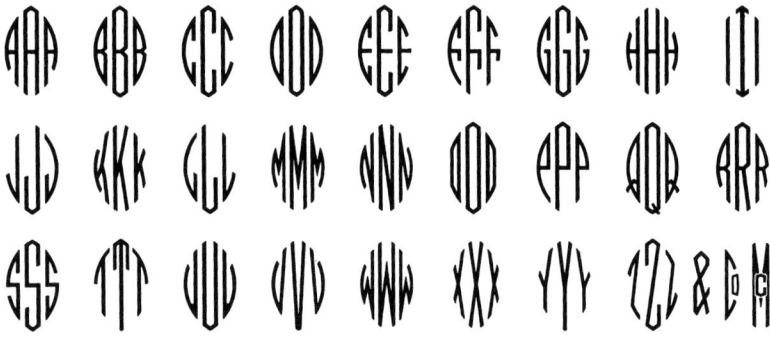

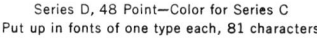

Series C, 48 Point	Series D, 48 Point—Color for Series C
Put up in fonts of one type each, 81 characters	Put up in fonts of one type each, 81 characters

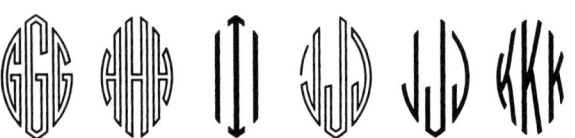

Series A, 60 Point	Series B, 60 Point—Color for Series A
Put up in fonts of one type each, 81 characters	Put up in fonts of one type each, 81 characters

VIRKOTYPE FRAMES
Series EF, to be used with Series E or F Virkotype Combination Monograms

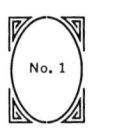 No. 1 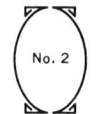 No. 2 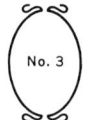 No. 3  No. 4

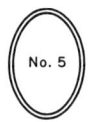 No. 5 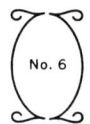 No. 6  No. 7 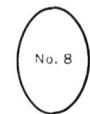 No. 8

 Series CD, to be used with Series C or D Virkotype Combination Monograms

All characters cast on 72 Point body

 Series AB, to be used with Series A or B Virkotype Combination Monograms

All fonts contain all designs shown in Series EF
When ordering specify Series and Number of frame desired

VIRKOTYPE TINT BLOCKS
Four sizes: for use with two, three, four and five letter combinations
Series No. 3, for use with 36 Point

No. 25   No. 24   No. 23   No. 22

Series No. 2, for 48 Point   Series No. 1, for 60 Point

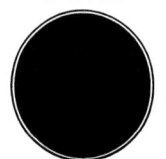 Series Nos. 1 and 2 contain all characters shown in Series No. 3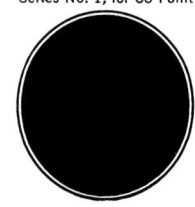

PRINCESS COMBINATION MONOGRAMS—For One Color

A font contains one each of the smaller characters A to Z (right and left), and one each of the larger characters A to Z

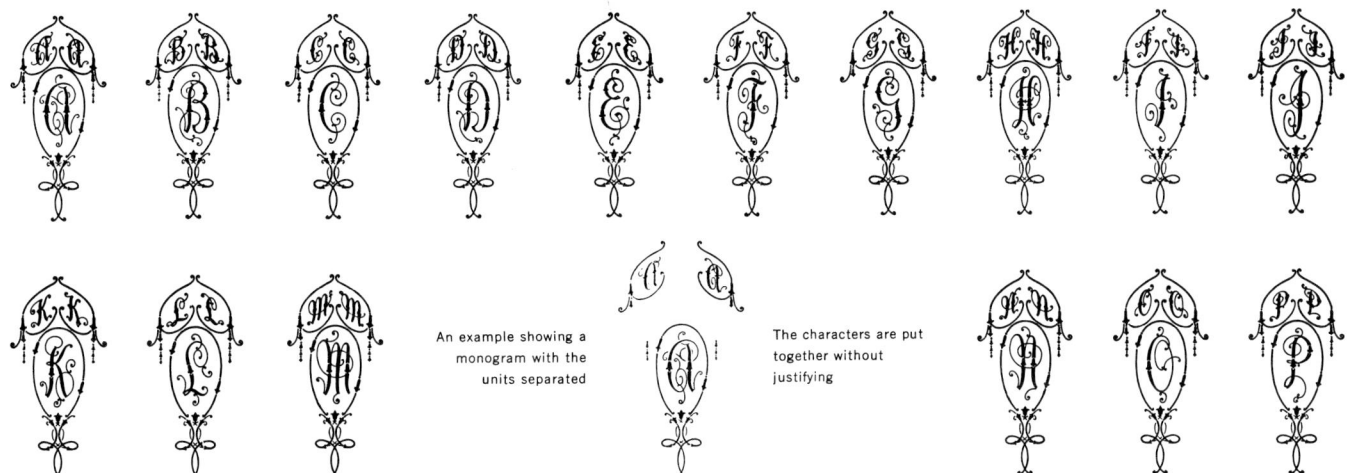

An example showing a monogram with the units separated

The characters are put together without justifying

PRINCESS COMBINATION MONOGRAMS—For Two Colors

In this series the decoration is cast separately, otherwise the font is made up the same as the one color font. Six type of the decorative piece are included in a font

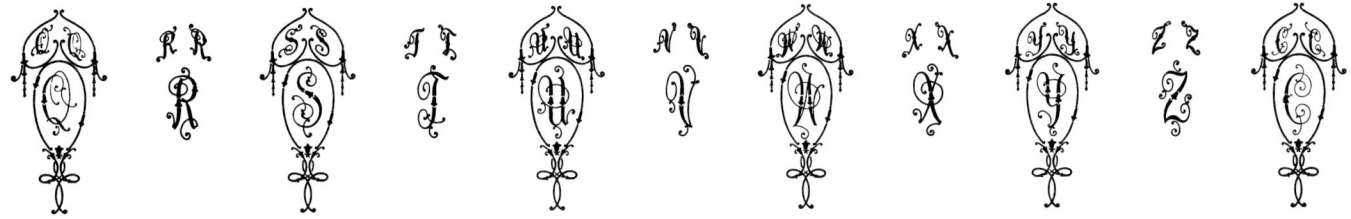

Fonts contain three of each character, which may be arranged in a variety of ways, the initial of the family name always being last

NEWPORT MONOGRAMS

Cast on 36 Point body

Characters are cast on 12 point set, except the I (9 point) and M and W (18 point). All cast to register for two color printing

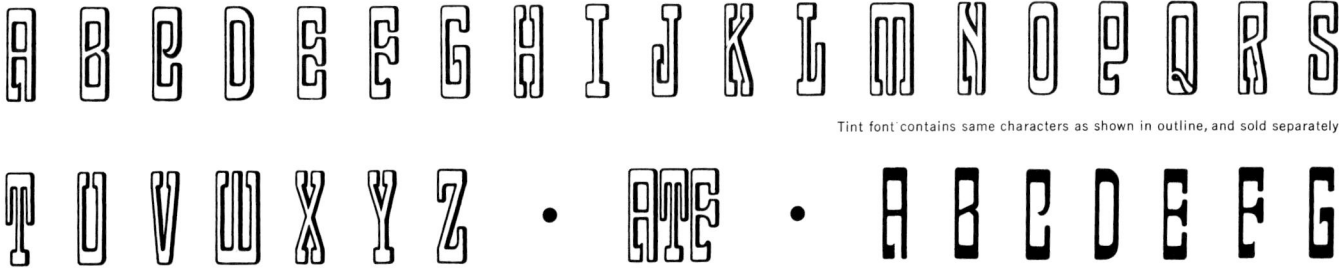

Tint font contains same characters as shown in outline, and sold separately

ELITE MONOGRAM INITIALS

Series C, 36 Point

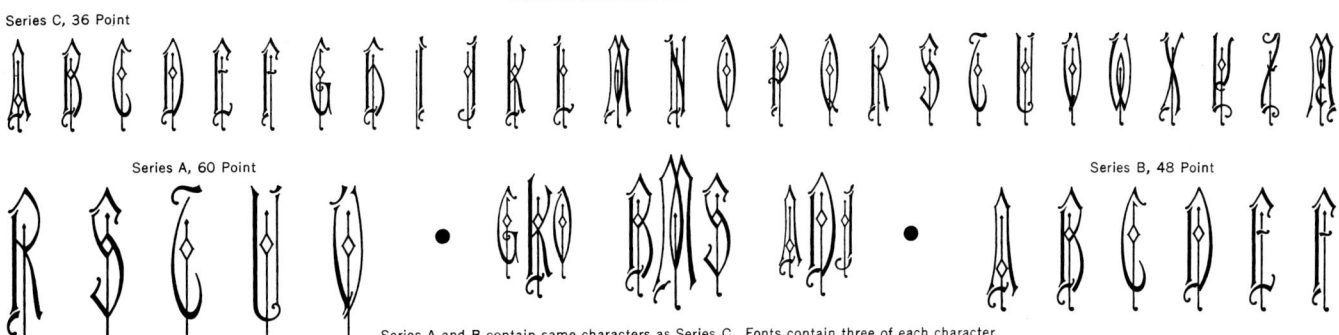

Series A, 60 Point

Series B, 48 Point

Series A and B contain same characters as Series C. Fonts contain three of each character

BROADWAY MONOGRAM INITIALS

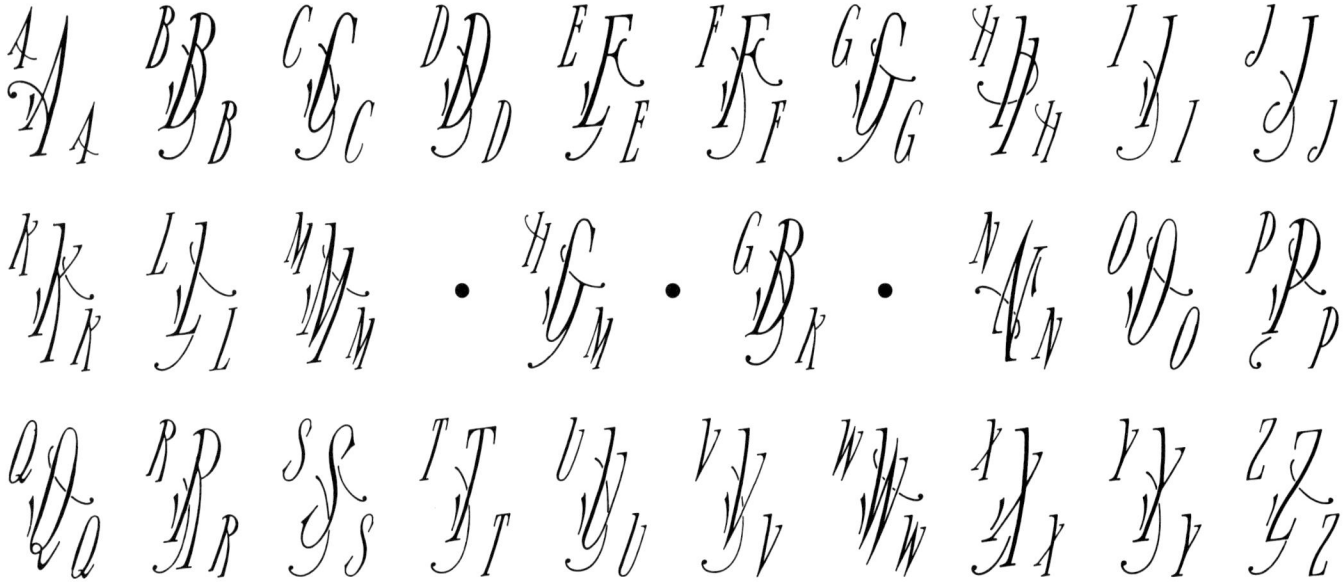

Fonts contain one each of the larger letters A to Z and two each of the small letters. Large letter should be used for the family name. The larger letters are cast recessed at top and bottom, which permits the insertion of the small characters without justification. Very effective results may be obtained by printing these monograms in more than one color.

HOLLYWOOD COMBINATION INITIALS

EXAMPLES

Color Characters for Hollywood Combination Initials shown below, are fonted and sold separately

A font of Hollywood Combination Initials contains three characters of every letter in the alphabet and an Mc and Mac. The same character is cast in three different positions on the type body. With the exception of M, W, Mc and Mac (cast 12 point set) all characters are cast 8 point set and require no justification. The M, W, Mc and Mac, when used with 8 point set characters require slight justification in order to give the desired slope.

FIFTH AVENUE MONOGRAM INITIALS

A font contains three type of each character cast on 54 point body, and three type of each character cast on 24 point body. The M and W of both sizes are cast on 8 point set; all other characters are cast on 6 point set. Very effective results may be obtained by printing these monograms in more than one color.

FIFTH AVENUE INITIAL FRAMES

Made in seven sizes (two pieces, right and left), to accommodate the different combinations which may be made with the letters by simple justification

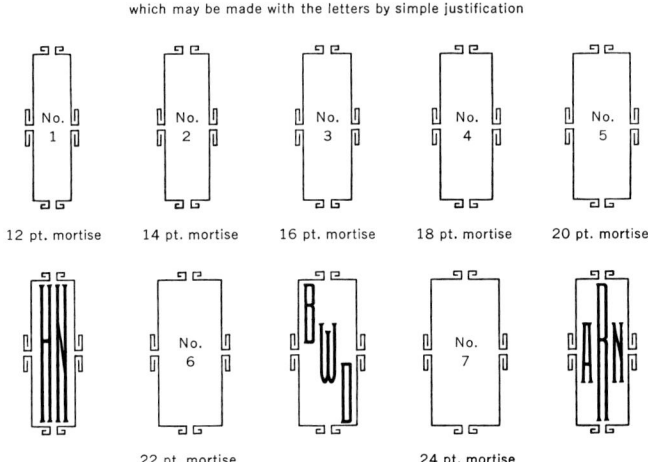

:[200]:

VOGUE INITIALS

Made in six sizes; each size has 28 letters, four of which are made in two styles (see Series F). Sold in sets containing one of each character, or by individual character; when ordering duplicate characters mention Series and Number of letter desired. The range of sizes and weights of faces may be observed by studying the lines below showing at least one letter of each size.

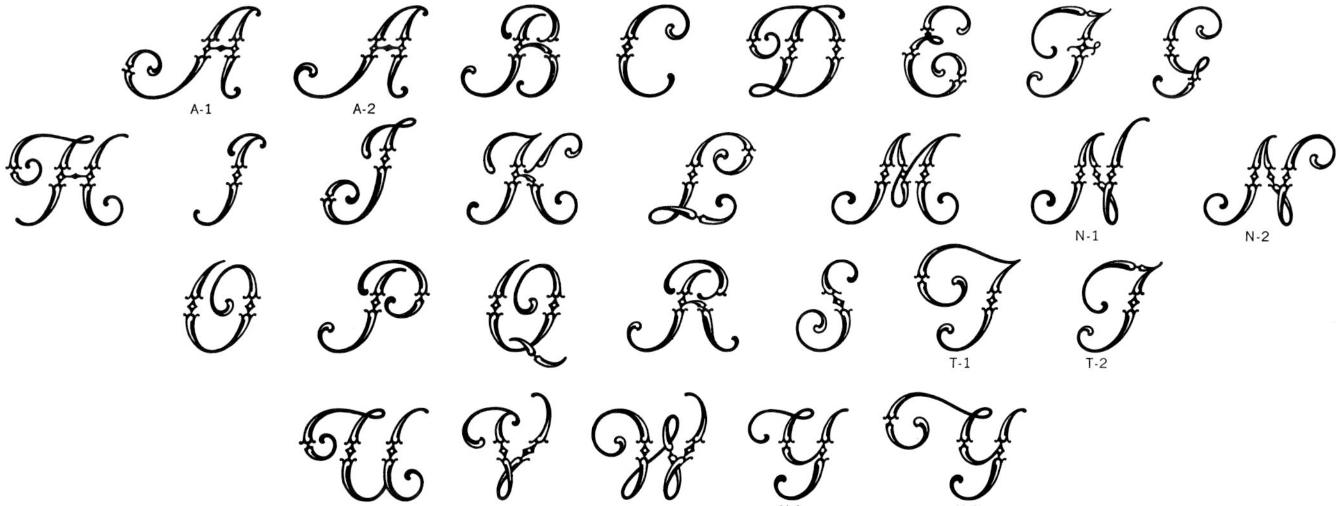

LIBERTY INITIALS

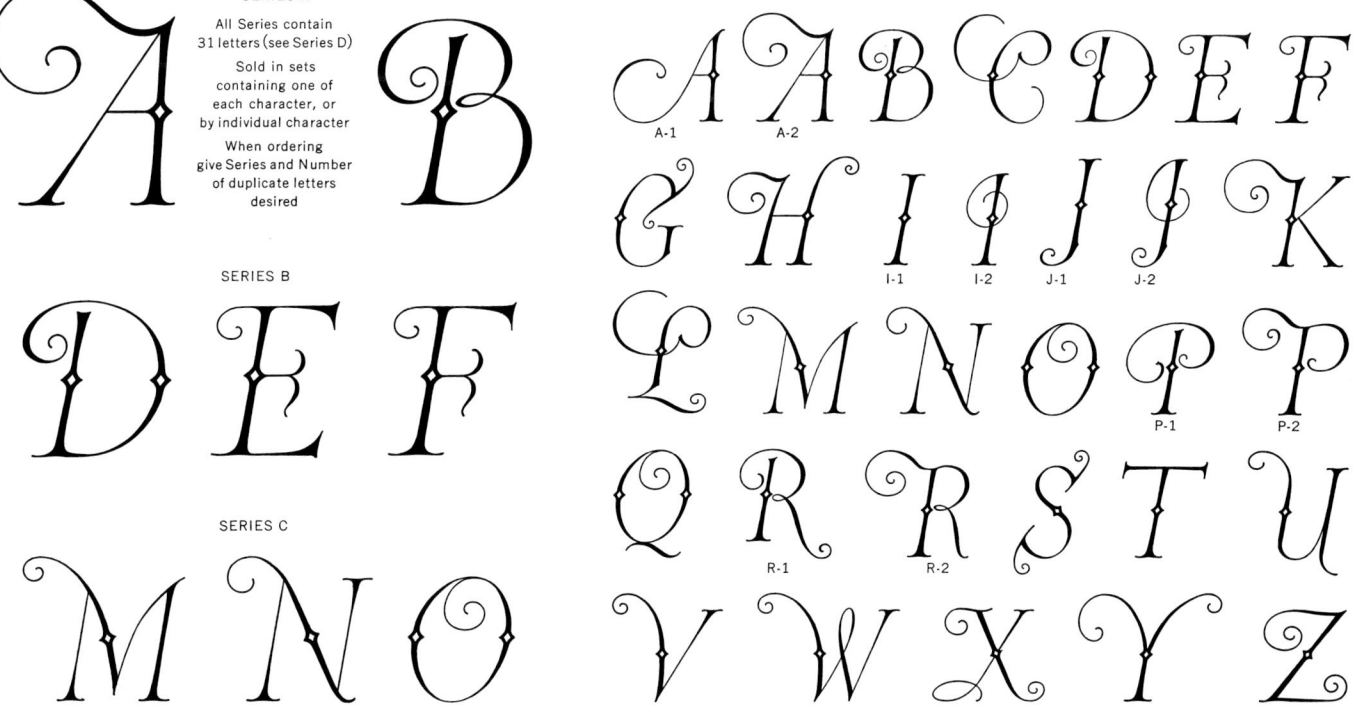

GEORGIAN INITIALS—Series A

ABCDEF
GHIKLM
NOPRST
UV
WX
YZ
QJ

Set Contains 26 Characters

All characters except Q and J cast on 72 Point Body

Q and J are cast on 96 Point Body

24 POINT STATIONERS INITIALS

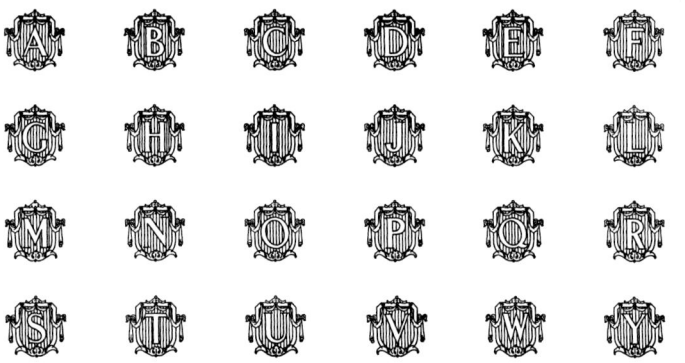

For One or Two Colors—Sold by the Set or Individual Character
One Color Set Contains 24 Characters   Two Color Set Contains 48 Characters

36 POINT STATIONERS INITIALS

48 POINT STATIONERS INITIALS

36 and 48 Point Sets Contain Same Characters as Shown in 24 Point

Made in Twenty-four Characters   72 POINT CALLIGRAPH INITIALS   Sold by the Set or Individual Character

ABCDEF
GHIJKL
MNOPQR
STUVWY

96 POINT CALLIGRAPH INITIALS

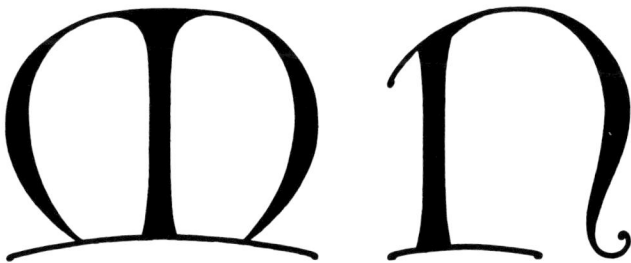

120 POINT CALLIGRAPH INITIALS

All Sets Contain Same Characters as Shown in 72 Point Size

24 POINT UNIVERSITY INITIALS

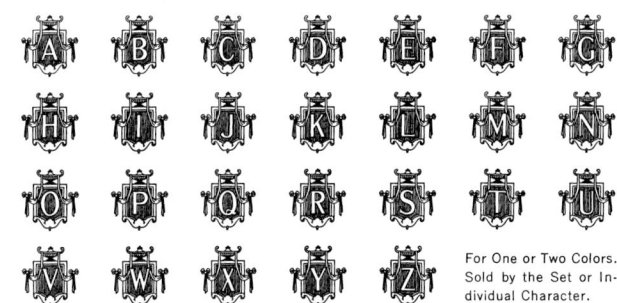

For One or Two Colors. Sold by the Set or Individual Character.

One Color Set contains 26 Characters   Two Color Set contains 52 Characters

36 POINT UNIVERSITY INITIALS

48 POINT UNIVERSITY INITIALS

All Sets Contain Same Characters as Shown in 24 Point Size

VANITY INITIALS

Cast full body and are not mortised

A-3 72 Point
other sizes { A-2 60 Point / A-1 48 Point

A-6 72 Point
other sizes { A-5 60 Point / A-4 48 Point

A-9 96 Point; other sizes { A-8 72 Point / A-7 60 Point

B-1 60 Point
other sizes { B-2 48 Point / B-3 36 Point

C-2 60 Point
other sizes { C-1 48 Point / C-3 36 Point

D-3 72 Point
other sizes { D-2 60 Point / D-1 48 Point

E-3 72 Point
other sizes { E-2 60 Point / E-1 48 Point

SF-4 48 Point

SF-1 60 Point; other sizes { SF-2 48 Point / SF-3 30 Point

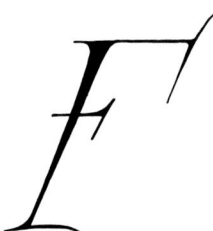
F-3 96 Point
other sizes { F-2 72 Point / F-1 54 Point

G-9 84 Point
other sizes { G-8 72 Point / G-7 54 Point

G-6 96 Point
other sizes { G-5 72 Point / G-4 54 Point

G-3 120 Point
other sizes { G-2 72 Point / G-1 48 Point

H-3 144 Point
other sizes { H-2 120 Point / H-1 96 Point

H-6 72 Point
other sizes { H-5 60 Point / H-4 48 Point

I-3 96 Point
other size: I-2 72 Point

J-3 84 Point
other sizes { J-2 72 Point / J-1 54 Point

K-3 60 Point
other sizes { K-2 48 Point / K-1 36 Point

L-3 60 Point
other sizes { L-2 48 Point / L-1 36 Point

L-6 60 Point
other sizes { L-5 48 Point / L-4 36 Point

M-3 96 Point
other sizes { M-2 72 Point / M-1 48 Point

M-6 120 Point; other sizes { M-5 96 Point / M-4 72 Point

N-3 120 Point; other sizes { N-2 96 Point / N-1 72 Point

P-3 60 Point
other sizes { P-2 48 Point / P-1 36 Point

VANITY INITIALS

Cast full body and are not mortised

R-3 108 Point
other sizes { R-2 84 Point / R-1 54 Point

S-3 72 Point
other sizes { S-2 48 Point / S-1 36 Point

S-6 120 Point; other sizes { S-5 84 Point / S-4 60 Point

ST-13 34 Point; other size ST-5 24 Point

ST-8 72 Point; other sizes { ST-9 48 Point / ST-3 36 Point

ST-6 60 Point
other sizes { ST-10 48 Point / ST-2 30 Point

ST-4 54 Point; other size ST-11 36 Point

ST-7 36 Point

ST-12 36 Point

ST-1 48 Point

U-3 60 Point
other sizes { U-2 48 Point / U-1 36 Point

V-3 72 Point
other sizes { V-2 60 Point / V-1 48 Point

W-10 60 Point; other sizes { W-9 48 Point / W-8 36 Point

W-7 60 Point; other sizes { W-6 48 Point / W-5 36 Point

W-4 84 Point
other sizes { W-3 72 Point / W-2 54 Point / W-1 42 Point

Y-3 84 Point
other sizes { Y-2 60 Point / Y-1 36 Point

Y-5 96 Point
other size Y-4 72 Point

LT-6 48 Point
other sizes { LT-7 42 Point / LT-8 36 Point / LT-9 30 Point / LT-10 24 Point

LT-4 24 Point

LT-1 36 Point
other size LT-5 24 Point

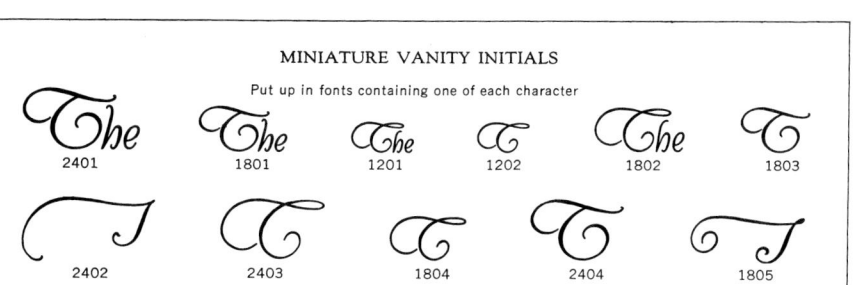

MINIATURE VANITY INITIALS
Put up in fonts containing one of each character

2401 · 1801 · 1201 · 1202 · 1802 · 1803
2402 · 2403 · 1804 · 2404 · 1805

LT-2 36 Point

LT-3 36 Point

[205]

Cloister Initials and Bradley Ultra Modern Initials

CLOISTER INITIALS—Designed by F. W. Goudy

36 Point For one or two colors

96 Point

BRADLEY ULTRA MODERN INITIALS

Designed by Will Bradley

Sold singly, and in sets containing one of each character shown in the 36 Point size

84 Point

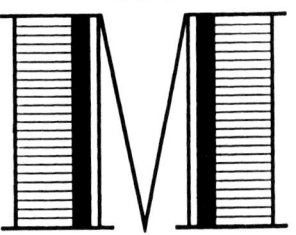

60 Point

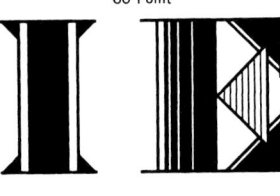

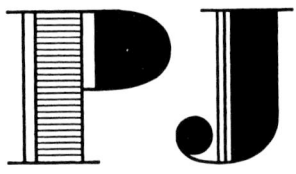

84 Point

72 Point

48 Point

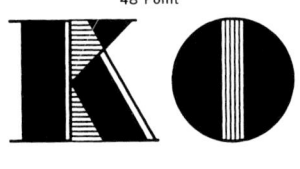

Cloister Initials sold singly, and in sets containing one of each character
Tint blocks are available for all sizes except 36 Point

120 Point

48 Point

60 Point

144 Point

Characters in Complete Font · 36 Point BRADLEY ULTRA MODERN INITIALS · Mention Size and Number when ordering single characters

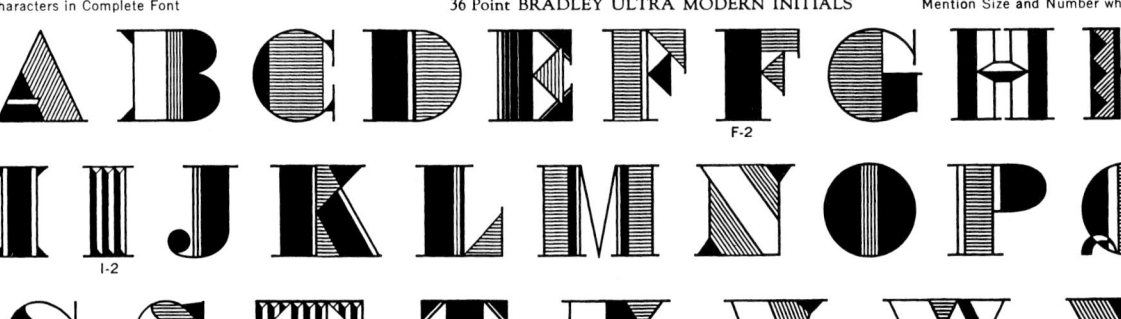

:[206]: